AVENGERS

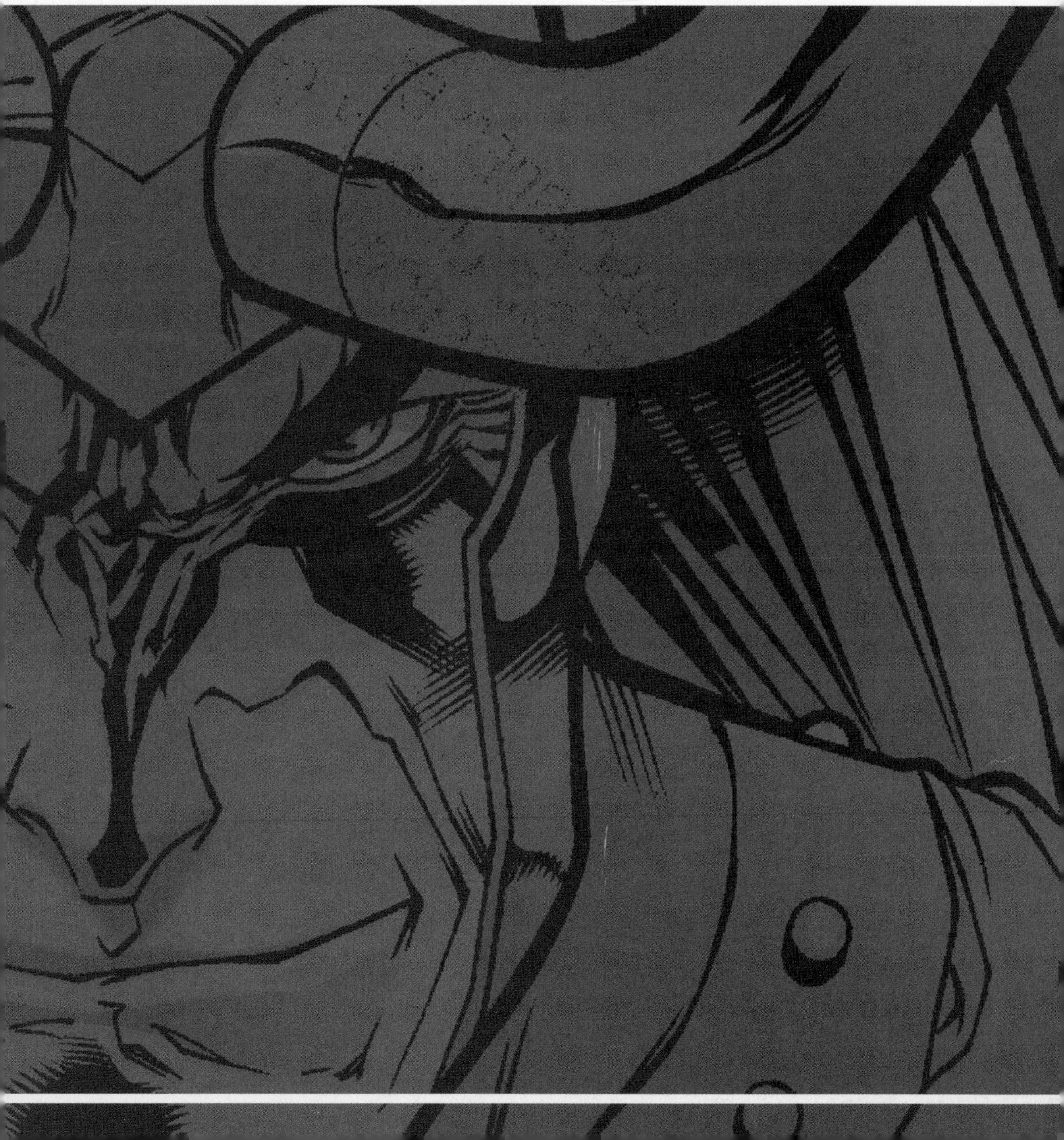

COLLECTION EDITOR: **JENNIFER GRÜNWALD**
ASSISTANT EDITOR: **CAITLIN O'CONNELL**
ASSOCIATE MANAGING EDITOR: **KATERI WOODY**
EDITOR, SPECIAL PROJECTS: **MARK D. BEAZLEY**
VP PRODUCTION & SPECIAL PROJECTS: **JEFF YOUNGQUIST**
SVP PRINT, SALES & MARKETING: **DAVID GABRIEL**
BOOK DESIGN: **JEFF POWELL**

EDITOR IN CHIEF: **C.B. CEBULSKI**
CHIEF CREATIVE OFFICER: **JOE QUESADA**
PRESIDENT: **DAN BUCKLEY**
EXECUTIVE PRODUCER: **ALAN FINE**

AVENGERS: MIGHTY ORIGINS. Contains material originally published in magazine form as AVENGERS: SEASON ONE and AVENGERS #1. First printing 2018. ISBN 978-0-7851-8525-3. Published by MARVEL WORLDW INC., a subsidiary of MARVEL ENTERTAINMENT, LLC. OFFICE OF PUBLICATION: 135 West 50th Street, New York, NY 10020. **Printed in the U.S.A.** DAN BUCKLEY, President, Ma Entertainment; JOHN NEE, Publisher; JOE QUESADA, Chief Creative Officer; TOM BREVOORT, SVP of Publishing; DAVID BOGART, SVP of Business Affairs & Operations, Publishing & Partnership; DAVID GABRIEL, SVP of S & Marketing, Publishing; JEFF YOUNGQUIST, VP of Production & Special Projects; DAN CARR, Executive Director of Publishing Technology; ALEX MORALES, Director of Publishing Operations; SUSAN CRESPI, Produc Manager; STAN LEE, Chairman Emeritus. For information regarding advertising in Marvel Comics or on Marvel.com, please contact Vit DeBellis, Custom Solutions & Integrated Advertising Manager, at vdebellis@ma com. For Marvel subscription inquiries, please call 888-511-5480. **Manufactured between 2/9/2018 and 3/13/2018 by LSC COMMUNICATIONS INC., KENDALLVILLE, IN, USA.**

10 9 8 7 6 5 4 3 2 1

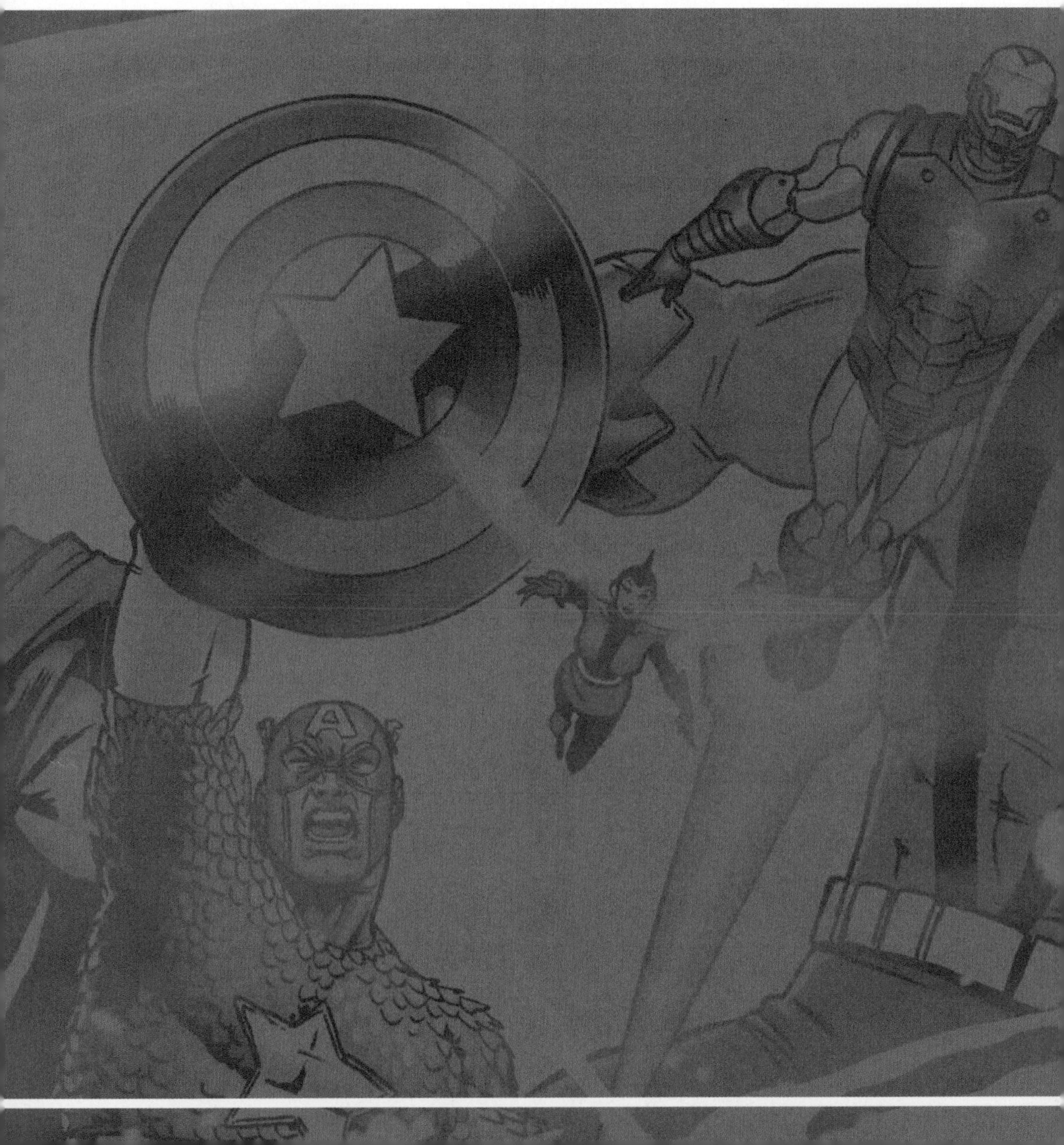

AVENGERS

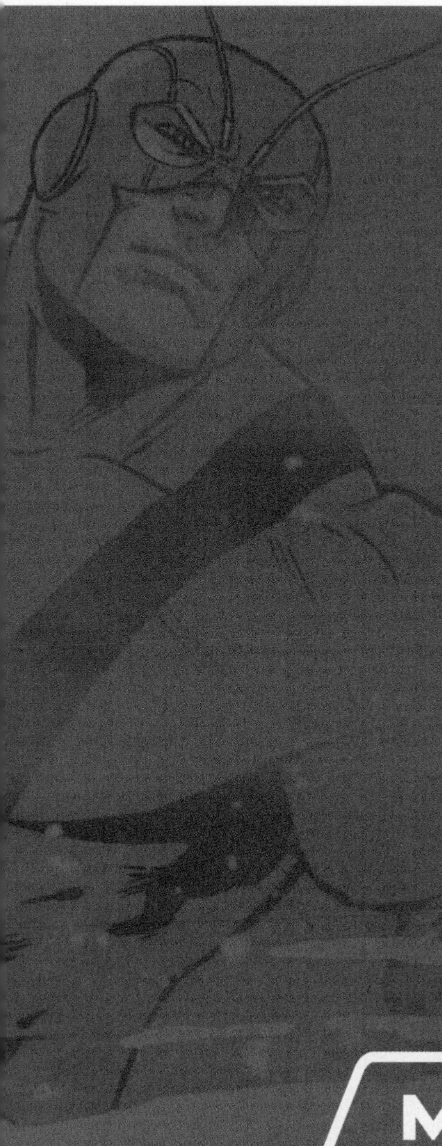

WRITER
PETER DAVID

ARTISTS
ANDREA Di VITO (PAGES 1-21 & 80-100)
JON BURAN (PAGES 22-41)
NIGEL RAYNOR (PAGES 42-59)
MIKE BOWDEN &
WALDEN WONG (PAGES 60-79)

COLOR ARTIST
WIL QUINTANA

LETTERER
VC'S CLAYTON COWLES

COVER ART
JULIAN TOTINO TEDESCO

ASSISTANT EDITOR
JAKE THOMAS

ASSOCIATE EDITOR
LAUREN SANKOVITCH

EXECUTIVE EDITOR
TOM BREVOORT

AVENGERS CREATED BY STAN LEE & JACK KIRBY

MIGHTY ORIGINS

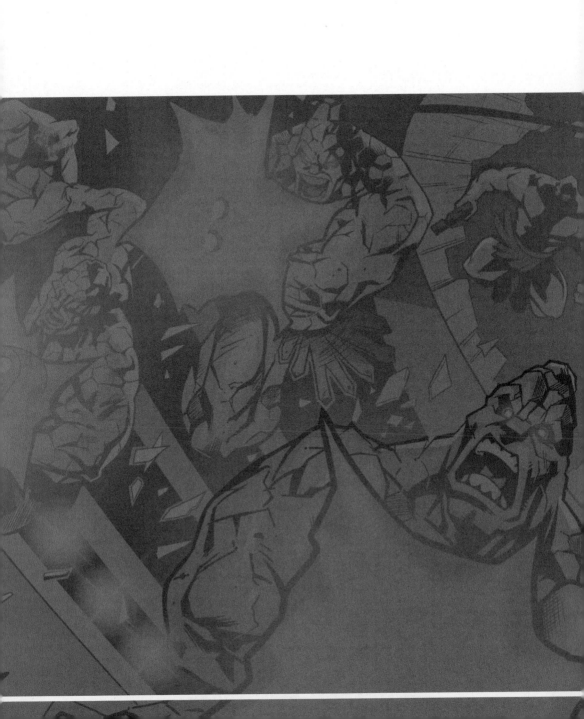

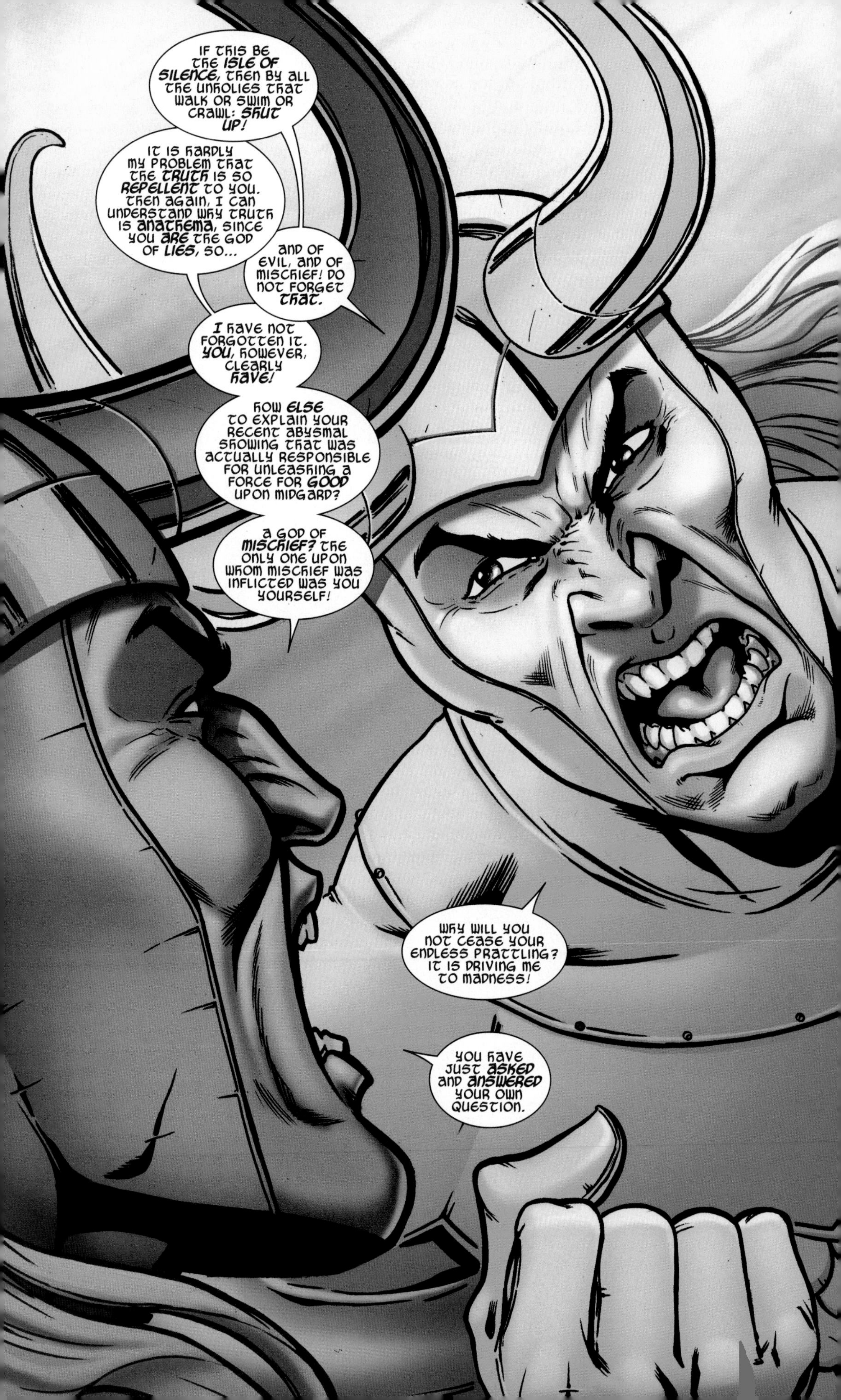
IF THIS BE THE ISLE OF SILENCE, THEN BY ALL THE UNHOLIES THAT WALK OR SWIM OR CRAWL: SHUT UP!
IT IS HARDLY MY PROBLEM THAT THE TRUTH IS SO REPELLENT TO YOU. THEN AGAIN, I CAN UNDERSTAND WHY TRUTH IS ANATHEMA, SINCE YOU ARE THE GOD OF LIES, SO...
AND OF EVIL, AND OF MISCHIEF! DO NOT FORGET THAT.
I HAVE NOT FORGOTTEN IT. YOU, HOWEVER, CLEARLY HAVE!
HOW ELSE TO EXPLAIN YOUR RECENT ABYSMAL SHOWING THAT WAS ACTUALLY RESPONSIBLE FOR UNLEASHING A FORCE FOR GOOD UPON MIDGARD?
A GOD OF MISCHIEF? THE ONLY ONE UPON WHOM MISCHIEF WAS INFLICTED WAS YOU YOURSELF!
WHY WILL YOU NOT CEASE YOUR ENDLESS PRATTLING? IT IS DRIVING ME TO MADNESS!
YOU HAVE JUST ASKED AND ANSWERED YOUR OWN QUESTION.

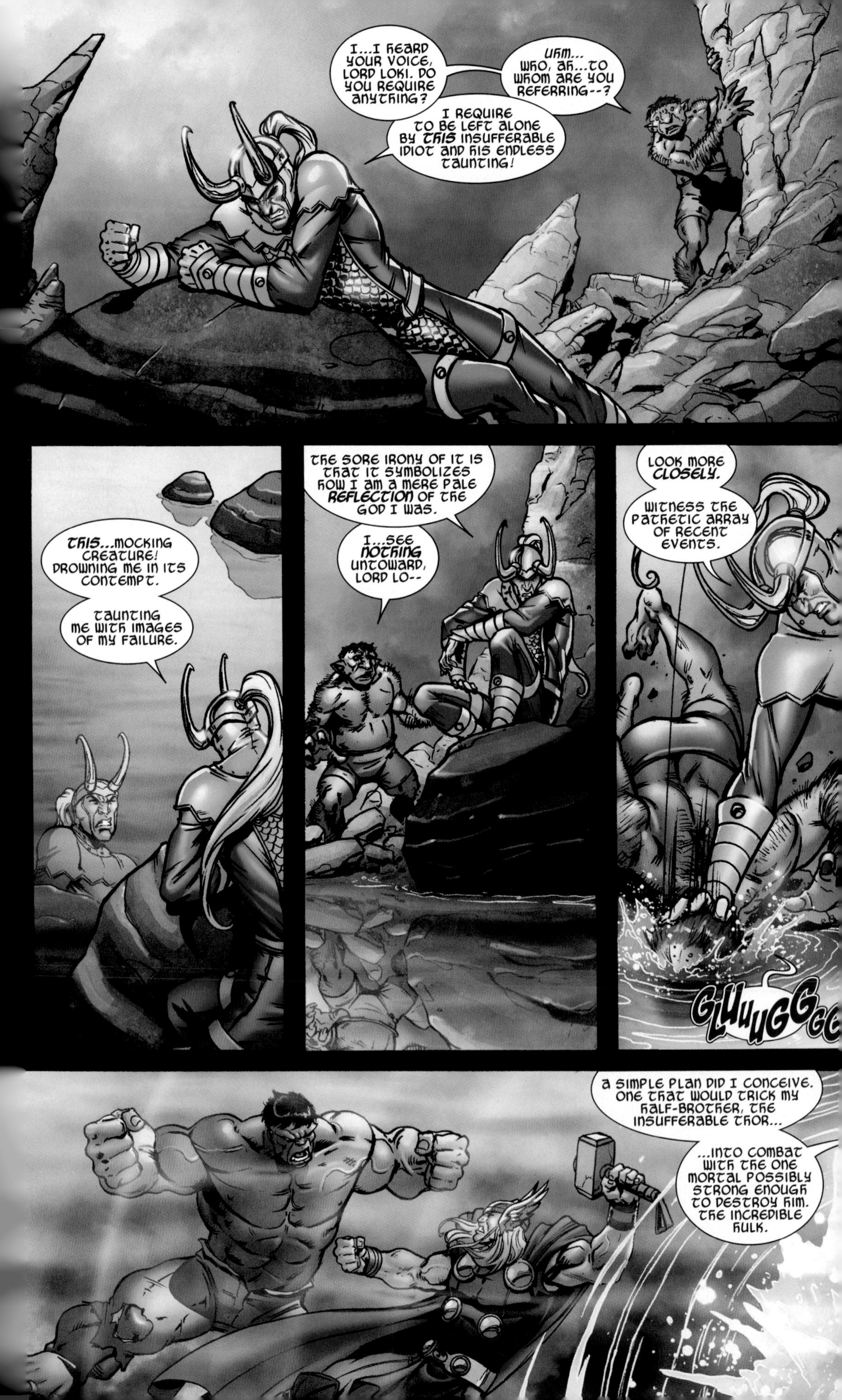

I...I HEARD YOUR VOICE, LORD LOKI. DO YOU REQUIRE ANYTHING?
UHM... WHO, AH...TO WHOM ARE YOU REFERRING--?
I REQUIRE TO BE LEFT ALONE BY THIS INSUFFERABLE IDIOT AND HIS ENDLESS TAUNTING!
THIS...MOCKING CREATURE! DROWNING ME IN ITS CONTEMPT.
TAUNTING ME WITH IMAGES OF MY FAILURE.
THE SORE IRONY OF IT IS THAT IT SYMBOLIZES HOW I AM A MERE PALE REFLECTION OF THE GOD I WAS.
I...SEE NOTHING UNTOWARD, LORD LO--
LOOK MORE CLOSELY.
WITNESS THE PATHETIC ARRAY OF RECENT EVENTS.
GLUUUGGGG
A SIMPLE PLAN DID I CONCEIVE. ONE THAT WOULD TRICK MY HALF-BROTHER, THE INSUFFERABLE THOR...
...INTO COMBAT WITH THE ONE MORTAL POSSIBLY STRONG ENOUGH TO DESTROY HIM. THE INCREDIBLE HULK.

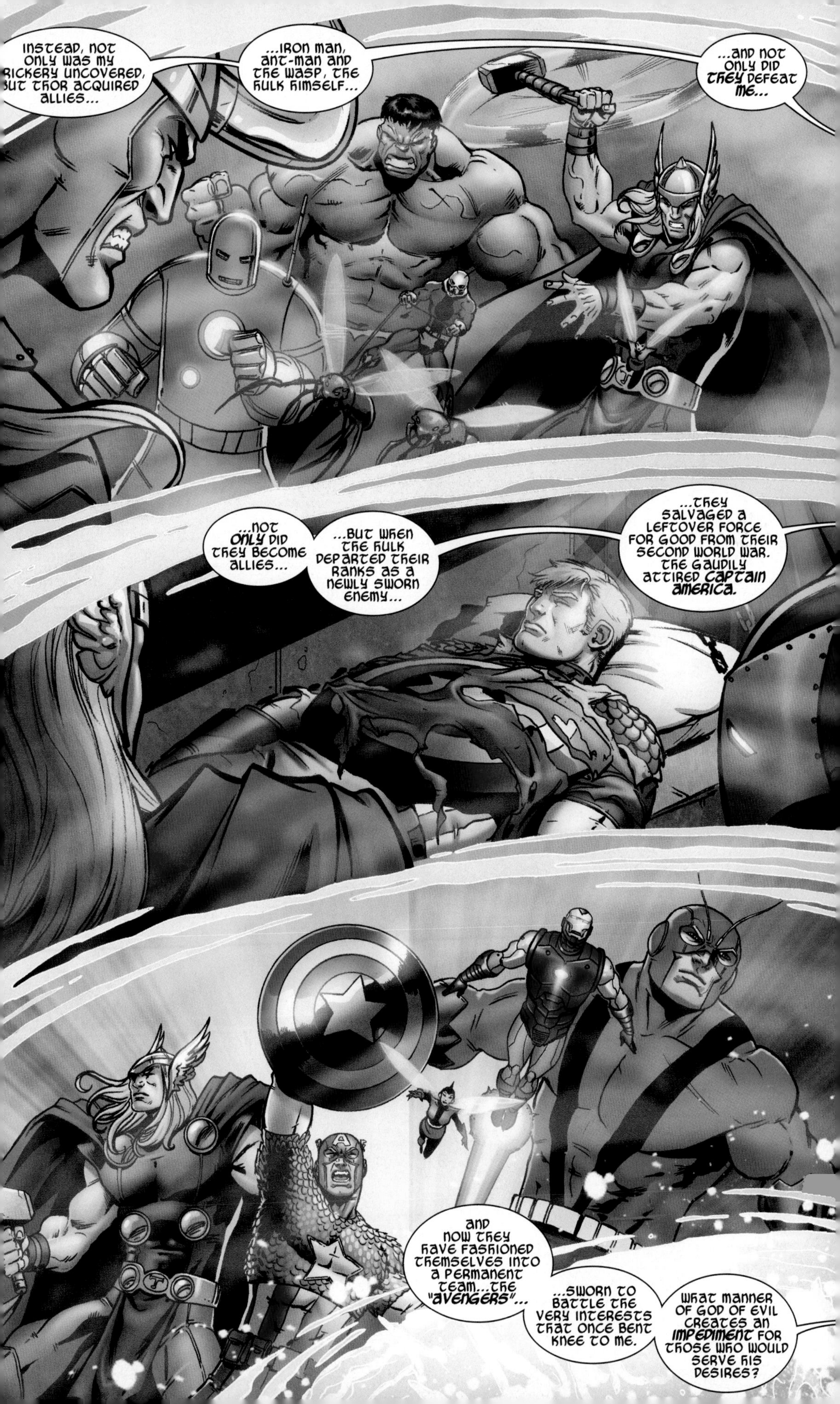

INSTEAD, NOT ONLY WAS MY RICKERY UNCOVERED, UT THOR ACQUIRED ALLIES...
...IRON MAN, ANT-MAN AND THE WASP, THE HULK HIMSELF...
...AND NOT ONLY DID THEY DEFEAT ME...
...NOT ONLY DID THEY BECOME ALLIES...
...BUT WHEN THE HULK DEPARTED THEIR RANKS AS A NEWLY SWORN ENEMY...
...THEY SALVAGED A LEFTOVER FORCE FOR GOOD FROM THEIR SECOND WORLD WAR. THE GAUDILY ATTIRED CAPTAIN AMERICA.
AND NOW THEY HAVE FASHIONED THEMSELVES INTO A PERMANENT TEAM...THE "AVENGERS"...
...SWORN TO BATTLE THE VERY INTERESTS THAT ONCE BENT KNEE TO ME.
WHAT MANNER OF GOD OF EVIL CREATES AN IMPEDIMENT FOR THOSE WHO WOULD SERVE HIS DESIRES?

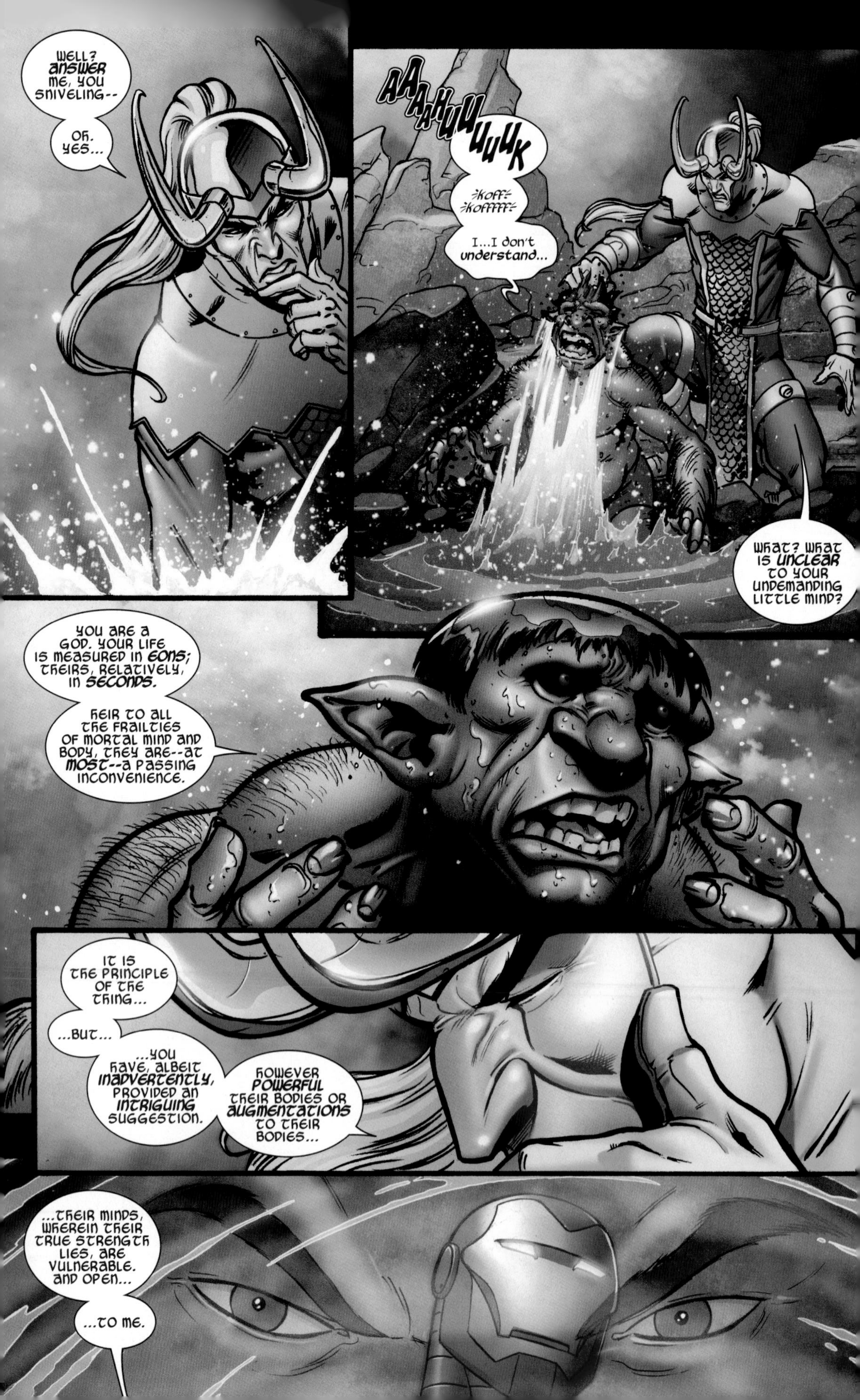

WELL? ANSWER ME, YOU SNIVELING--
OH. YES...
AAAAHUUUUUK
KOFF KOFFFFF
I...I don't understand...
WHAT? WHAT IS UNCLEAR TO YOUR UNDEMANDING LITTLE MIND?
YOU ARE A GOD. YOUR LIFE IS MEASURED IN EONS; THEIRS, RELATIVELY, IN SECONDS.
HEIR TO ALL THE FRAILTIES OF MORTAL MIND AND BODY, THEY ARE--AT MOST--A PASSING INCONVENIENCE.
IT IS THE PRINCIPLE OF THE THING...
...BUT...
...YOU HAVE, ALBEIT INADVERTENTLY, PROVIDED AN INTRIGUING SUGGESTION.
HOWEVER POWERFUL THEIR BODIES OR AUGMENTATIONS TO THEIR BODIES...
...THEIR MINDS, WHEREIN THEIR TRUE STRENGTH LIES, ARE VULNERABLE. AND OPEN...
...TO ME.

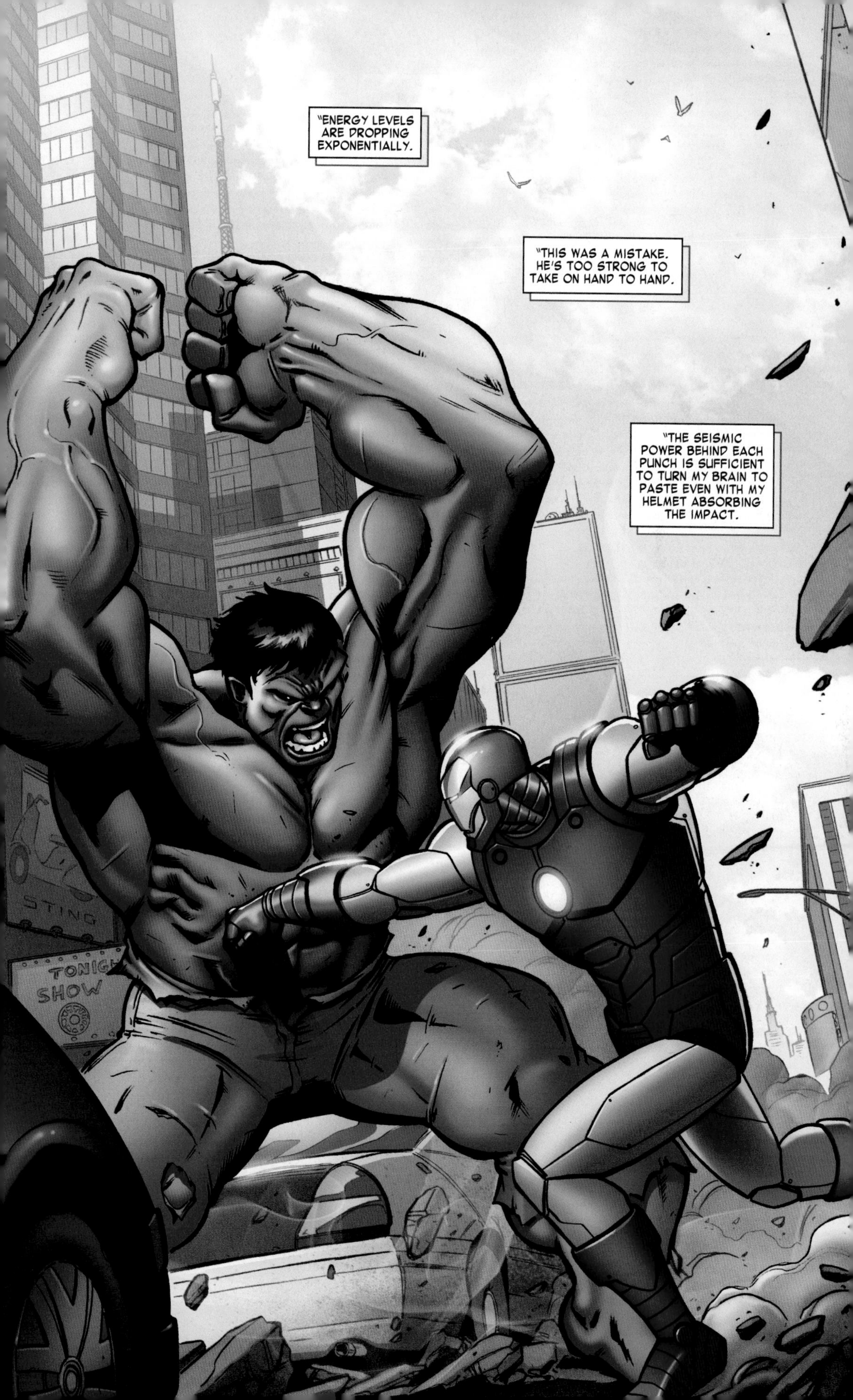
"ENERGY LEVELS ARE DROPPING EXPONENTIALLY.
"THIS WAS A MISTAKE. HE'S TOO STRONG TO TAKE ON HAND TO HAND.
"THE SEISMIC POWER BEHIND EACH PUNCH IS SUFFICIENT TO TURN MY BRAIN TO PASTE EVEN WITH MY HELMET ABSORBING THE IMPACT.
STING
TONIGH
SHOW

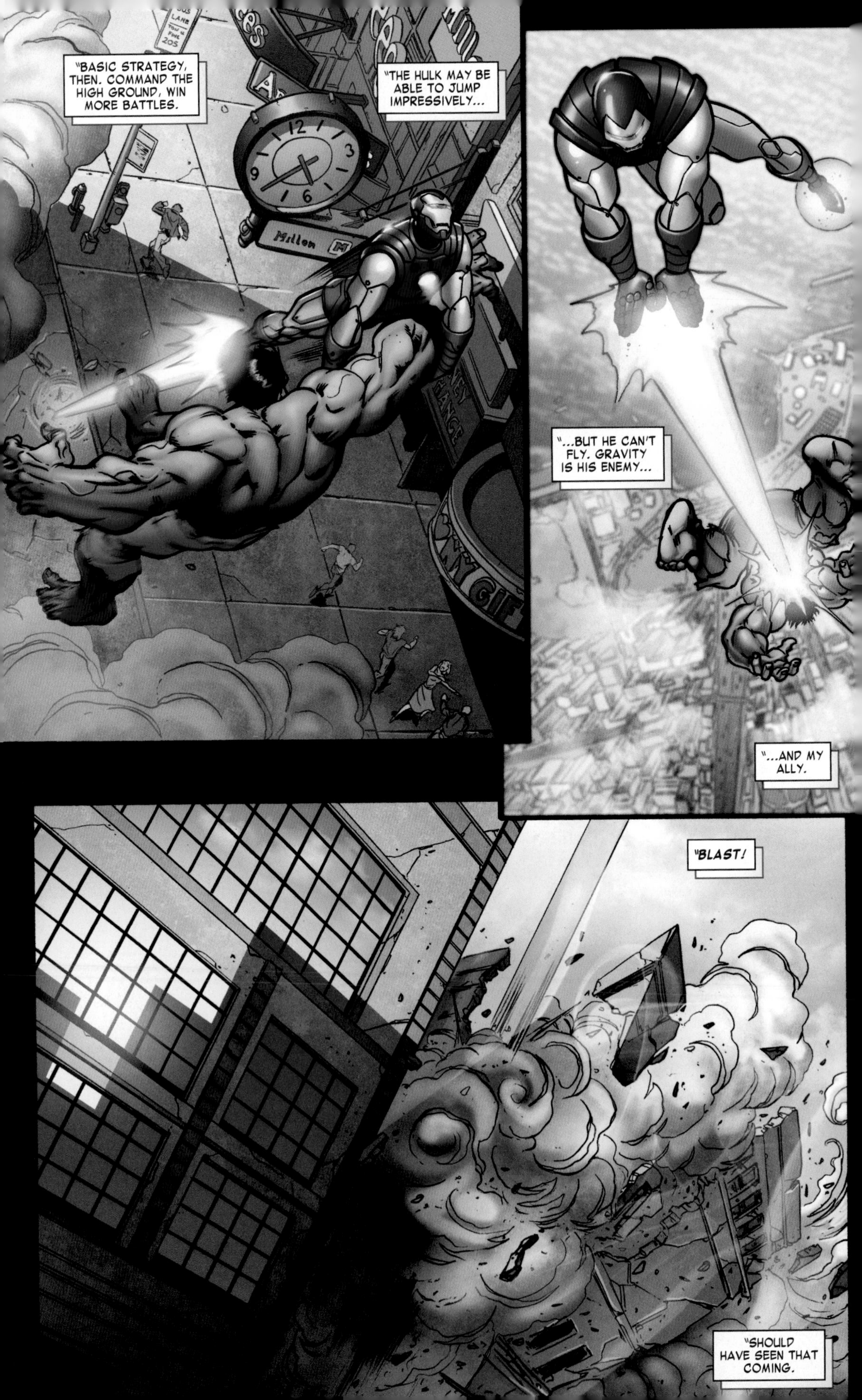
"BASIC STRATEGY, THEN. COMMAND THE HIGH GROUND, WIN MORE BATTLES.
"THE HULK MAY BE ABLE TO JUMP IMPRESSIVELY...
"...BUT HE CAN'T FLY. GRAVITY IS HIS ENEMY...
"...AND MY ALLY.
"BLAST!
"SHOULD HAVE SEEN THAT COMING.

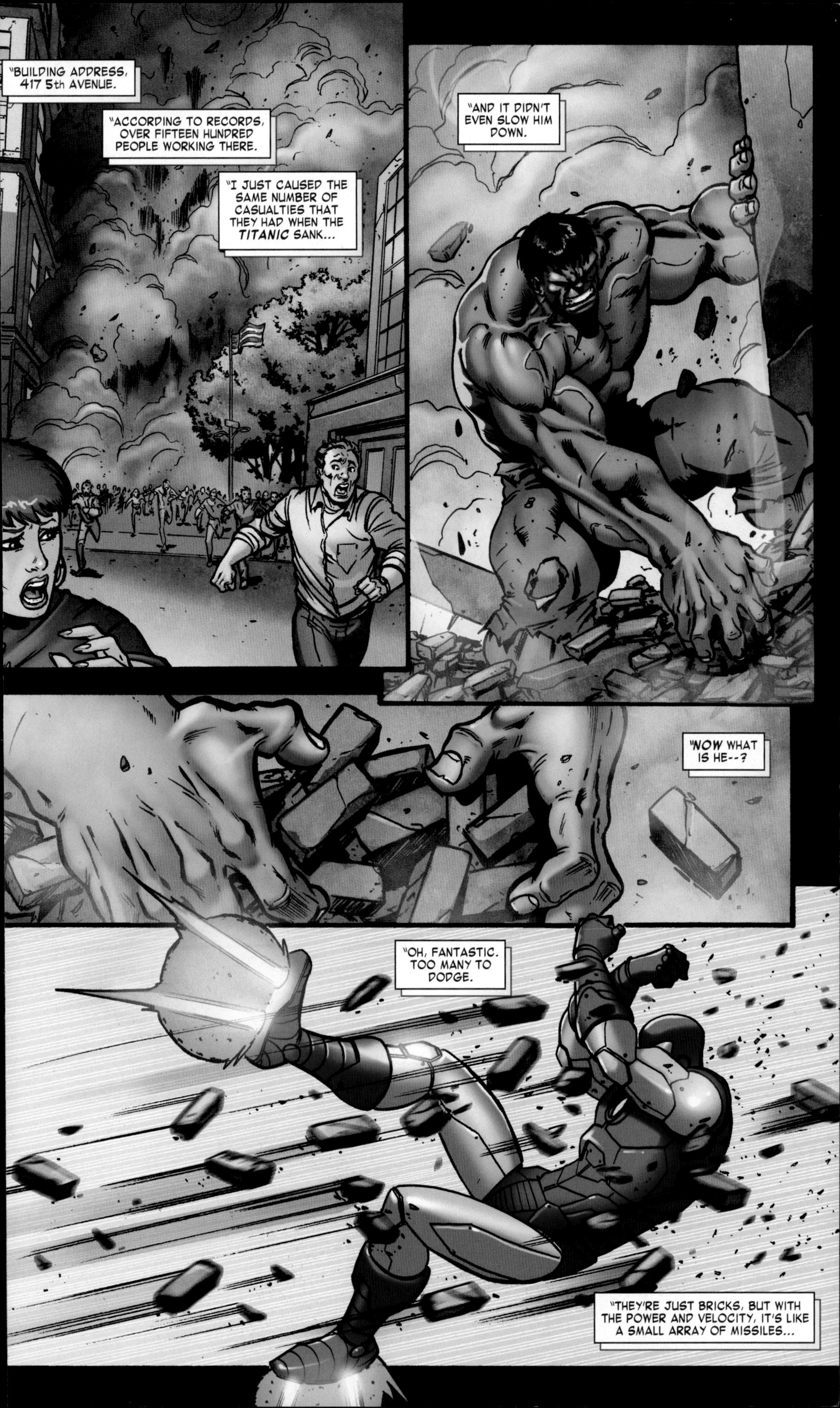
"BUILDING ADDRESS, 417 5th AVENUE.
"ACCORDING TO RECORDS, OVER FIFTEEN HUNDRED PEOPLE WORKING THERE.
"I JUST CAUSED THE SAME NUMBER OF CASUALTIES THAT THEY HAD WHEN THE *TITANIC* SANK...
"AND IT DIDN'T EVEN SLOW HIM DOWN.
"*NOW* WHAT IS HE--?
"OH, FANTASTIC. TOO MANY TO DODGE.
"THEY'RE JUST BRICKS, BUT WITH THE POWER AND VELOCITY, IT'S LIKE A SMALL ARRAY OF MISSILES...

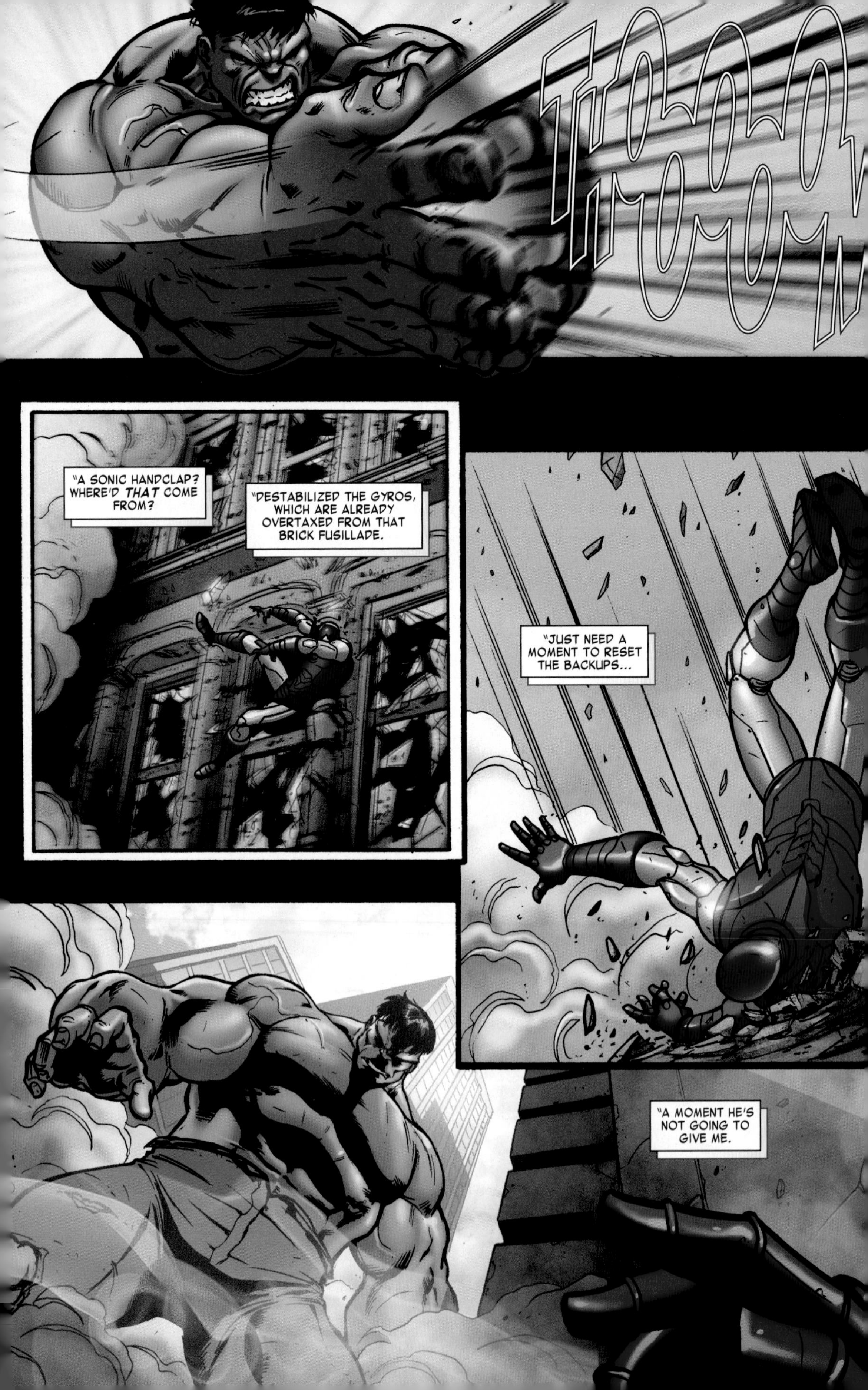
"A SONIC HANDCLAP? WHERE'D *THAT* COME FROM?
"DESTABILIZED THE GYROS, WHICH ARE ALREADY OVERTAXED FROM THAT BRICK FUSILLADE.
"JUST NEED A MOMENT TO RESET THE BACKUPS...
"A MOMENT HE'S NOT GOING TO GIVE ME.

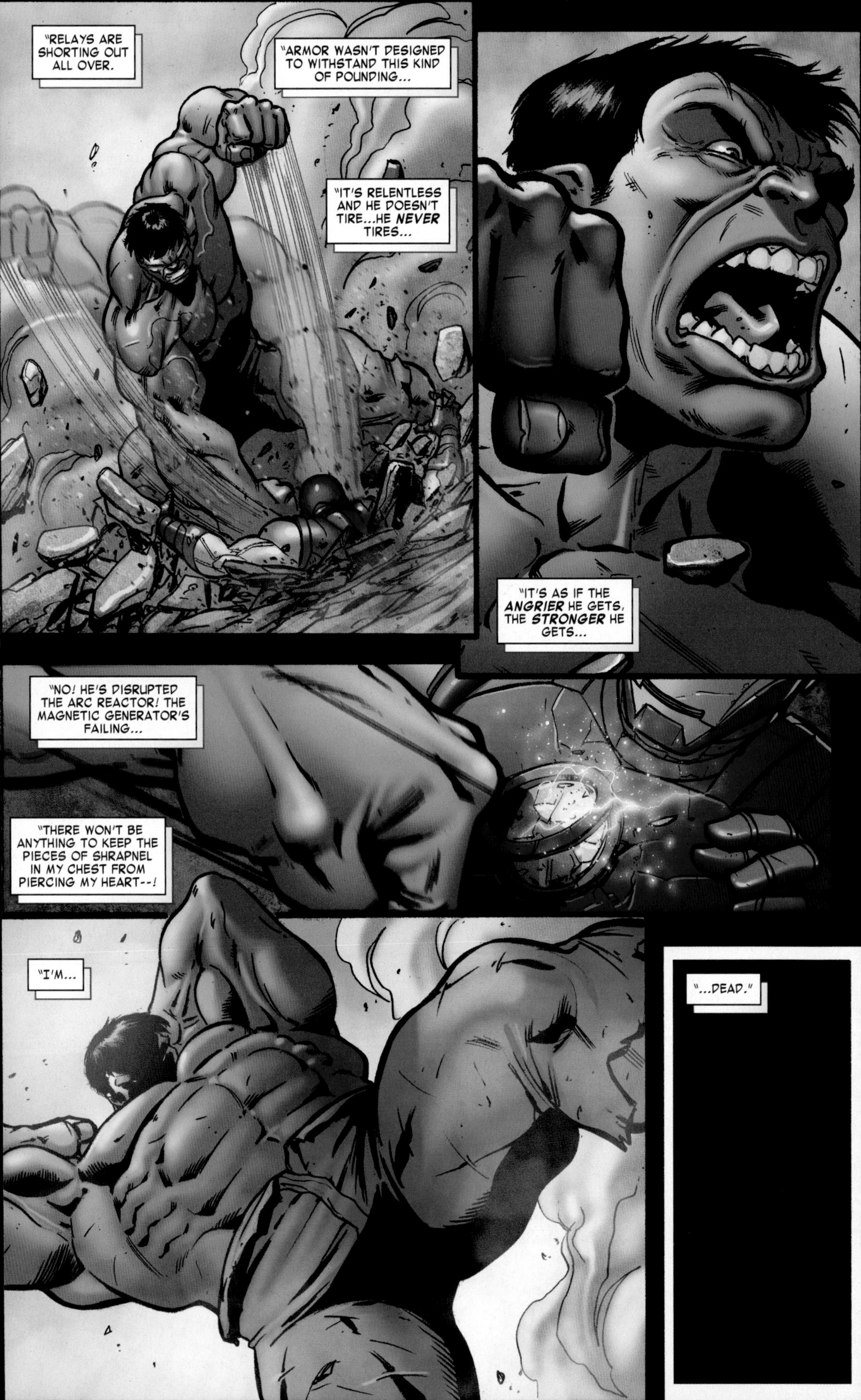
"RELAYS ARE SHORTING OUT ALL OVER.
"ARMOR WASN'T DESIGNED TO WITHSTAND THIS KIND OF POUNDING...
"IT'S RELENTLESS AND HE DOESN'T TIRE...HE NEVER TIRES...
"IT'S AS IF THE ANGRIER HE GETS, THE STRONGER HE GETS...
"NO! HE'S DISRUPTED THE ARC REACTOR! THE MAGNETIC GENERATOR'S FAILING...
"THERE WON'T BE ANYTHING TO KEEP THE PIECES OF SHRAPNEL IN MY CHEST FROM PIERCING MY HEART--!
"I'M...
"...DEAD."

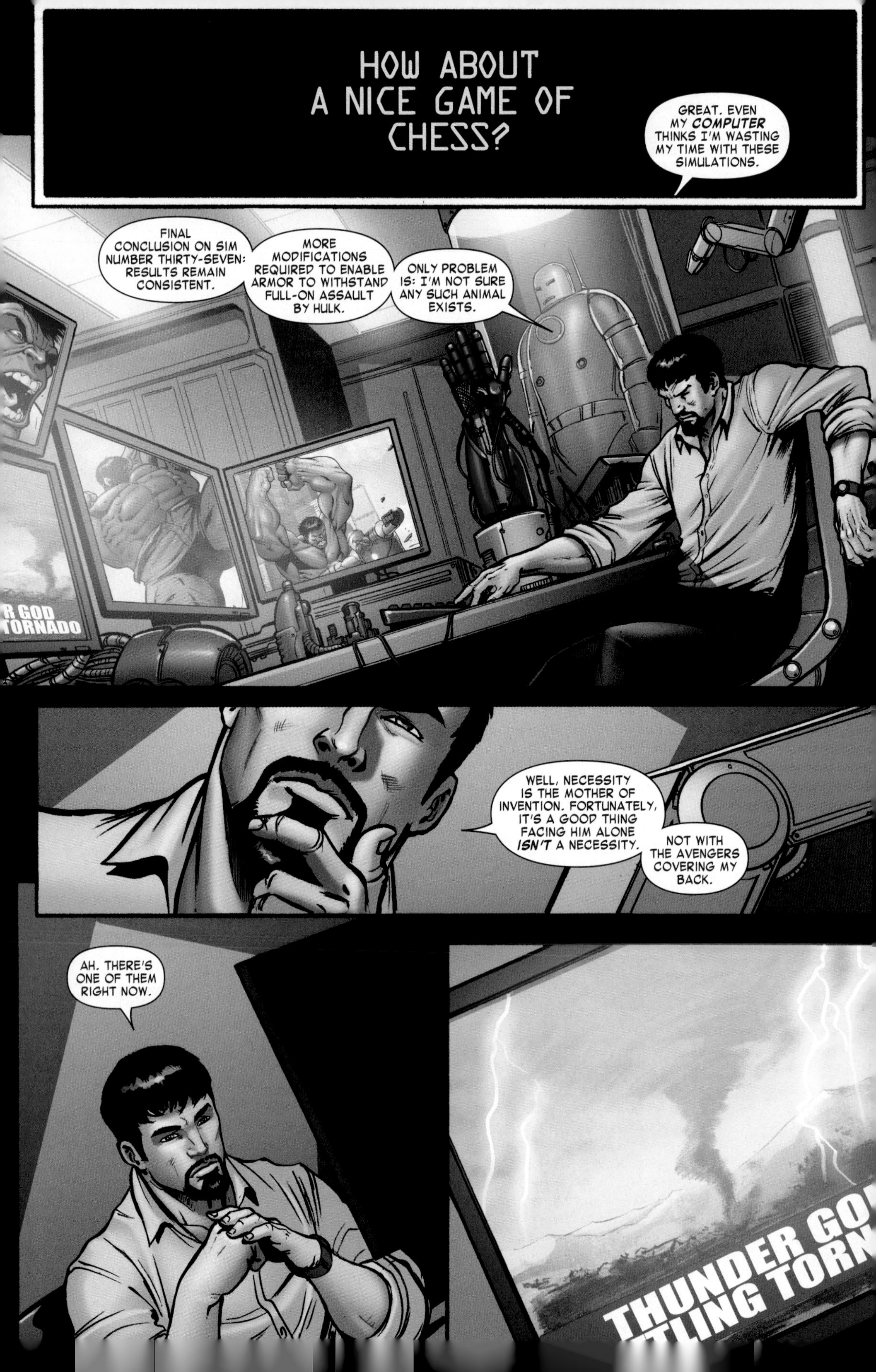
HOW ABOUT A NICE GAME OF CHESS?
GREAT. EVEN MY COMPUTER THINKS I'M WASTING MY TIME WITH THESE SIMULATIONS.
FINAL CONCLUSION ON SIM NUMBER THIRTY-SEVEN: RESULTS REMAIN CONSISTENT.
MORE MODIFICATIONS REQUIRED TO ENABLE ARMOR TO WITHSTAND FULL-ON ASSAULT BY HULK.
ONLY PROBLEM IS: I'M NOT SURE ANY SUCH ANIMAL EXISTS.
R GOD TORNADO
WELL, NECESSITY IS THE MOTHER OF INVENTION. FORTUNATELY, IT'S A GOOD THING FACING HIM ALONE ISN'T A NECESSITY.
NOT WITH THE AVENGERS COVERING MY BACK.
AH. THERE'S ONE OF THEM RIGHT NOW.
THUNDER GO
TLING TORN

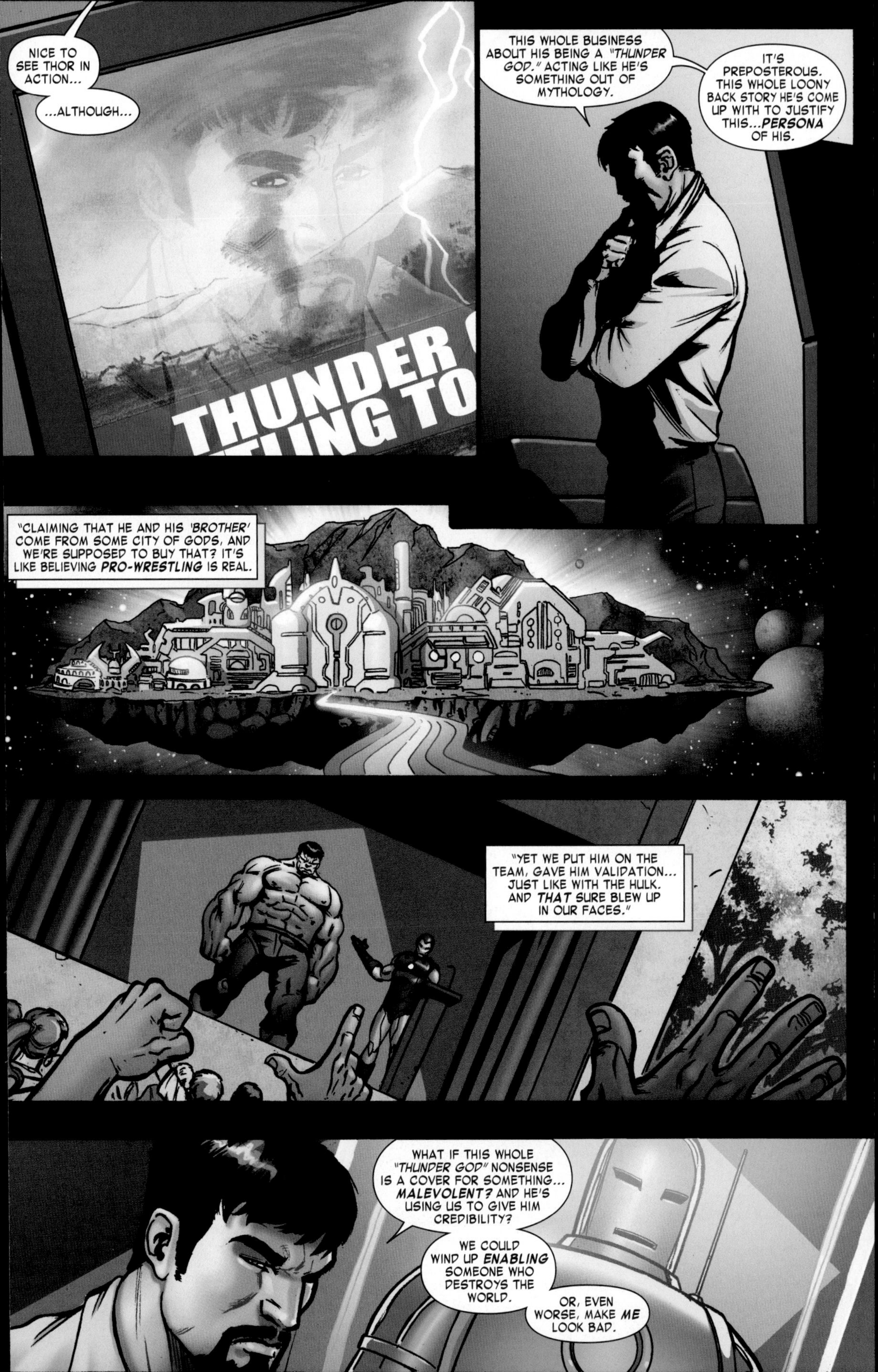
NICE TO SEE THOR IN ACTION...
...ALTHOUGH...
THUNDER
TLING TO
THIS WHOLE BUSINESS ABOUT HIS BEING A "THUNDER GOD." ACTING LIKE HE'S SOMETHING OUT OF MYTHOLOGY.
IT'S PREPOSTEROUS. THIS WHOLE LOONY BACK STORY HE'S COME UP WITH TO JUSTIFY THIS...PERSONA OF HIS.
"CLAIMING THAT HE AND HIS 'BROTHER' COME FROM SOME CITY OF GODS, AND WE'RE SUPPOSED TO BUY THAT? IT'S LIKE BELIEVING PRO-WRESTLING IS REAL.
"YET WE PUT HIM ON THE TEAM, GAVE HIM VALIDATION... JUST LIKE WITH THE HULK. AND THAT SURE BLEW UP IN OUR FACES."
WHAT IF THIS WHOLE "THUNDER GOD" NONSENSE IS A COVER FOR SOMETHING... MALEVOLENT? AND HE'S USING US TO GIVE HIM CREDIBILITY?
WE COULD WIND UP ENABLING SOMEONE WHO DESTROYS THE WORLD.
OR, EVEN WORSE, MAKE ME LOOK BAD.

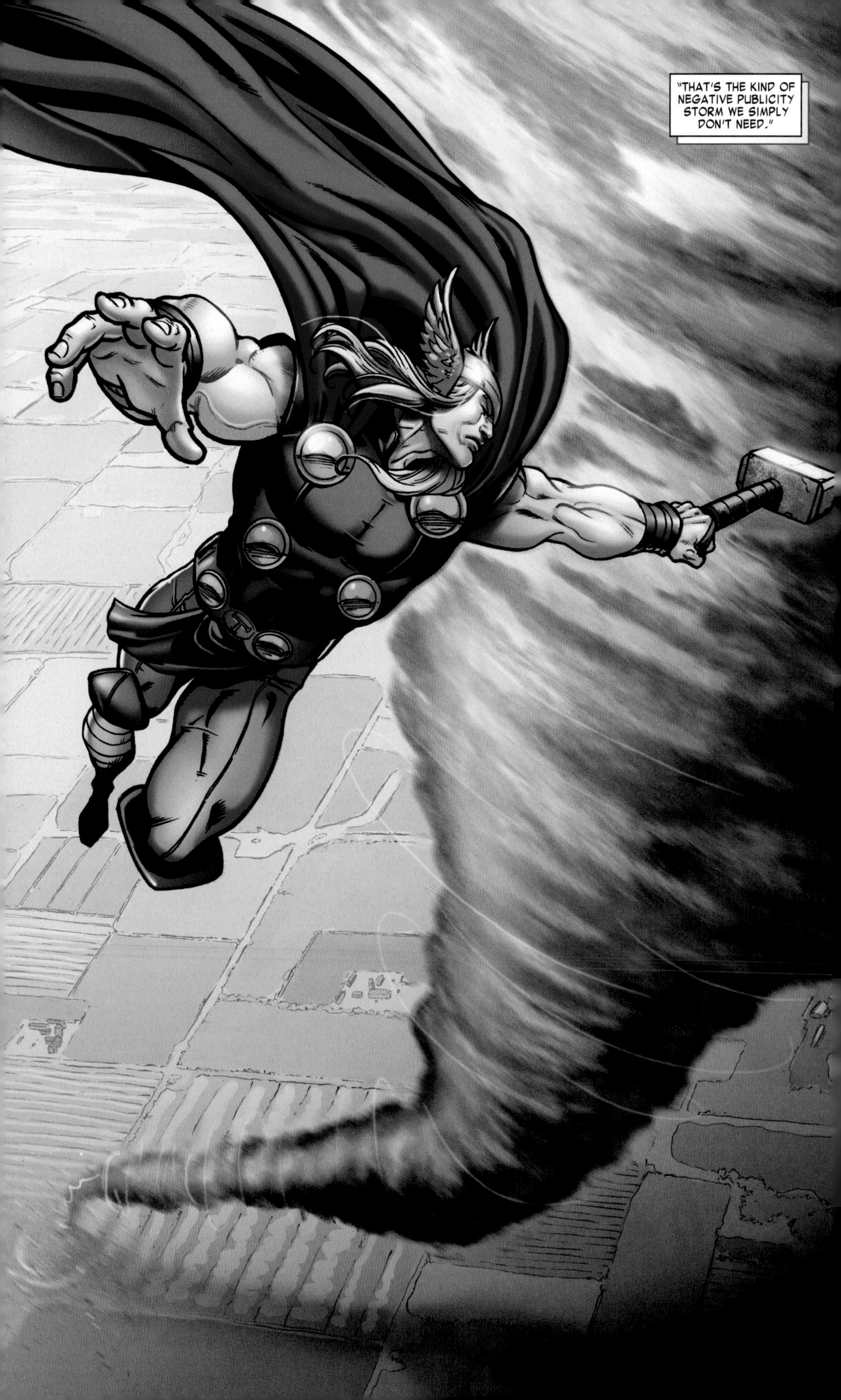
"THAT'S THE KIND OF NEGATIVE PUBLICITY STORM WE SIMPLY DON'T NEED."

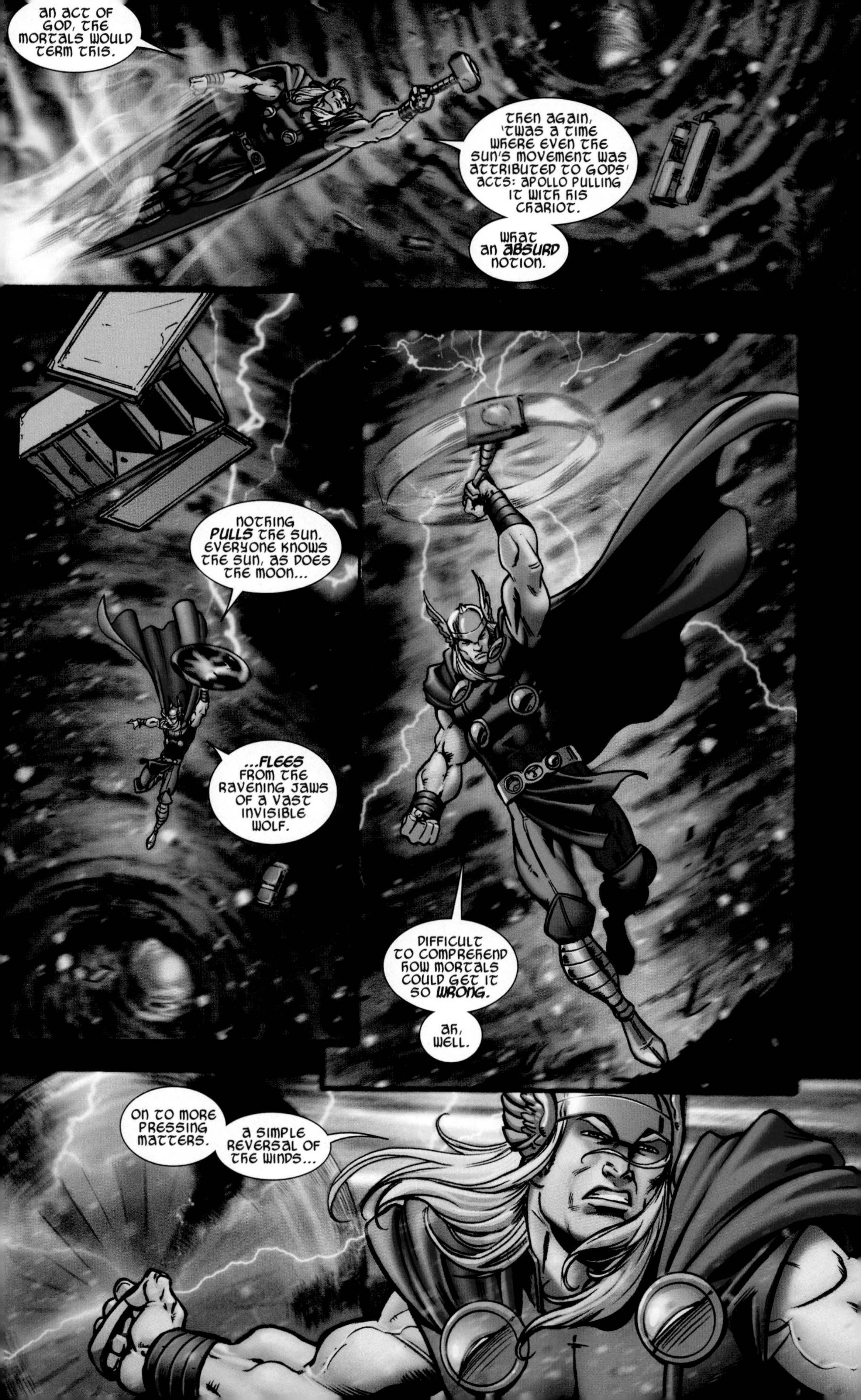
AN ACT OF GOD, THE MORTALS WOULD TERM THIS.
THEN AGAIN, 'TWAS A TIME WHERE EVEN THE SUN'S MOVEMENT WAS ATTRIBUTED TO GODS' ACTS: APOLLO PULLING IT WITH HIS CHARIOT.
WHAT AN ABSURD NOTION.
NOTHING PULLS THE SUN. EVERYONE KNOWS THE SUN, AS DOES THE MOON...
...FLEES FROM THE RAVENING JAWS OF A VAST INVISIBLE WOLF.
DIFFICULT TO COMPREHEND HOW MORTALS COULD GET IT SO WRONG.
AH, WELL.
ON TO MORE PRESSING MATTERS.
A SIMPLE REVERSAL OF THE WINDS...

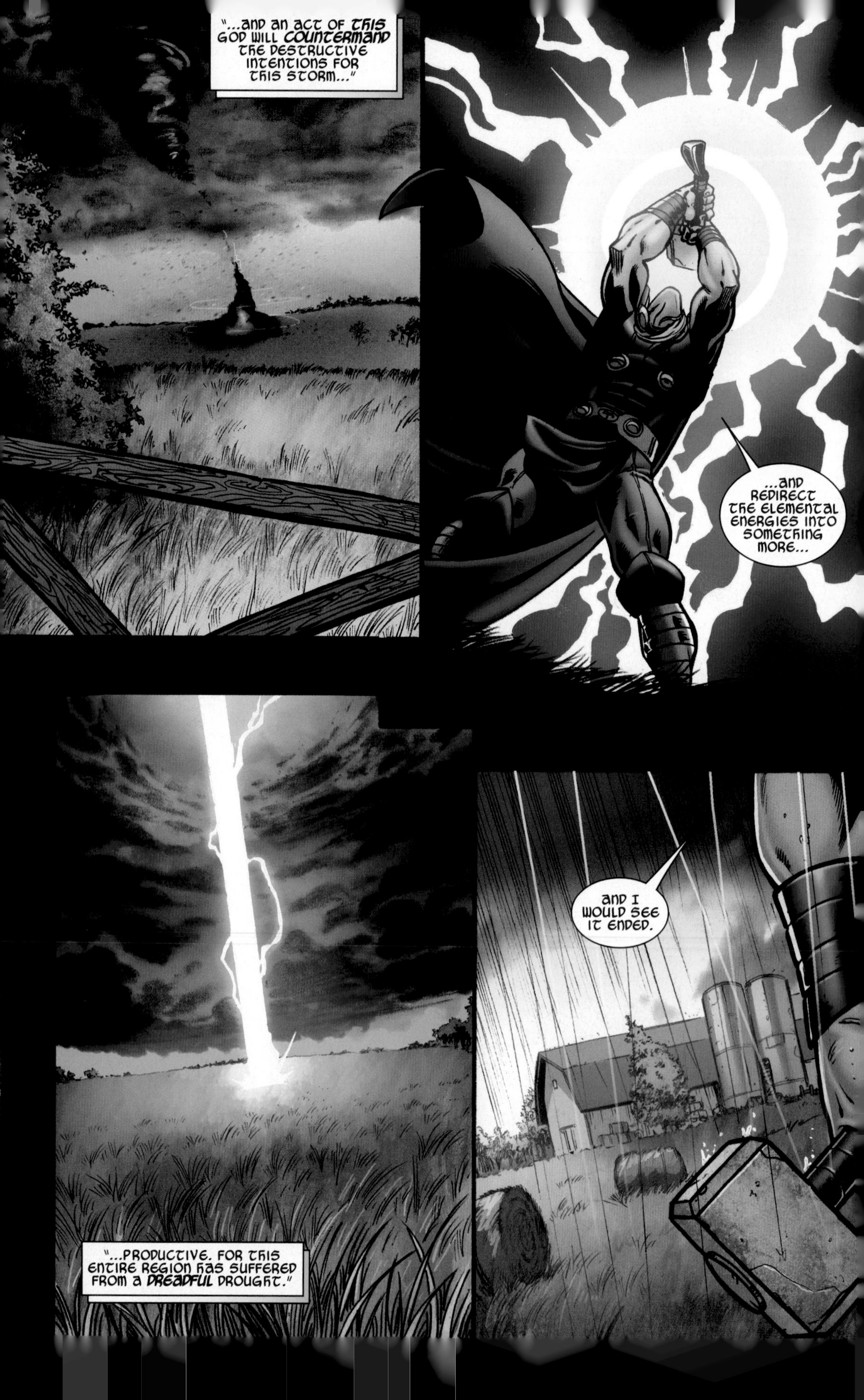
"...AND AN ACT OF THIS GOD WILL COUNTERMAND THE DESTRUCTIVE INTENTIONS FOR THIS STORM..."
...AND REDIRECT THE ELEMENTAL ENERGIES INTO SOMETHING MORE...
"...PRODUCTIVE. FOR THIS ENTIRE REGION HAS SUFFERED FROM A DREADFUL DROUGHT."
AND I WOULD SEE IT ENDED.

AN *EXCELLENT* RAIN, IF I SAY SO MYSELF.

DID...DID *YOU* DO THIS? GET RID OF THE TORNADO? MAKE IT RAIN?

YES, OLD ONE, 'TWAS I.

WE WERE HIDING DOWN IN OUR STORM CELLAR! THEN WE HEARD IT ALL JUST...JUST STOP--!

AND IMAGINE! A GOD STEPPED IN AND--!

EASY, GRANDPA. WE SHOULD GET YOU BACK INSIDE. WEATHER'S STILL ROUGH...

FORGET THAT! I COME FROM HARDY STOCK! MY DAD FOUGHT IN THE WAR TO END ALL WARS...

RAGNAROK?

AND *I* WAS IN DUBBYA DUBBYA TWO! EVEN SAW CAPTAIN AMERICA IN ACTION!

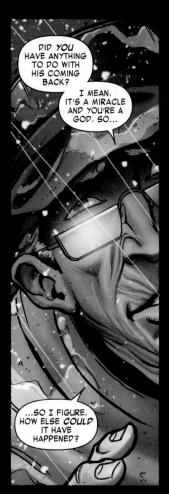

DID *YOU* HAVE ANYTHING TO DO WITH HIS COMING BACK?

I MEAN, IT'S A MIRACLE AND YOU'RE A GOD, SO...

...SO I FIGURE, HOW ELSE *COULD* IT HAVE HAPPENED?

INDEED...'TWOULD SEEM TO HAVE REQUIRED DIVINE INTERVENTION.

YOUR *PARDON*, OLD ONE. I MUST NEEDS *DEPART*.

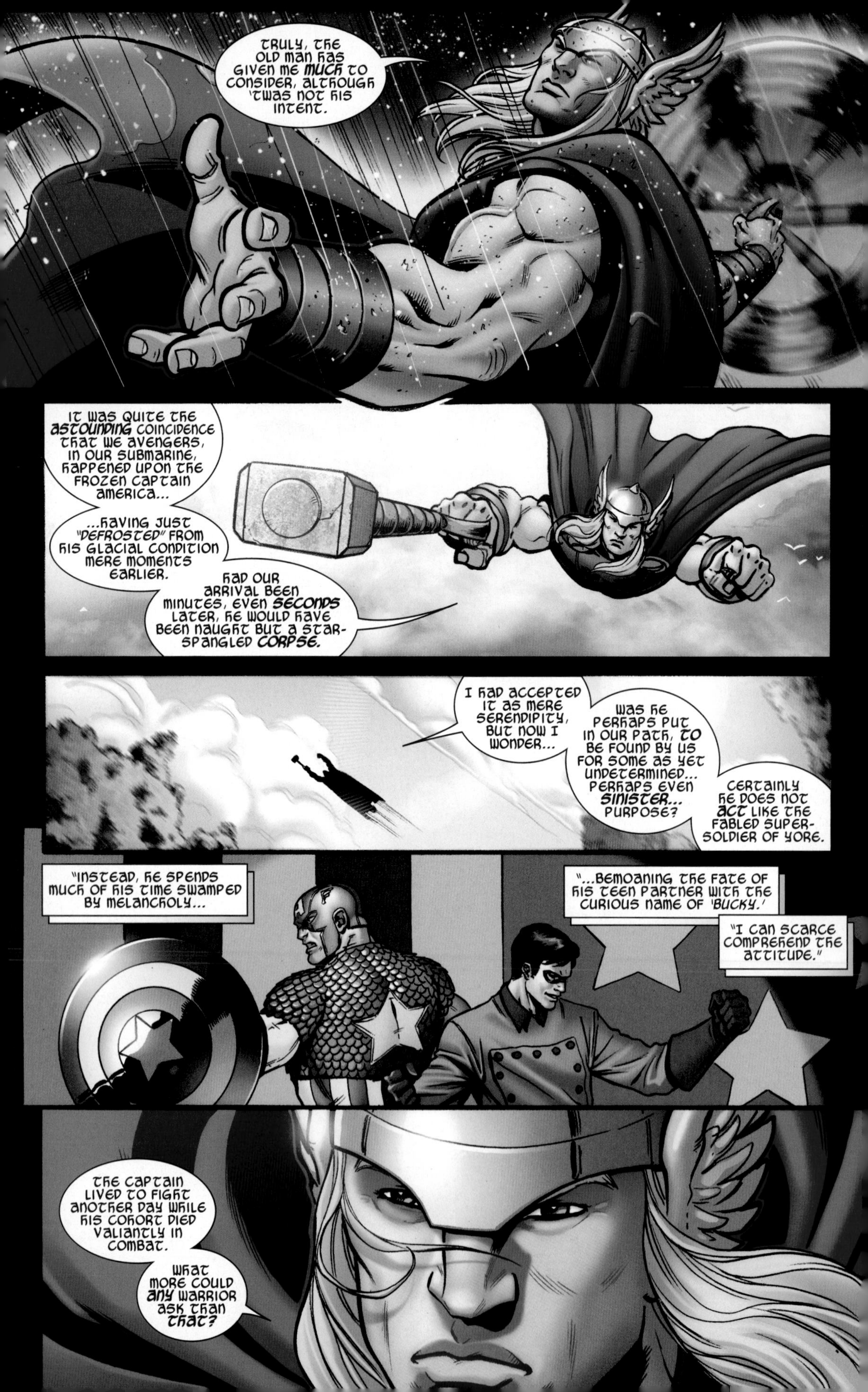
TRULY, THE OLD MAN HAS GIVEN ME MUCH TO CONSIDER, ALTHOUGH 'TWAS NOT HIS INTENT.
IT WAS QUITE THE ASTOUNDING COINCIDENCE THAT WE AVENGERS, IN OUR SUBMARINE, HAPPENED UPON THE FROZEN CAPTAIN AMERICA...
...HAVING JUST "DEFROSTED" FROM HIS GLACIAL CONDITION MERE MOMENTS EARLIER.
HAD OUR ARRIVAL BEEN MINUTES, EVEN SECONDS LATER, HE WOULD HAVE BEEN NAUGHT BUT A STAR-SPANGLED CORPSE.
I HAD ACCEPTED IT AS MERE SERENDIPITY, BUT NOW I WONDER...
WAS HE PERHAPS PUT IN OUR PATH, TO BE FOUND BY US FOR SOME AS YET UNDETERMINED... PERHAPS EVEN SINISTER... PURPOSE?
CERTAINLY HE DOES NOT ACT LIKE THE FABLED SUPER-SOLDIER OF YORE.
"INSTEAD, HE SPENDS MUCH OF HIS TIME SWAMPED BY MELANCHOLY...
"...BEMOANING THE FATE OF HIS TEEN PARTNER WITH THE CURIOUS NAME OF 'BUCKY.'
"I CAN SCARCE COMPREHEND THE ATTITUDE."
THE CAPTAIN LIVED TO FIGHT ANOTHER DAY WHILE HIS COHORT DIED VALIANTLY IN COMBAT.
WHAT MORE COULD ANY WARRIOR ASK THAN THAT?

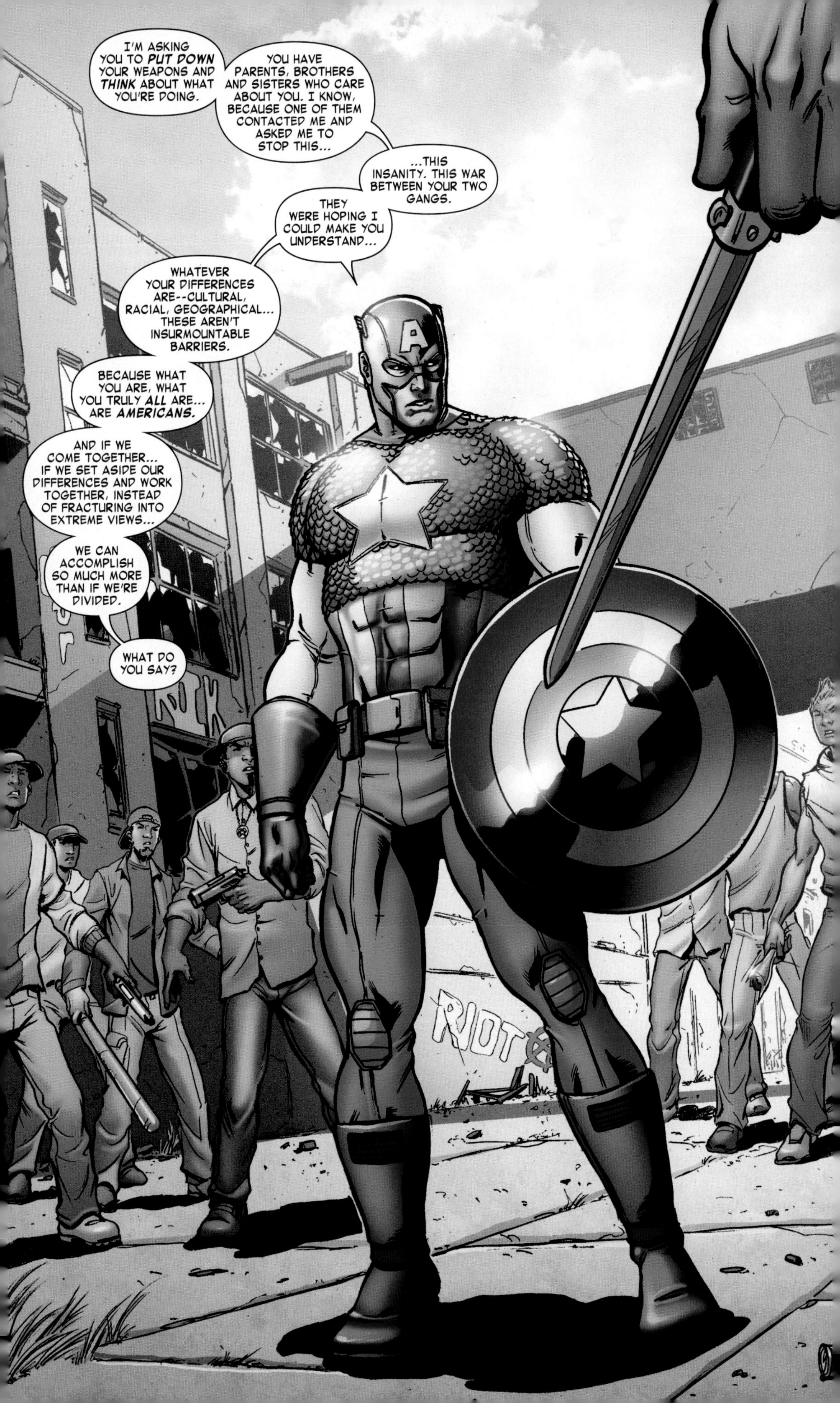
I'M ASKING YOU TO PUT DOWN YOUR WEAPONS AND THINK ABOUT WHAT YOU'RE DOING.
YOU HAVE PARENTS, BROTHERS AND SISTERS WHO CARE ABOUT YOU. I KNOW, BECAUSE ONE OF THEM CONTACTED ME AND ASKED ME TO STOP THIS...
...THIS INSANITY. THIS WAR BETWEEN YOUR TWO GANGS.
THEY WERE HOPING I COULD MAKE YOU UNDERSTAND...
WHATEVER YOUR DIFFERENCES ARE--CULTURAL, RACIAL, GEOGRAPHICAL... THESE AREN'T INSURMOUNTABLE BARRIERS.
BECAUSE WHAT YOU ARE, WHAT YOU TRULY ALL ARE... ARE AMERICANS.
AND IF WE COME TOGETHER... IF WE SET ASIDE OUR DIFFERENCES AND WORK TOGETHER, INSTEAD OF FRACTURING INTO EXTREME VIEWS...
WE CAN ACCOMPLISH SO MUCH MORE THAN IF WE'RE DIVIDED.
WHAT DO YOU SAY?
RIOT

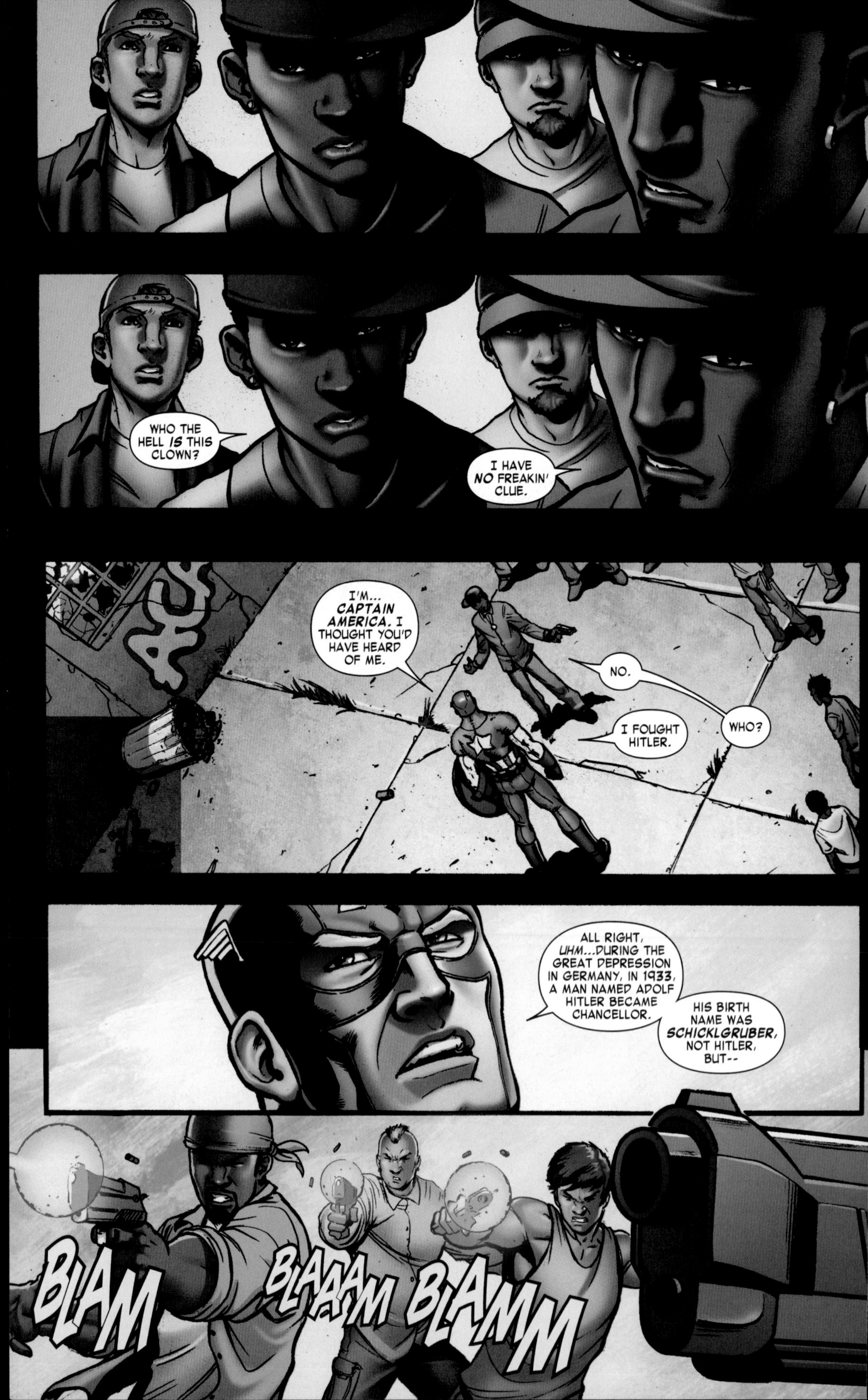
WHO THE HELL *IS* THIS CLOWN?
I HAVE *NO* FREAKIN' CLUE.
I'M... *CAPTAIN AMERICA.* I THOUGHT YOU'D HAVE HEARD OF ME.
NO.
WHO?
I FOUGHT HITLER.
ALL RIGHT, *UHM*...DURING THE GREAT DEPRESSION IN GERMANY, IN 1933, A MAN NAMED ADOLF HITLER BECAME CHANCELLOR.
HIS BIRTH NAME WAS *SCHICKLGRUBER*, NOT HITLER, BUT--
BLAM
BLAAAM
BLAMM

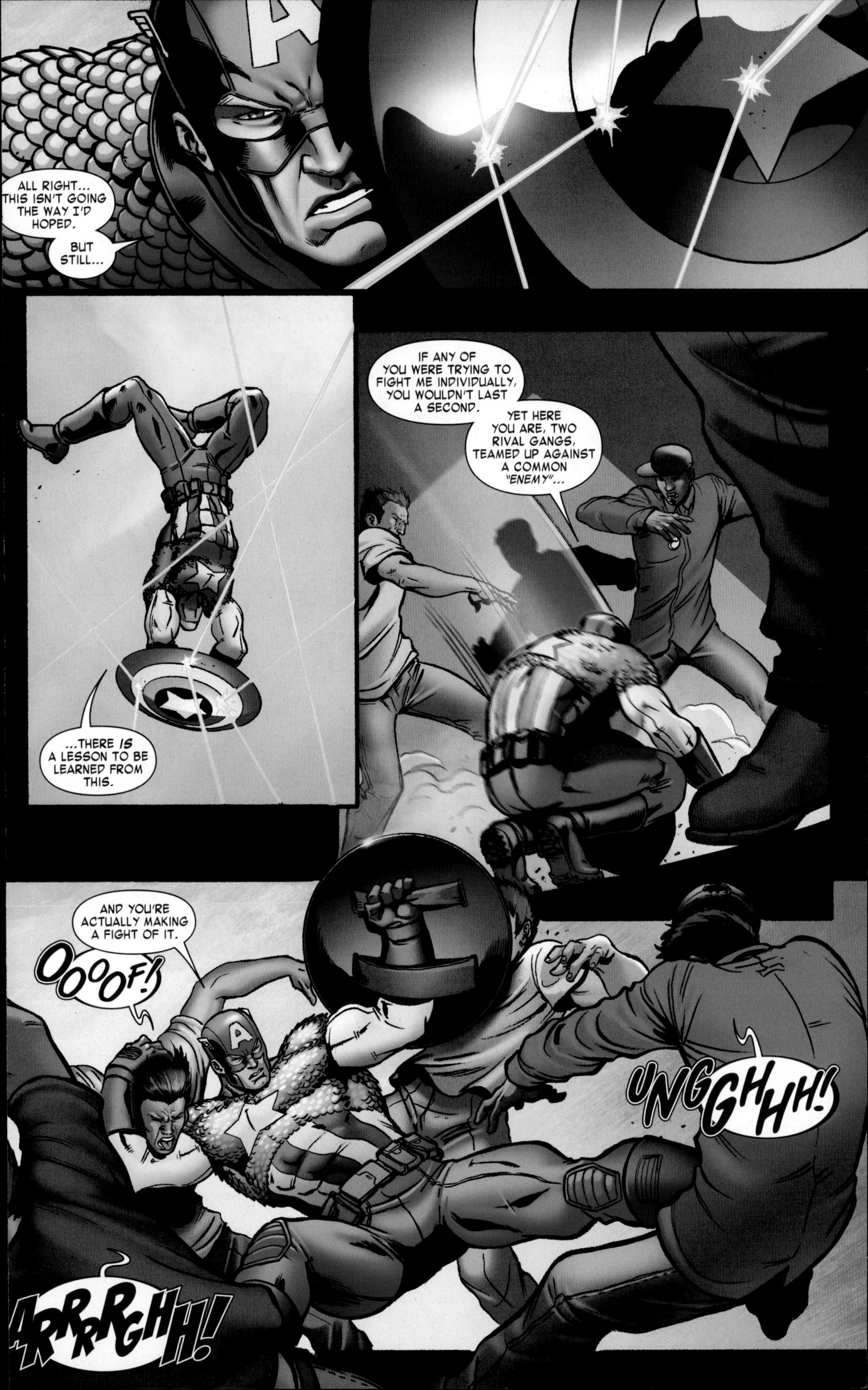
ALL RIGHT... THIS ISN'T GOING THE WAY I'D HOPED.
BUT STILL...
...THERE IS A LESSON TO BE LEARNED FROM THIS.
IF ANY OF YOU WERE TRYING TO FIGHT ME INDIVIDUALLY, YOU WOULDN'T LAST A SECOND.
YET HERE YOU ARE, TWO RIVAL GANGS, TEAMED UP AGAINST A COMMON "ENEMY"...
AND YOU'RE ACTUALLY MAKING A FIGHT OF IT.
OOOOF!
UNGGHHH!
ARRRRGHH!

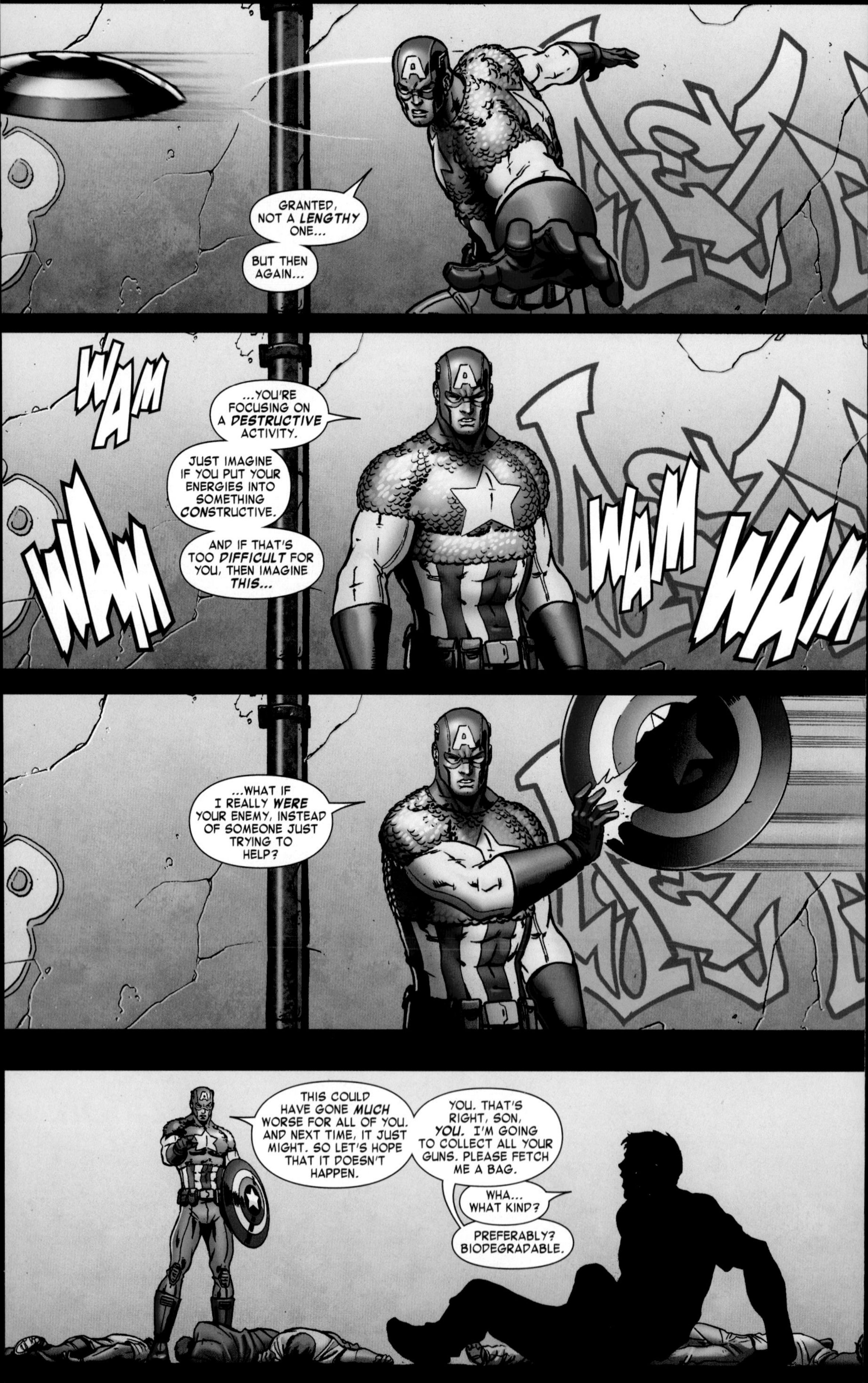
GRANTED, NOT A LENGTHY ONE...
BUT THEN AGAIN...
WAM
WAM
...YOU'RE FOCUSING ON A DESTRUCTIVE ACTIVITY.
JUST IMAGINE IF YOU PUT YOUR ENERGIES INTO SOMETHING CONSTRUCTIVE.
AND IF THAT'S TOO DIFFICULT FOR YOU, THEN IMAGINE THIS...
WAM
WAM
...WHAT IF I REALLY WERE YOUR ENEMY, INSTEAD OF SOMEONE JUST TRYING TO HELP?
THIS COULD HAVE GONE MUCH WORSE FOR ALL OF YOU. AND NEXT TIME, IT JUST MIGHT. SO LET'S HOPE THAT IT DOESN'T HAPPEN.
YOU. THAT'S RIGHT, SON, YOU. I'M GOING TO COLLECT ALL YOUR GUNS. PLEASE FETCH ME A BAG.
WHA... WHAT KIND?
PREFERABLY? BIODEGRADABLE.

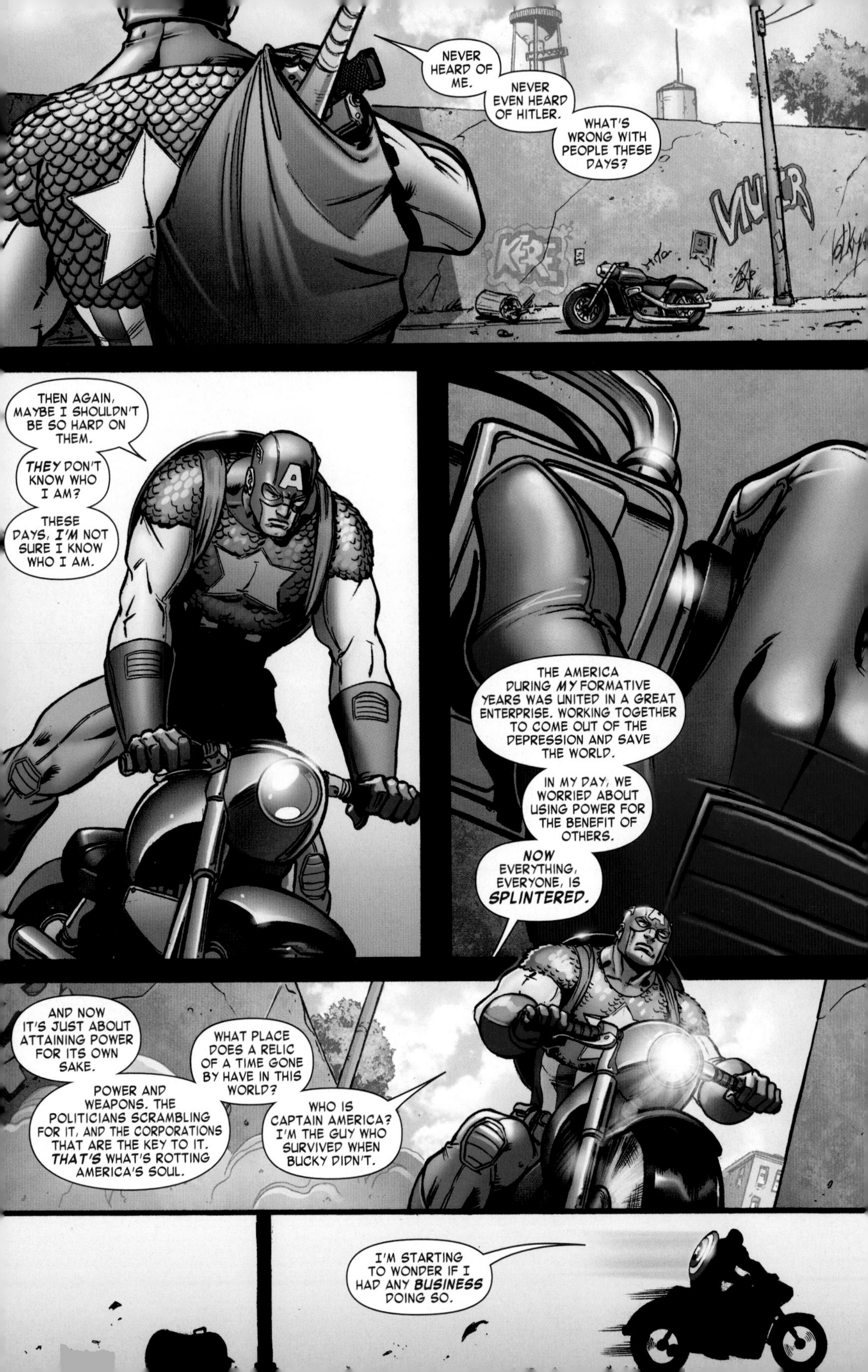

NEVER HEARD OF ME.
NEVER EVEN HEARD OF HITLER.
WHAT'S WRONG WITH PEOPLE THESE DAYS?
THEN AGAIN, MAYBE I SHOULDN'T BE SO HARD ON THEM.
THEY DON'T KNOW WHO I AM?
THESE DAYS, I'M NOT SURE I KNOW WHO I AM.
THE AMERICA DURING MY FORMATIVE YEARS WAS UNITED IN A GREAT ENTERPRISE. WORKING TOGETHER TO COME OUT OF THE DEPRESSION AND SAVE THE WORLD.
IN MY DAY, WE WORRIED ABOUT USING POWER FOR THE BENEFIT OF OTHERS.
NOW EVERYTHING, EVERYONE, IS SPLINTERED.
AND NOW IT'S JUST ABOUT ATTAINING POWER FOR ITS OWN SAKE.
POWER AND WEAPONS. THE POLITICIANS SCRAMBLING FOR IT, AND THE CORPORATIONS THAT ARE THE KEY TO IT. THAT'S WHAT'S ROTTING AMERICA'S SOUL.
WHAT PLACE DOES A RELIC OF A TIME GONE BY HAVE IN THIS WORLD?
WHO IS CAPTAIN AMERICA? I'M THE GUY WHO SURVIVED WHEN BUCKY DIDN'T.
I'M STARTING TO WONDER IF I HAD ANY BUSINESS DOING SO.

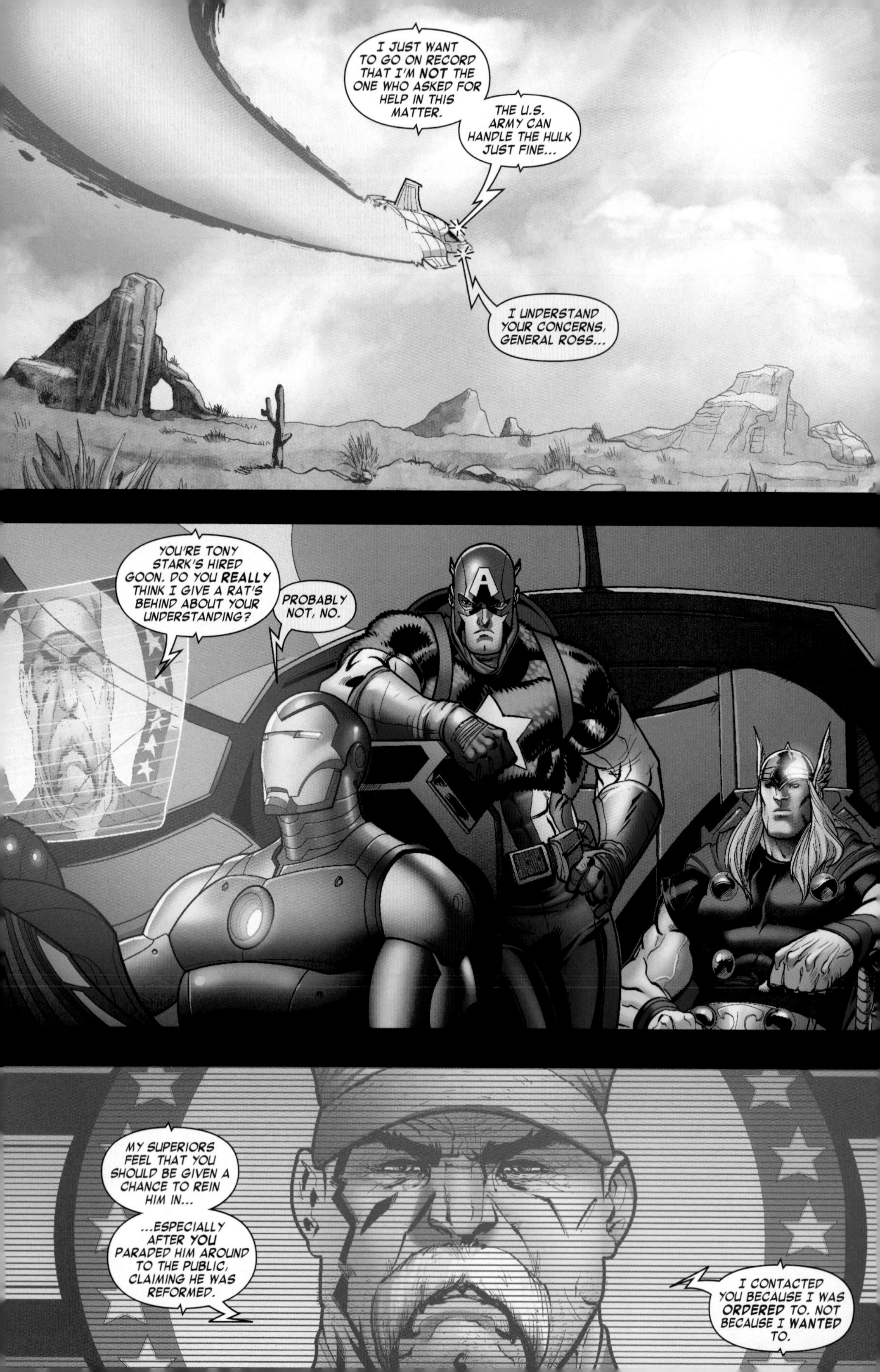
I JUST WANT TO GO ON RECORD THAT I'M NOT THE ONE WHO ASKED FOR HELP IN THIS MATTER.
THE U.S. ARMY CAN HANDLE THE HULK JUST FINE...
I UNDERSTAND YOUR CONCERNS, GENERAL ROSS...
YOU'RE TONY STARK'S HIRED GOON. DO YOU REALLY THINK I GIVE A RAT'S BEHIND ABOUT YOUR UNDERSTANDING?
PROBABLY NOT, NO.
MY SUPERIORS FEEL THAT YOU SHOULD BE GIVEN A CHANCE TO REIN HIM IN...
...ESPECIALLY AFTER YOU PARADED HIM AROUND TO THE PUBLIC, CLAIMING HE WAS REFORMED.
I CONTACTED YOU BECAUSE I WAS ORDERED TO. NOT BECAUSE I WANTED TO.

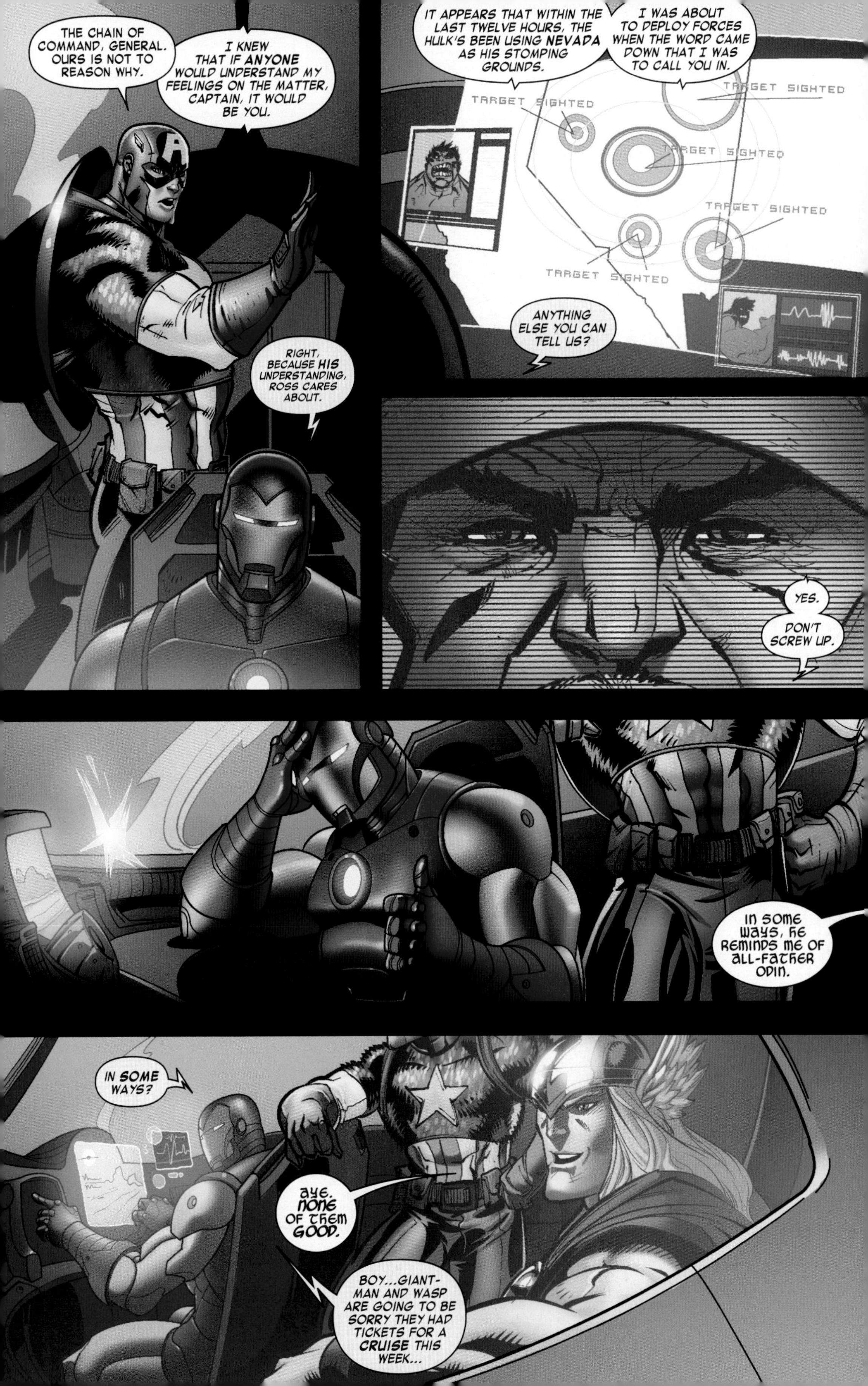
THE CHAIN OF COMMAND, GENERAL. OURS IS NOT TO REASON WHY.
I KNEW THAT IF ANYONE WOULD UNDERSTAND MY FEELINGS ON THE MATTER, CAPTAIN, IT WOULD BE YOU.
RIGHT, BECAUSE HIS UNDERSTANDING, ROSS CARES ABOUT.
IT APPEARS THAT WITHIN THE LAST TWELVE HOURS, THE HULK'S BEEN USING NEVADA AS HIS STOMPING GROUNDS.
I WAS ABOUT TO DEPLOY FORCES WHEN THE WORD CAME DOWN THAT I WAS TO CALL YOU IN.
TARGET SIGHTED
TARGET SIGHTED
TARGET SIGHTED
TARGET SIGHTED
TARGET SIGHTED
ANYTHING ELSE YOU CAN TELL US?
YES.
DON'T SCREW UP.
IN SOME WAYS, HE REMINDS ME OF ALL-FATHER ODIN.
IN SOME WAYS?
AYE. NONE OF THEM GOOD.
BOY...GIANT-MAN AND WASP ARE GOING TO BE SORRY THEY HAD TICKETS FOR A CRUISE THIS WEEK...

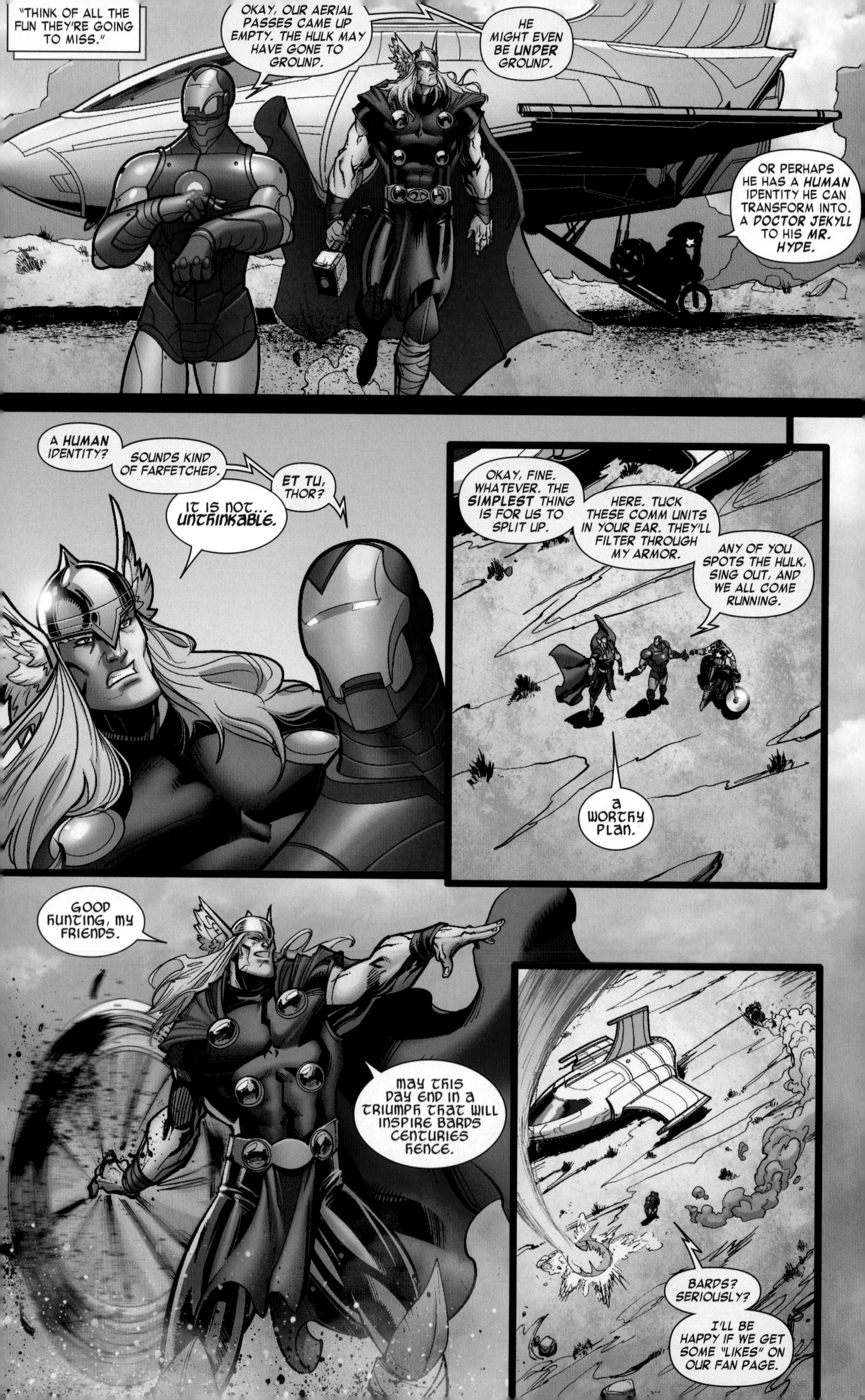
"THINK OF ALL THE FUN THEY'RE GOING TO MISS."
OKAY, OUR AERIAL PASSES CAME UP EMPTY. THE HULK MAY HAVE GONE TO GROUND.
HE MIGHT EVEN BE UNDER GROUND.
OR PERHAPS HE HAS A HUMAN IDENTITY HE CAN TRANSFORM INTO. A DOCTOR JEKYLL TO HIS MR. HYDE.
A HUMAN IDENTITY?
SOUNDS KIND OF FARFETCHED.
IT IS NOT... UNTHINKABLE.
ET TU, THOR?
OKAY, FINE. WHATEVER. THE SIMPLEST THING IS FOR US TO SPLIT UP.
HERE. TUCK THESE COMM UNITS IN YOUR EAR. THEY'LL FILTER THROUGH MY ARMOR.
ANY OF YOU SPOTS THE HULK, SING OUT, AND WE ALL COME RUNNING.
A WORTHY PLAN.
GOOD HUNTING, MY FRIENDS.
MAY THIS DAY END IN A TRIUMPH THAT WILL INSPIRE BARDS CENTURIES HENCE.
BARDS? SERIOUSLY?
I'LL BE HAPPY IF WE GET SOME "LIKES" ON OUR FAN PAGE.

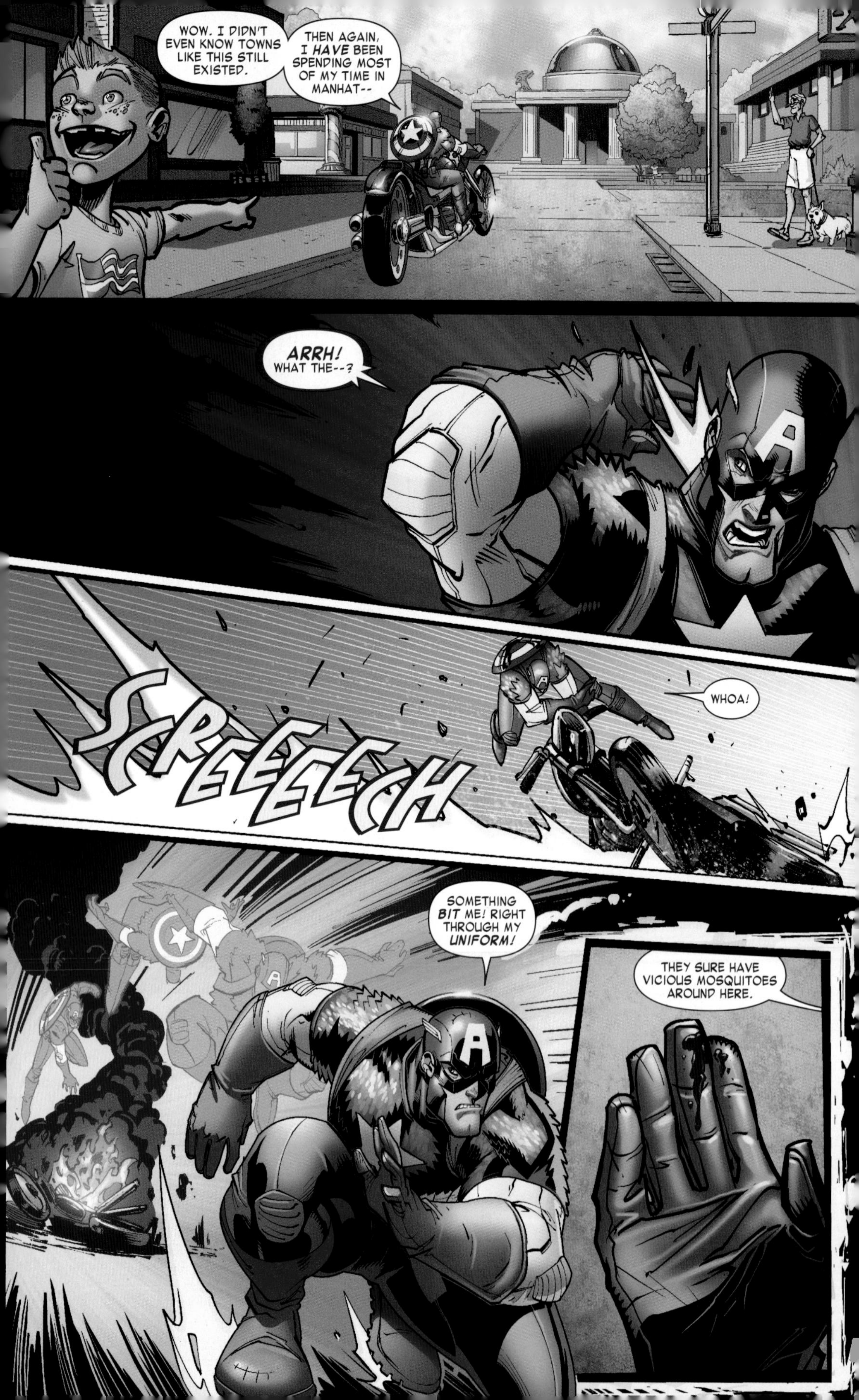
WOW. I DIDN'T EVEN KNOW TOWNS LIKE THIS STILL EXISTED.
THEN AGAIN, I *HAVE* BEEN SPENDING MOST OF MY TIME IN MANHAT--
ARRH! WHAT THE--?
SCREEEECH
WHOA!
SOMETHING *BIT* ME! RIGHT THROUGH MY *UNIFORM!*
THEY SURE HAVE VICIOUS MOSQUITOES AROUND HERE.

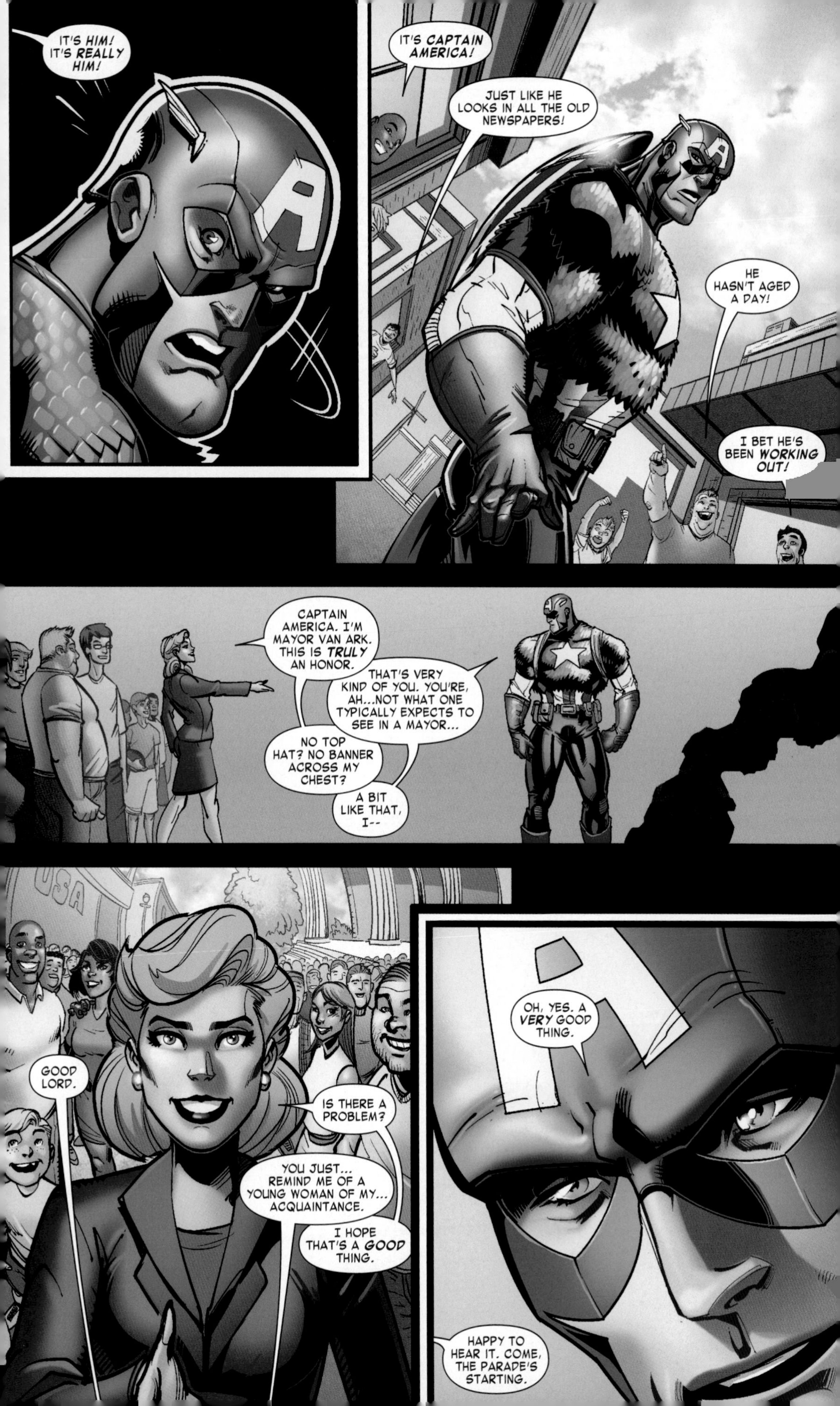

IT'S HIM! IT'S REALLY HIM!
IT'S CAPTAIN AMERICA!
JUST LIKE HE LOOKS IN ALL THE OLD NEWSPAPERS!
HE HASN'T AGED A DAY!
I BET HE'S BEEN WORKING OUT!
CAPTAIN AMERICA. I'M MAYOR VAN ARK. THIS IS TRULY AN HONOR.
THAT'S VERY KIND OF YOU. YOU'RE, AH...NOT WHAT ONE TYPICALLY EXPECTS TO SEE IN A MAYOR...
NO TOP HAT? NO BANNER ACROSS MY CHEST?
A BIT LIKE THAT, I--
GOOD LORD.
IS THERE A PROBLEM?
YOU JUST... REMIND ME OF A YOUNG WOMAN OF MY... ACQUAINTANCE.
I HOPE THAT'S A GOOD THING.
OH, YES. A VERY GOOD THING.
HAPPY TO HEAR IT. COME, THE PARADE'S STARTING.

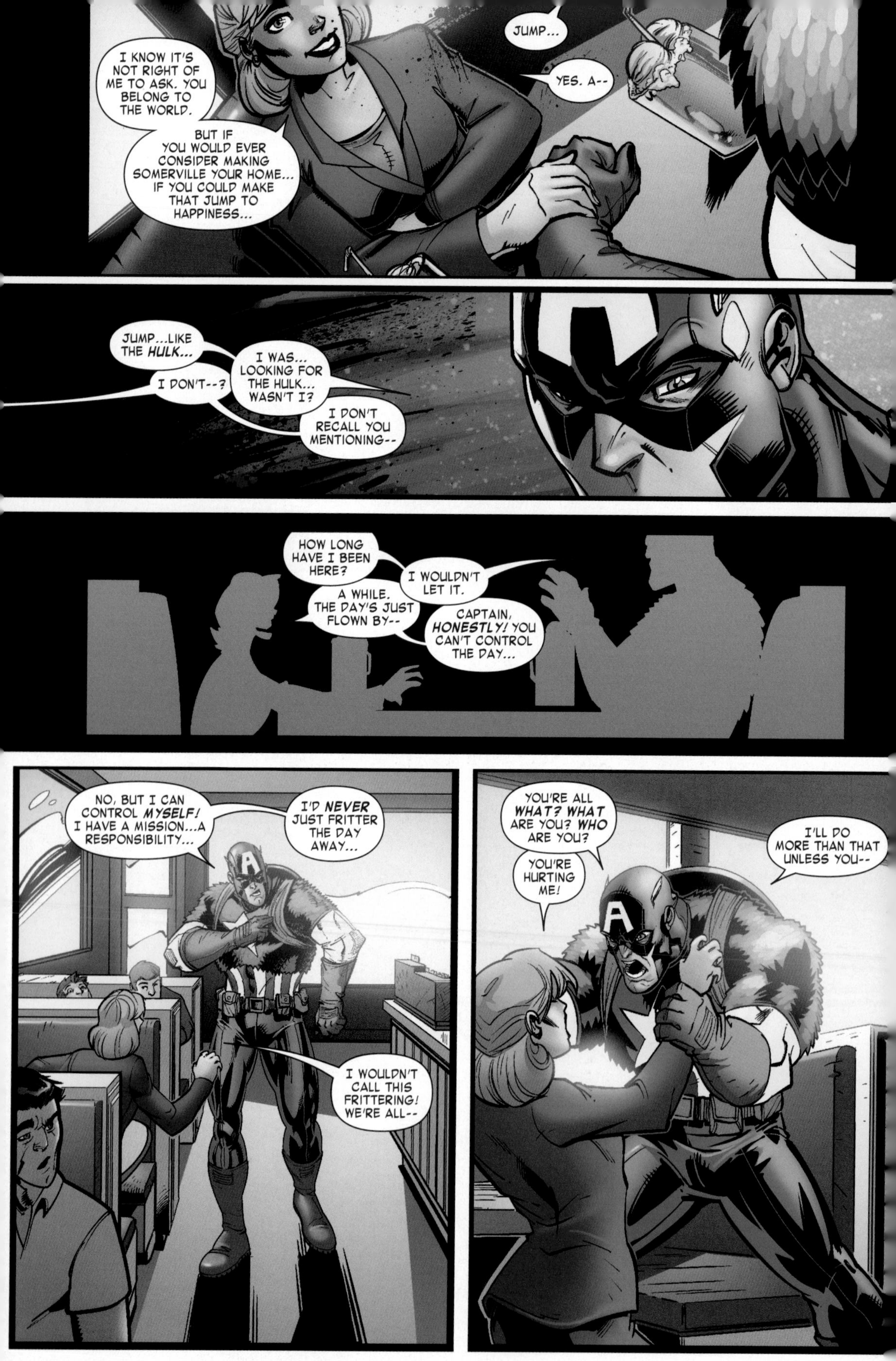
I KNOW IT'S NOT RIGHT OF ME TO ASK. YOU BELONG TO THE WORLD.
BUT IF YOU WOULD EVER CONSIDER MAKING SOMERVILLE YOUR HOME... IF YOU COULD MAKE THAT JUMP TO HAPPINESS...
JUMP...
YES. A--
JUMP...LIKE THE *HULK*...
I WAS... LOOKING FOR THE HULK... WASN'T I?
I DON'T--?
I DON'T RECALL YOU MENTIONING--
HOW LONG HAVE I BEEN HERE?
A WHILE. THE DAY'S JUST FLOWN BY--
I WOULDN'T LET IT.
CAPTAIN, *HONESTLY!* YOU CAN'T CONTROL THE DAY...
NO, BUT I CAN CONTROL *MYSELF!* I HAVE A MISSION...A RESPONSIBILITY...
I'D *NEVER* JUST FRITTER THE DAY AWAY...
I WOULDN'T CALL THIS FRITTERING! WE'RE ALL--
YOU'RE ALL *WHAT? WHAT* ARE YOU? *WHO* ARE YOU?
YOU'RE HURTING ME!
I'LL DO MORE THAN THAT UNLESS YOU--

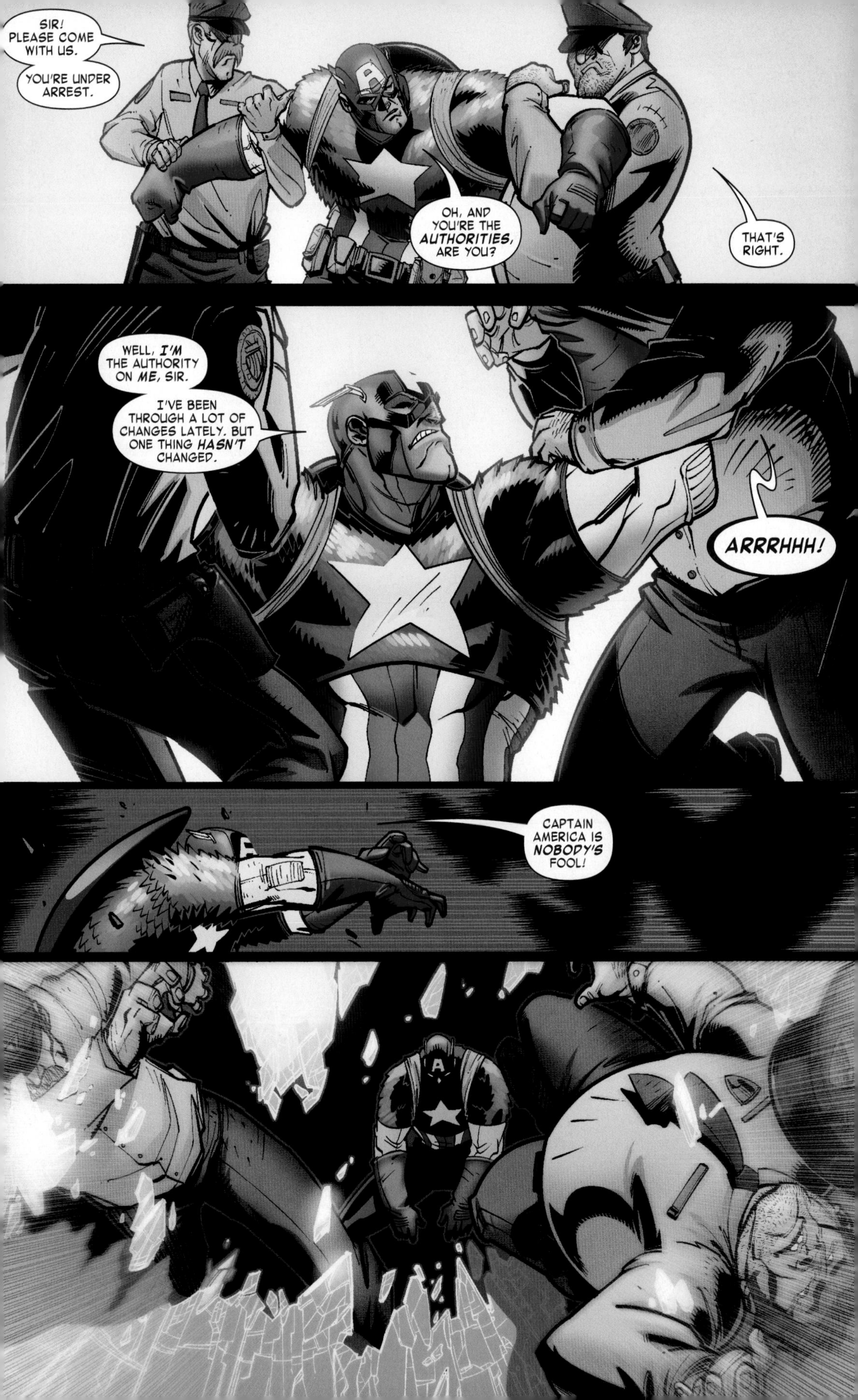
SIR! PLEASE COME WITH US.
YOU'RE UNDER ARREST.
OH, AND YOU'RE THE AUTHORITIES, ARE YOU?
THAT'S RIGHT.
WELL, I'M THE AUTHORITY ON ME, SIR.
I'VE BEEN THROUGH A LOT OF CHANGES LATELY. BUT ONE THING HASN'T CHANGED.
ARRRHHH!
CAPTAIN AMERICA IS NOBODY'S FOOL!

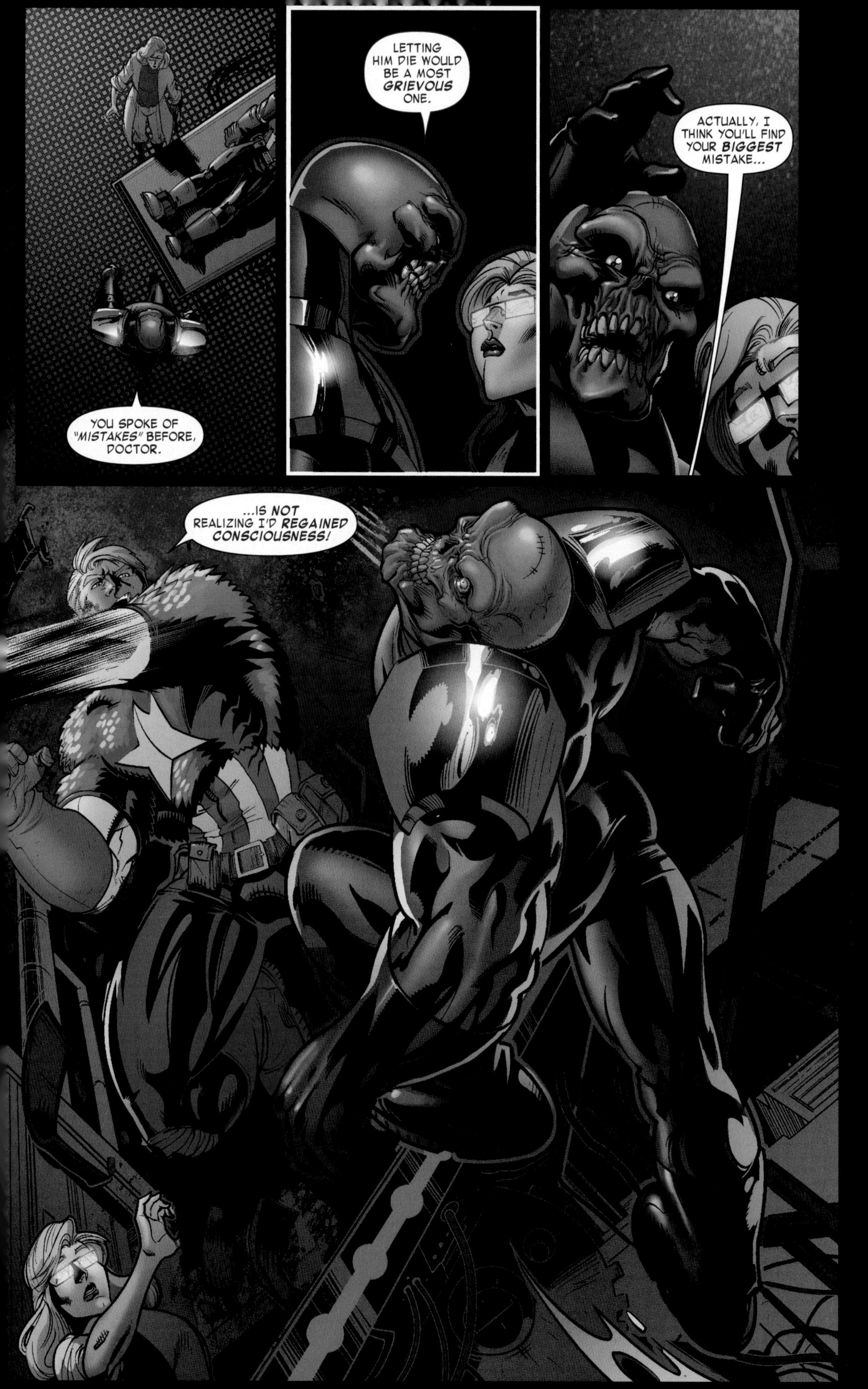
YOU SPOKE OF "MISTAKES" BEFORE, DOCTOR.
LETTING HIM DIE WOULD BE A MOST GRIEVOUS ONE.
ACTUALLY, I THINK YOU'LL FIND YOUR BIGGEST MISTAKE...
...IS NOT REALIZING I'D REGAINED CONSCIOUSNESS!

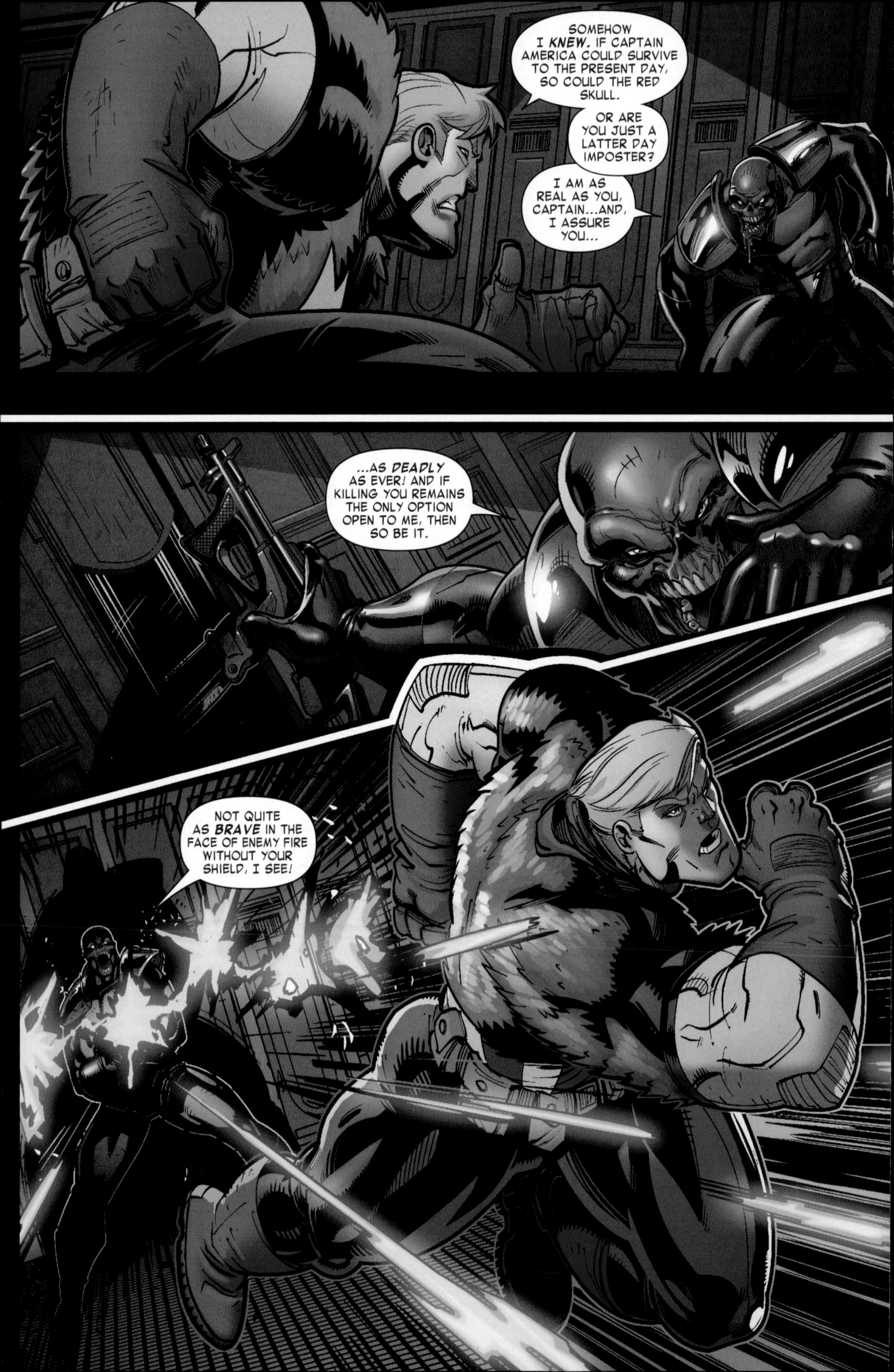
SOMEHOW I *KNEW.* IF CAPTAIN AMERICA COULD SURVIVE TO THE PRESENT DAY, SO COULD THE RED SKULL.
OR ARE YOU JUST A LATTER DAY IMPOSTER?
I AM AS REAL AS YOU, CAPTAIN...AND, I ASSURE YOU...
...AS *DEADLY* AS EVER! AND IF KILLING YOU REMAINS THE ONLY OPTION OPEN TO ME, THEN SO BE IT.
NOT QUITE AS *BRAVE* IN THE FACE OF ENEMY FIRE WITHOUT YOUR SHIELD, I SEE!

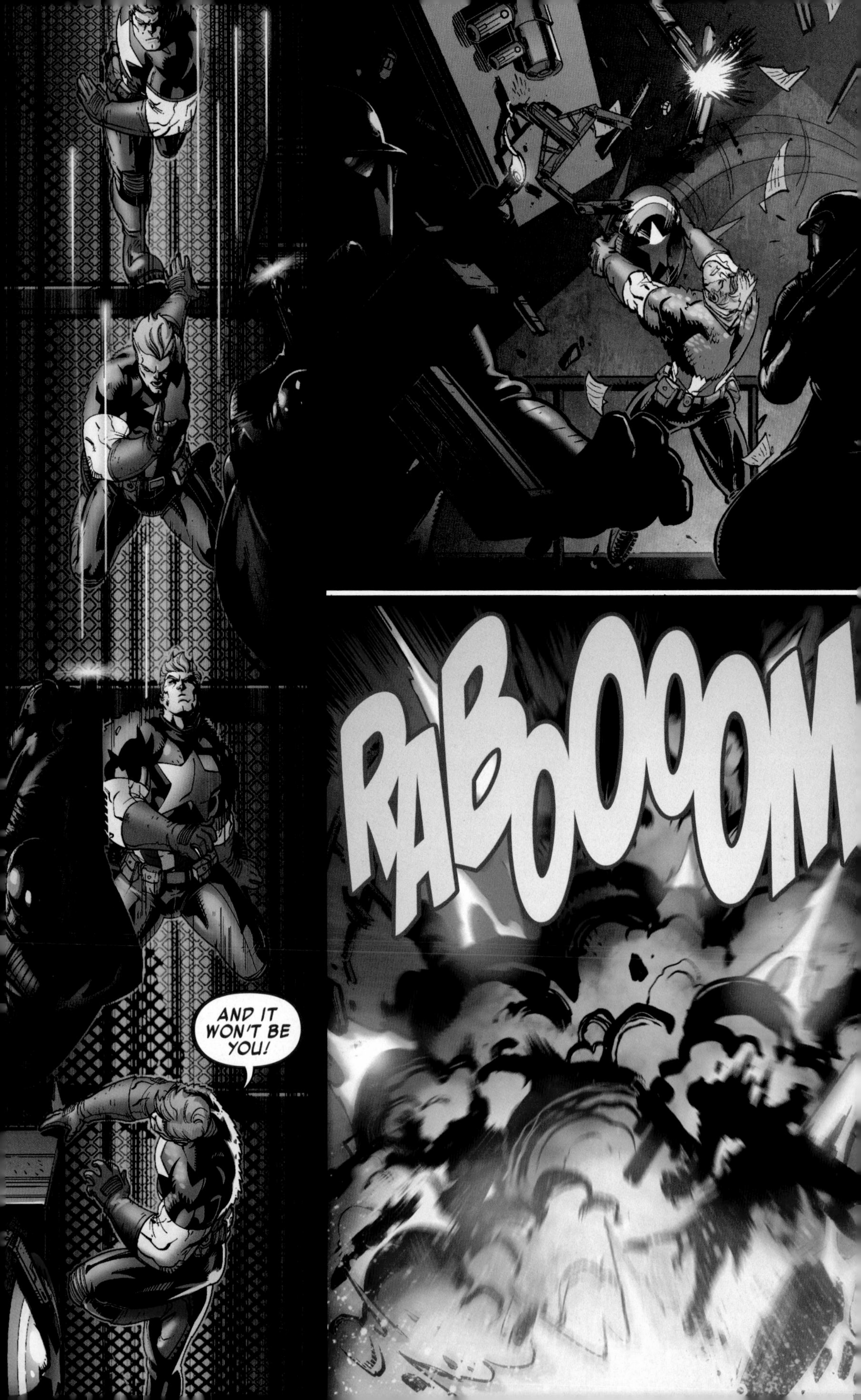
AND IT WON'T BE YOU!
RABOOOOM

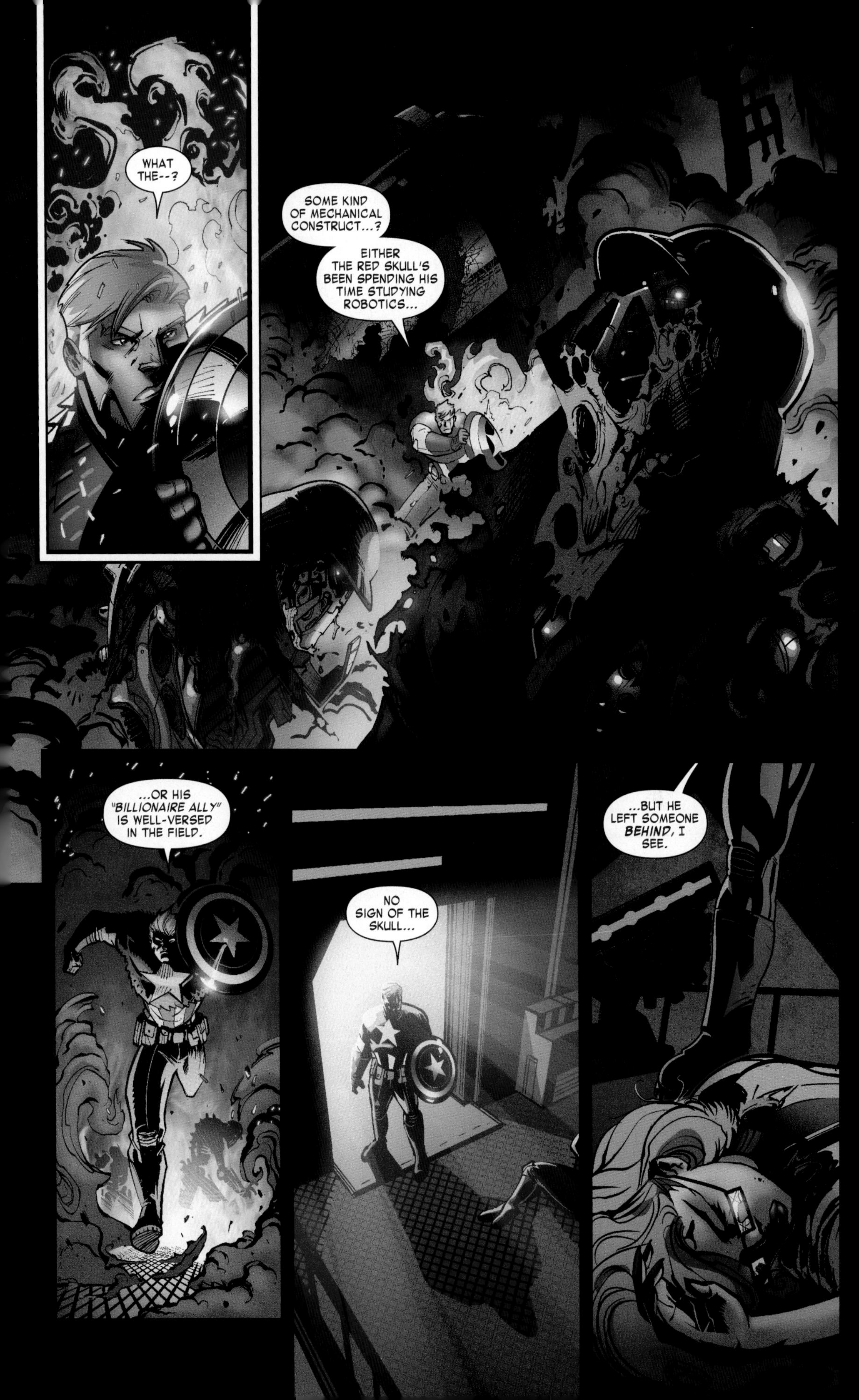
WHAT THE--?
SOME KIND OF MECHANICAL CONSTRUCT...?
EITHER THE RED SKULL'S BEEN SPENDING HIS TIME STUDYING ROBOTICS...
...OR HIS "BILLIONAIRE ALLY" IS WELL-VERSED IN THE FIELD.
NO SIGN OF THE SKULL...
...BUT HE LEFT SOMEONE BEHIND, I SEE.

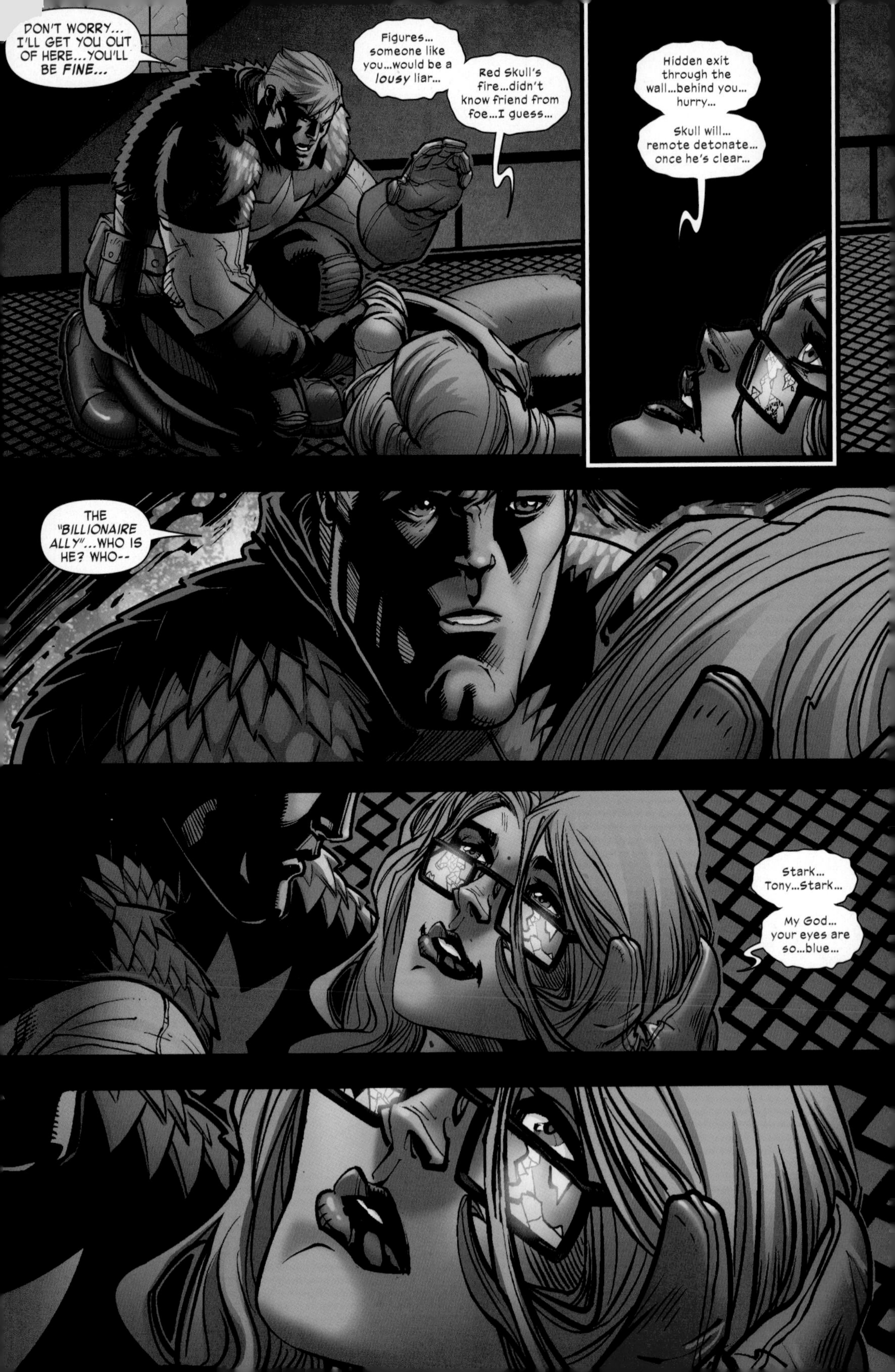
DON'T WORRY... I'LL GET YOU OUT OF HERE...YOU'LL BE FINE...
Figures... someone like you...would be a lousy liar...
Red Skull's fire...didn't know friend from foe...I guess...
Hidden exit through the wall...behind you... hurry...
Skull will... remote detonate... once he's clear...
THE "BILLIONAIRE ALLY"...WHO IS HE? WHO--
Stark... Tony...Stark...
My God... your eyes are so...blue...

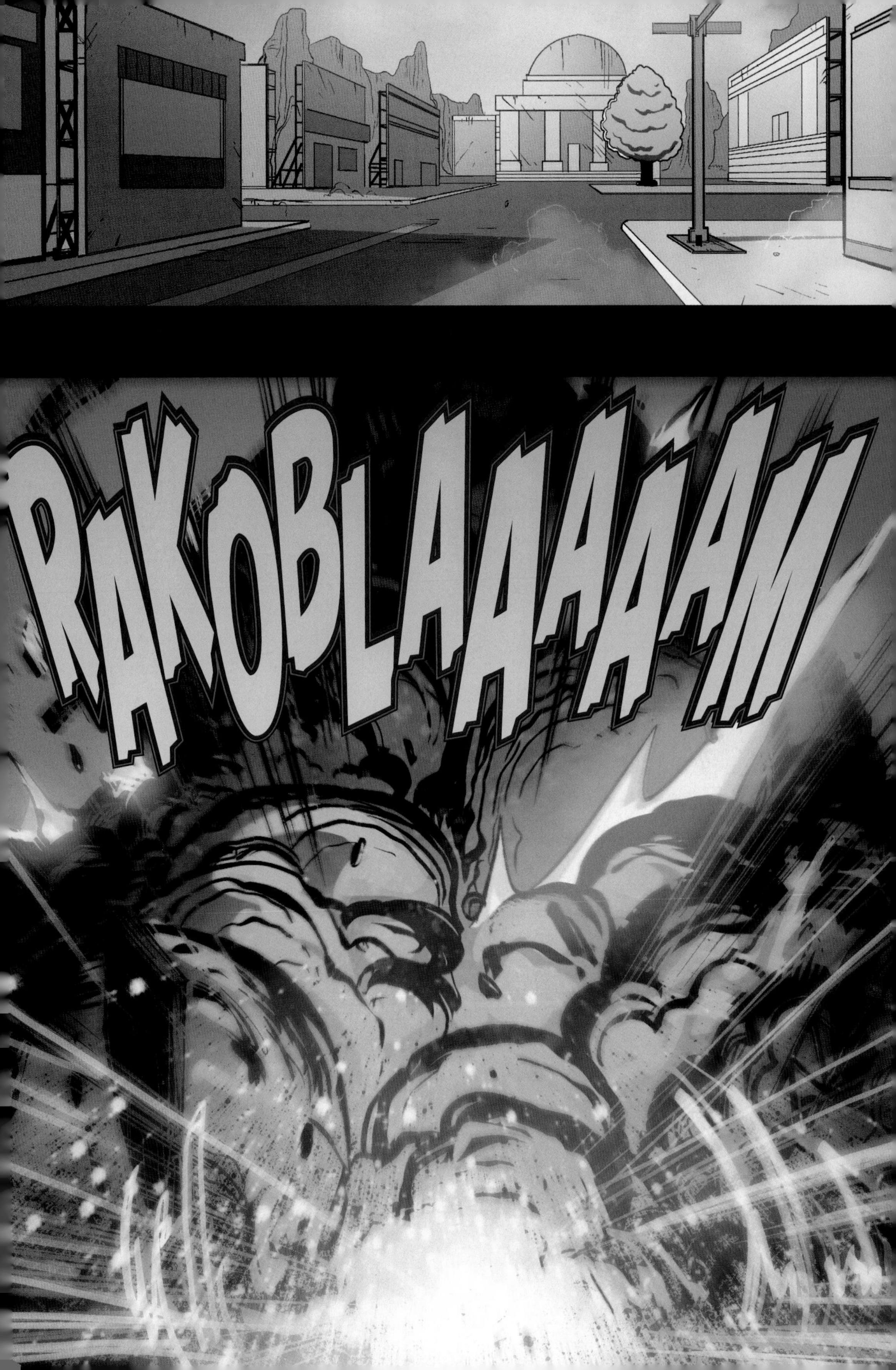
RAKOBLAAAAM

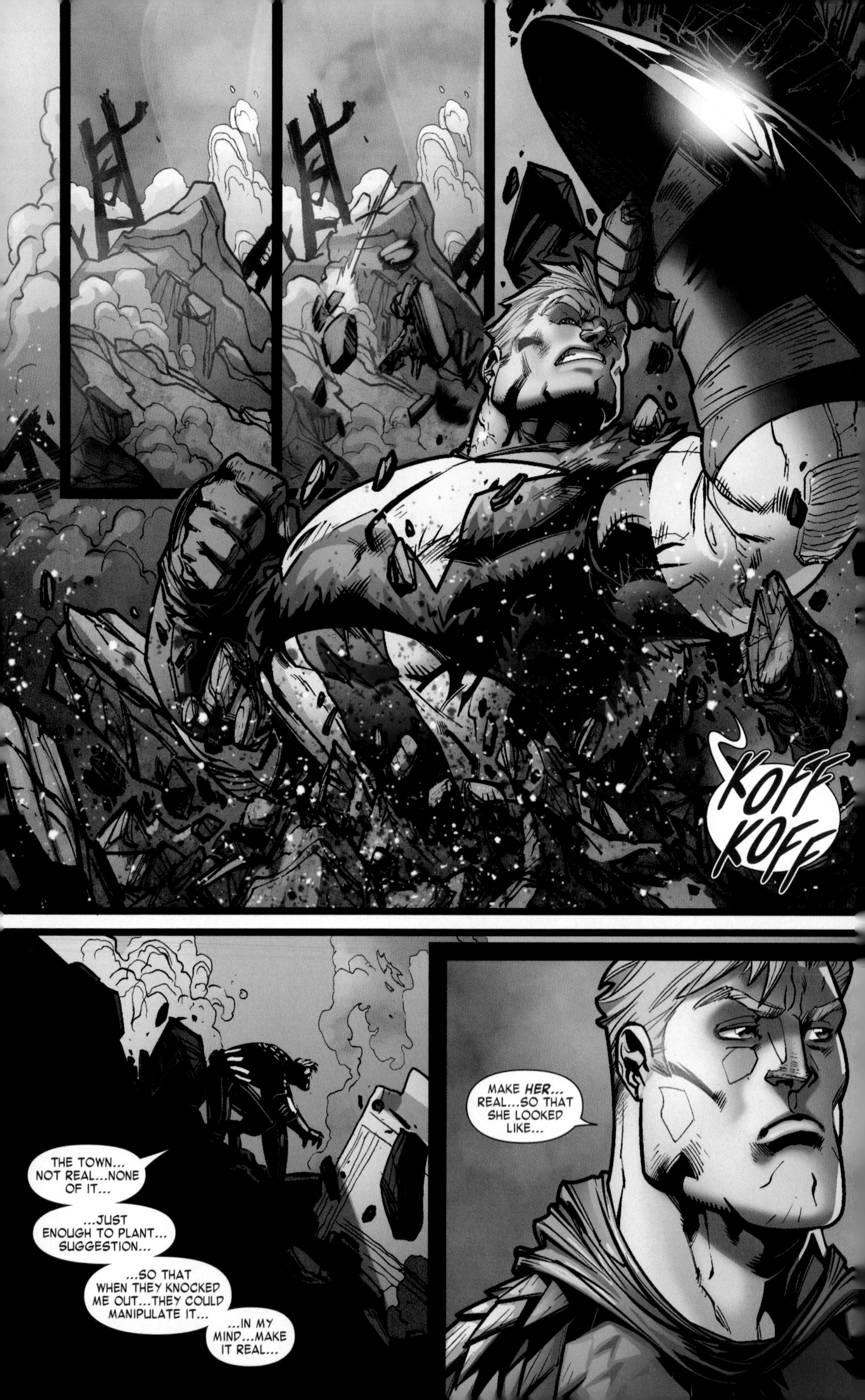
KOFF KOFF
THE TOWN... NOT REAL...NONE OF IT...
...JUST ENOUGH TO PLANT... SUGGESTION...
...SO THAT WHEN THEY KNOCKED ME OUT...THEY COULD MANIPULATE IT...
...IN MY MIND...MAKE IT REAL...
MAKE HER... REAL...SO THAT SHE LOOKED LIKE...

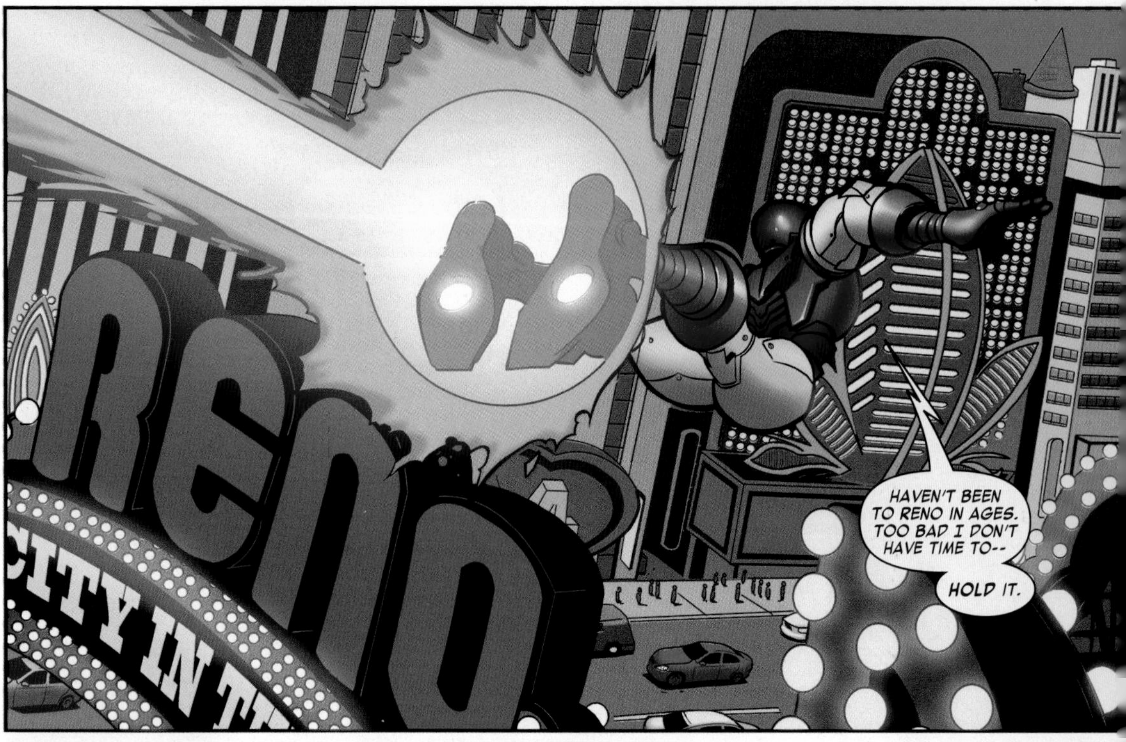
RENO
CITY IN TH
HAVEN'T BEEN TO RENO IN AGES. TOO BAD I DON'T HAVE TIME TO--
HOLD IT.

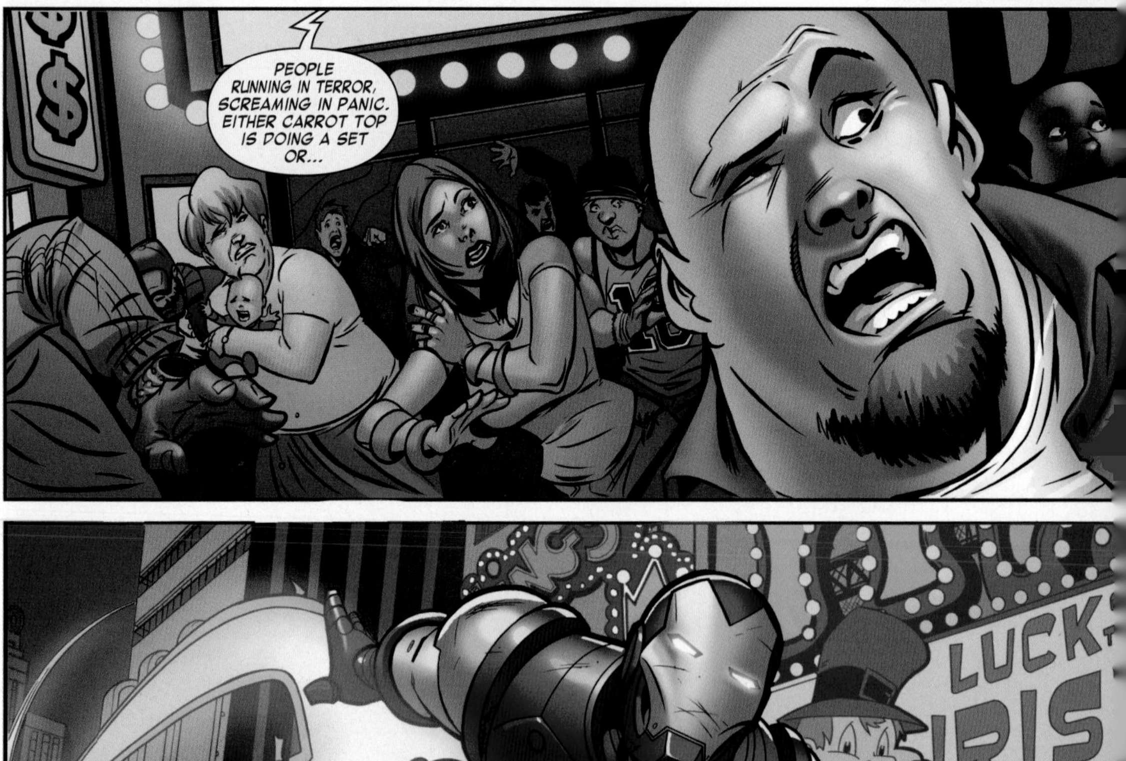
PEOPLE RUNNING IN TERROR, SCREAMING IN PANIC. EITHER CARROT TOP IS DOING A SET OR...

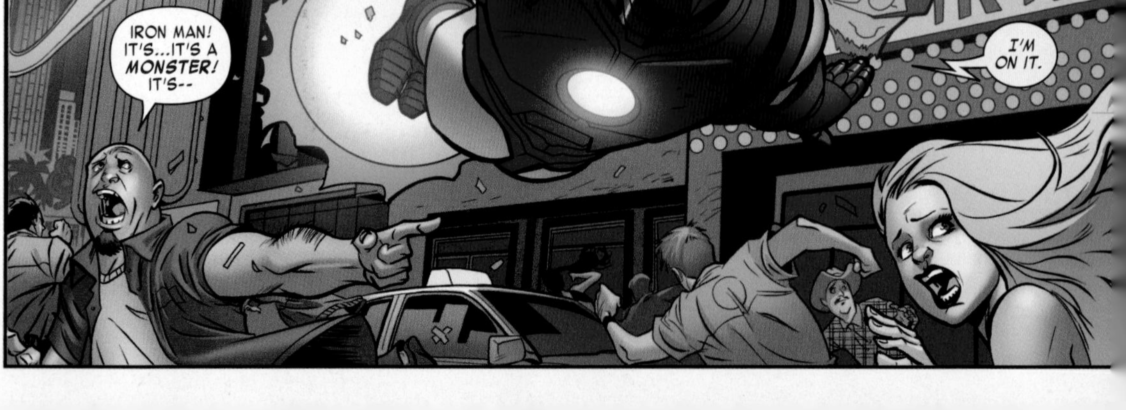
LUCK
IRIS
IRON MAN! IT'S...IT'S A MONSTER! IT'S--
I'M ON IT.

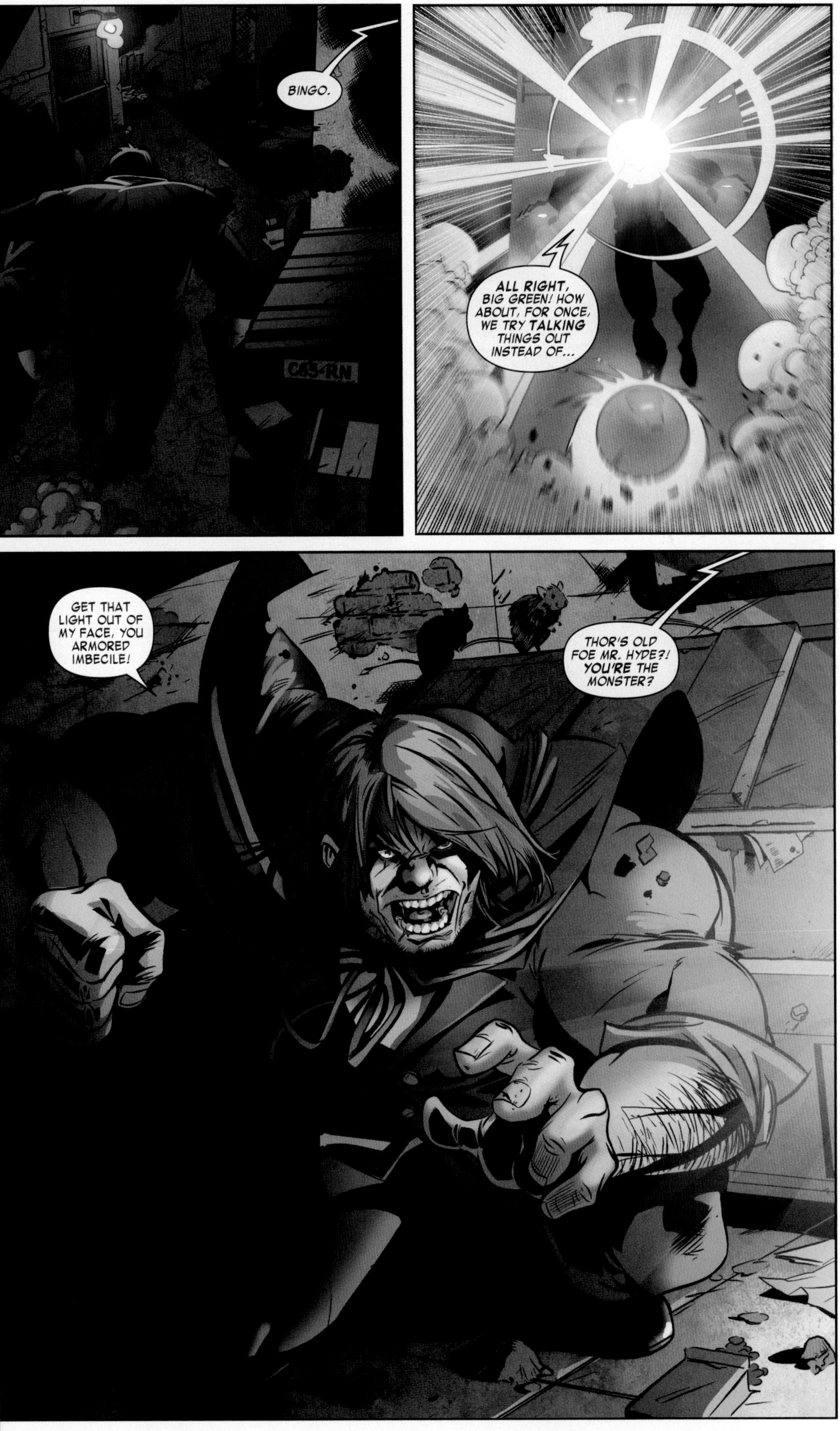
BINGO.
ALL RIGHT, BIG GREEN! HOW ABOUT, FOR ONCE, WE TRY TALKING THINGS OUT INSTEAD OF...
GET THAT LIGHT OUT OF MY FACE, YOU ARMORED IMBECILE!
THOR'S OLD FOE MR. HYDE?! YOU'RE THE MONSTER?

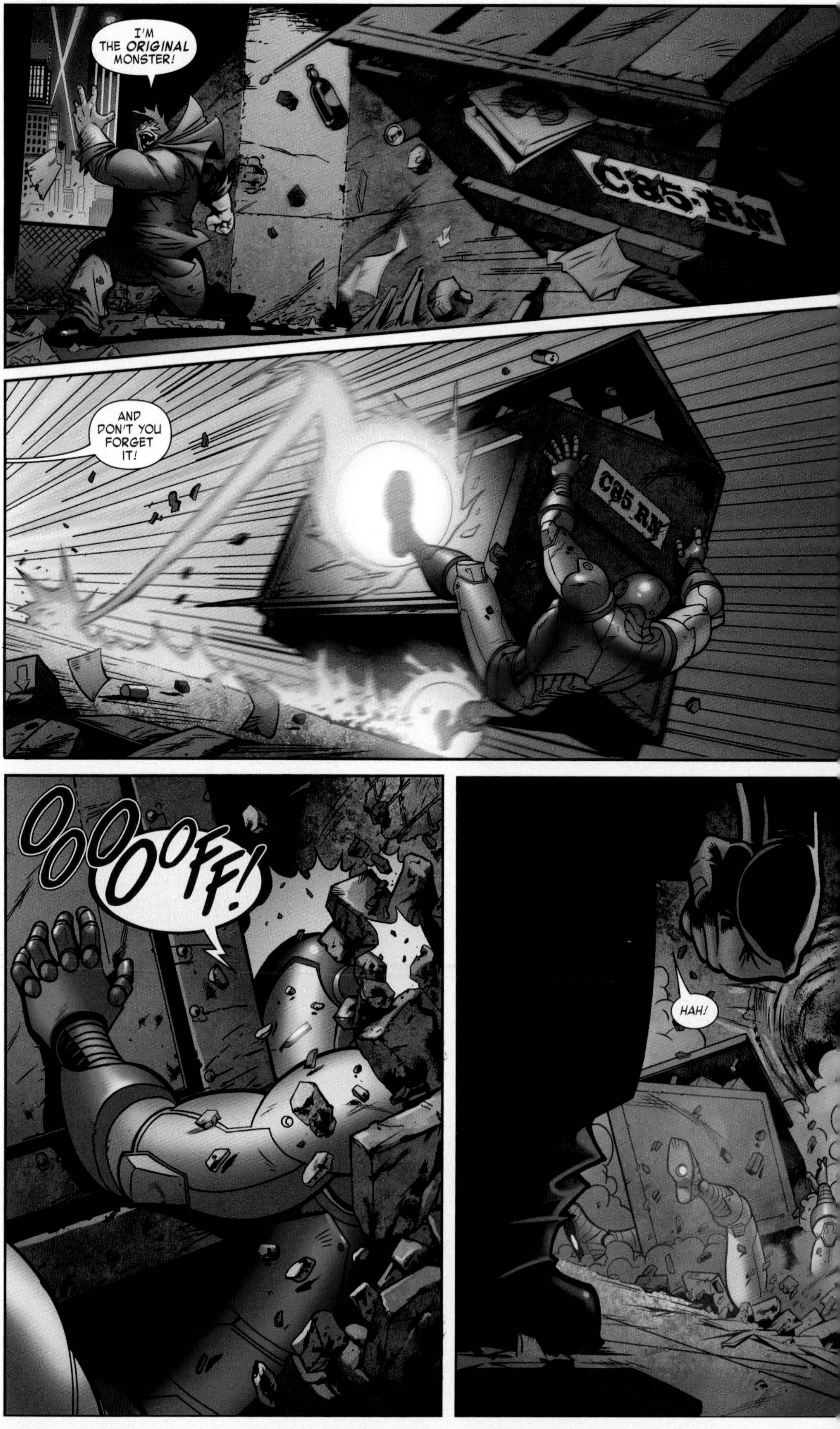
I'M THE ORIGINAL MONSTER!
C85-RN
AND DON'T YOU FORGET IT!
C85 RN
OOOOOFF!
HAH!

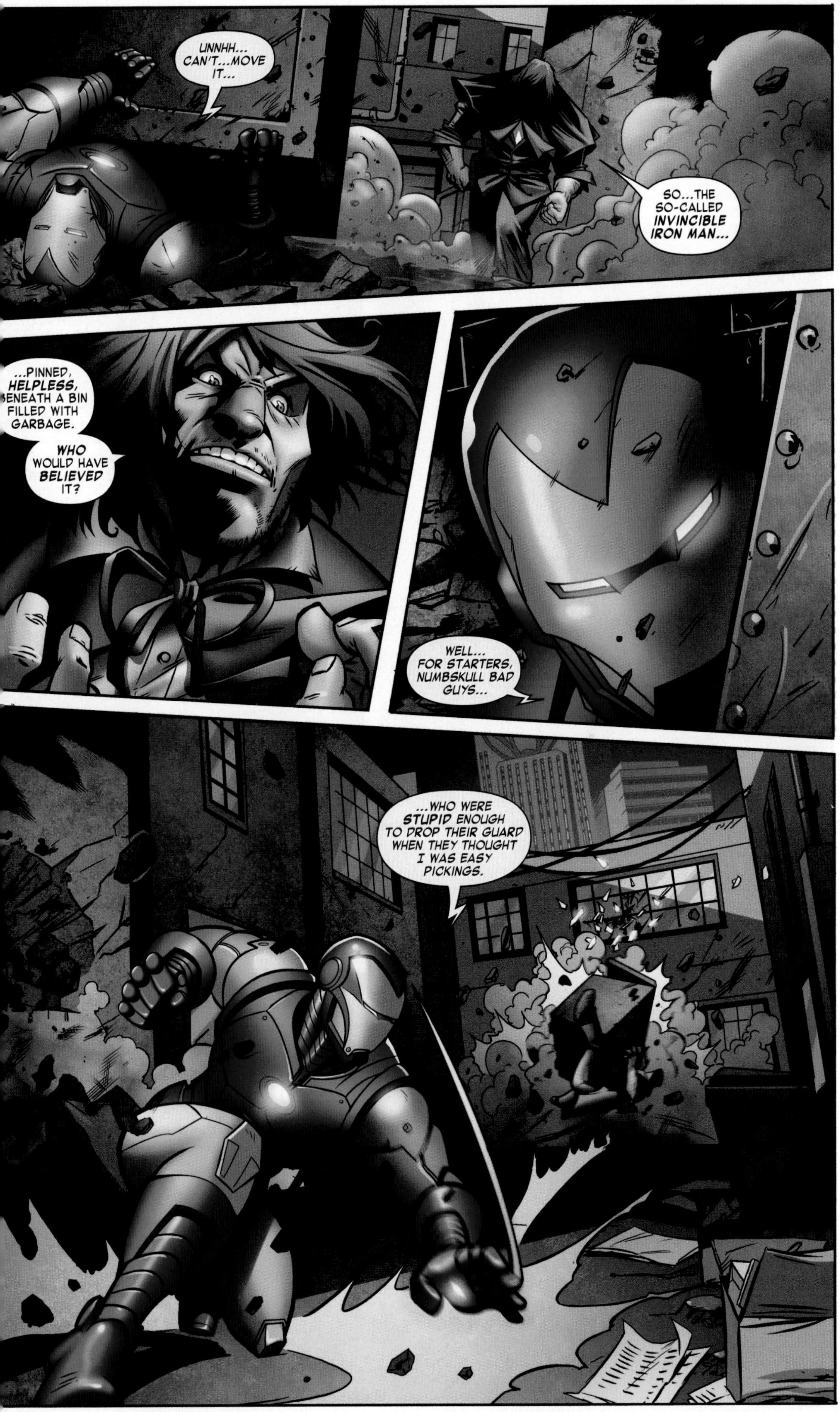

UNNHH... CAN'T...MOVE IT...
SO...THE SO-CALLED INVINCIBLE IRON MAN...
...PINNED, HELPLESS, BENEATH A BIN FILLED WITH GARBAGE.
WHO WOULD HAVE BELIEVED IT?
WELL... FOR STARTERS, NUMBSKULL BAD GUYS...
...WHO WERE STUPID ENOUGH TO DROP THEIR GUARD WHEN THEY THOUGHT I WAS EASY PICKINGS.

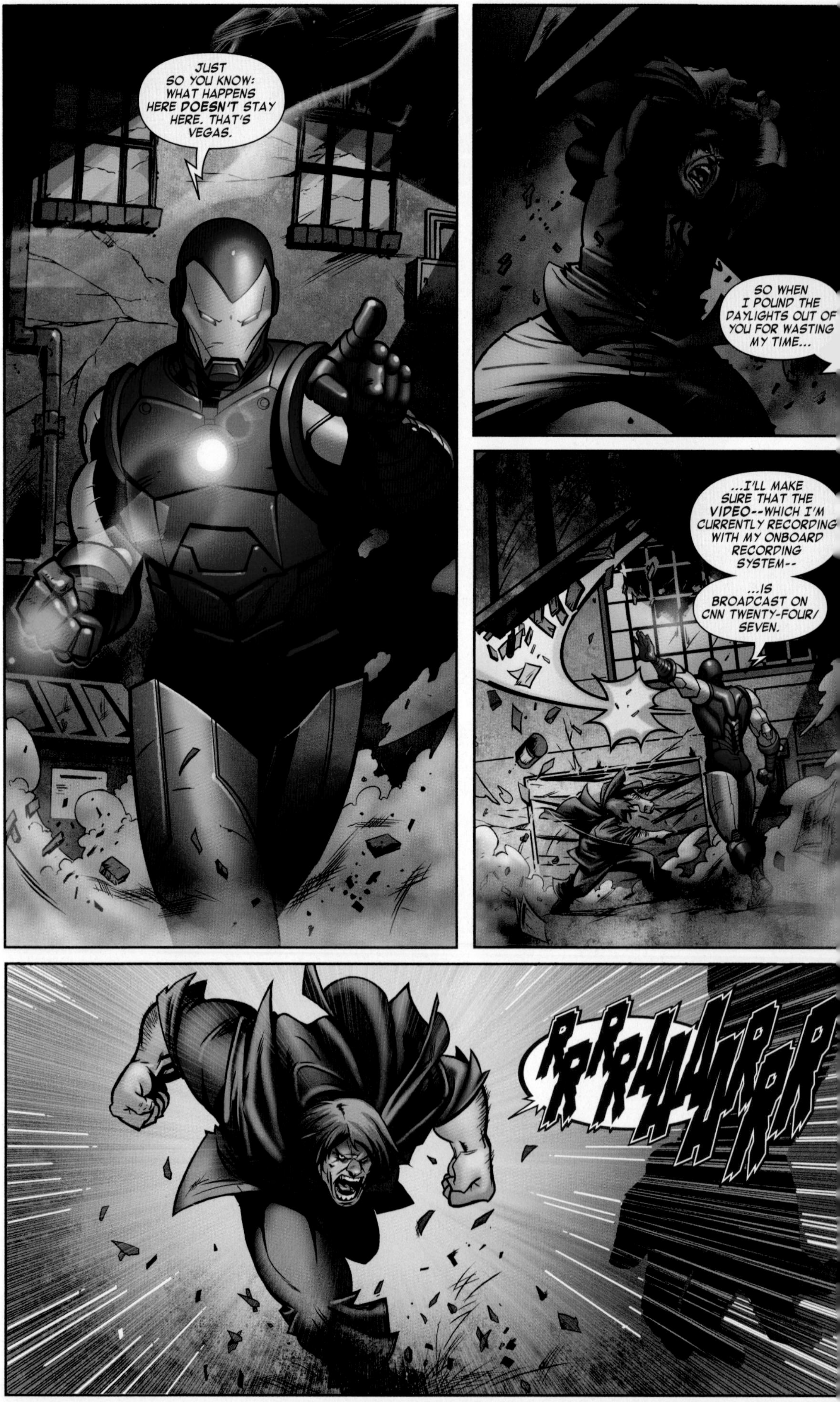
JUST SO YOU KNOW: WHAT HAPPENS HERE DOESN'T STAY HERE. THAT'S VEGAS.
SO WHEN I POUND THE DAYLIGHTS OUT OF YOU FOR WASTING MY TIME...
...I'LL MAKE SURE THAT THE VIDEO--WHICH I'M CURRENTLY RECORDING WITH MY ONBOARD RECORDING SYSTEM--
...IS BROADCAST ON CNN TWENTY-FOUR/ SEVEN.
RRRRAAAARRR

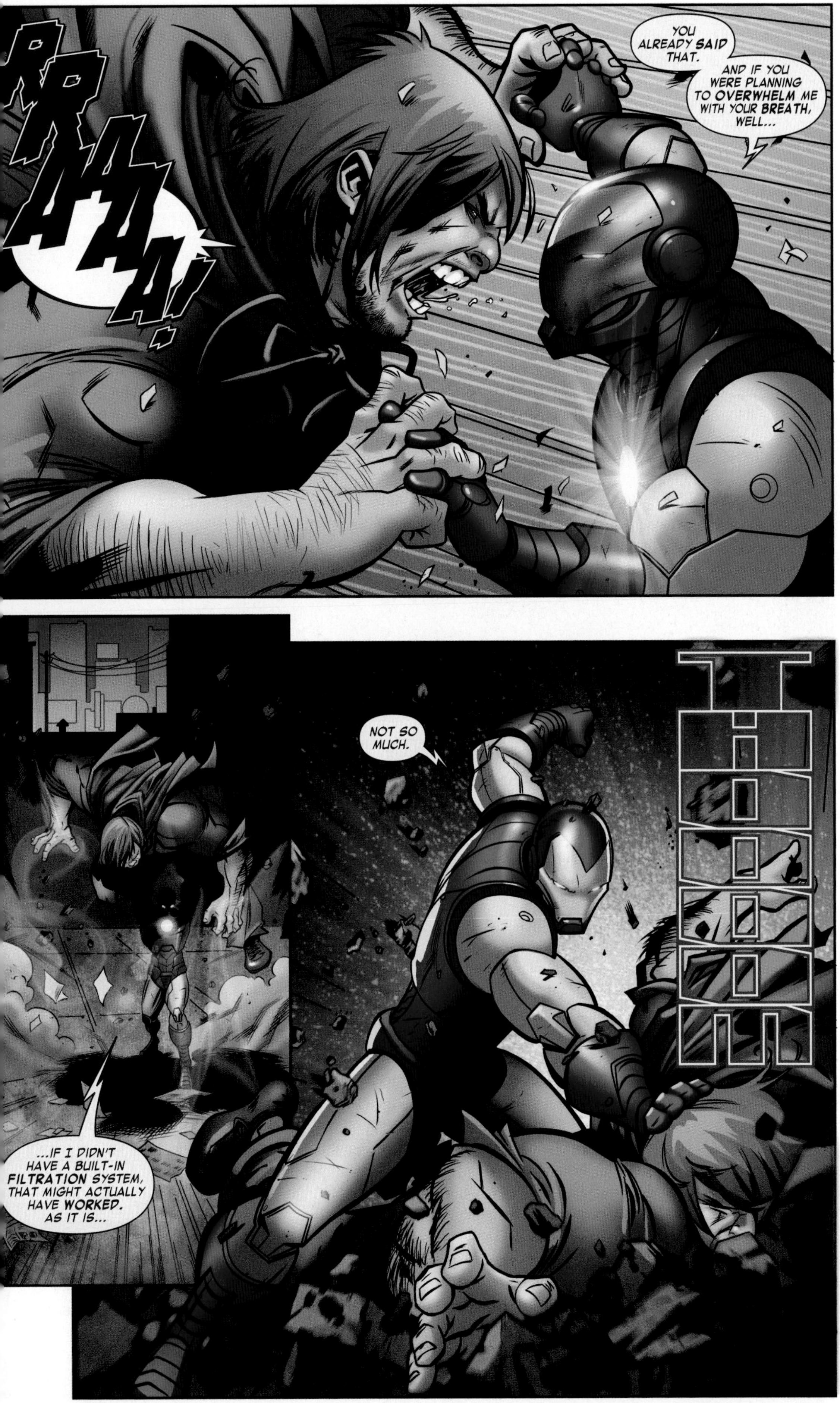
RRAAAAA!
YOU ALREADY SAID THAT.
AND IF YOU WERE PLANNING TO OVERWHELM ME WITH YOUR BREATH, WELL...
...IF I DIDN'T HAVE A BUILT-IN FILTRATION SYSTEM, THAT MIGHT ACTUALLY HAVE WORKED. AS IT IS...
NOT SO MUCH.
THOOOOM

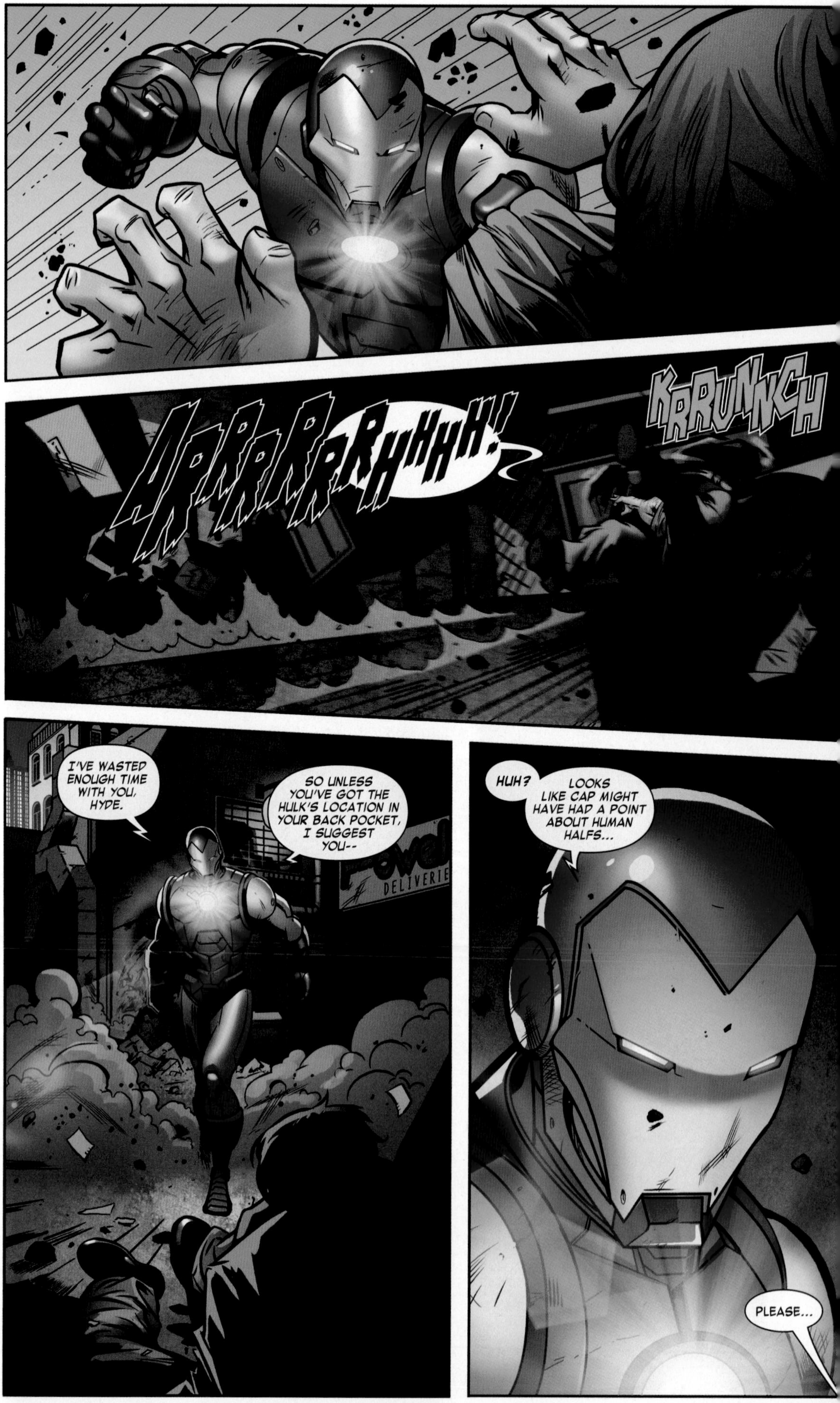

ARRRRRRRRHHHH!!
KRRUNNCH
I'VE WASTED ENOUGH TIME WITH YOU, HYDE.
SO UNLESS YOU'VE GOT THE HULK'S LOCATION IN YOUR BACK POCKET, I SUGGEST YOU--
DELIVERIE
HUH?
LOOKS LIKE CAP MIGHT HAVE HAD A POINT ABOUT HUMAN HALFS...
PLEASE...

PLEASE... DON'T...DON'T HURT ME...

I SWEAR, I WASN'T IN CONTROL. *HYDE* WAS! I'VE DONE NOTHING--! *THEY* CONTACTED HYDE...

...SAID THEY WERE WORKING WITH THE HULK TO LURE YOU HERE, AND HYDE WAS TO FINISH YOU--

I'VE NO IDEA WHAT YOU'RE TALKING ABOUT. FIRST OF ALL, WHO *ARE* YOU?

DOC...DOCTOR CALVIN ZABO. I DISCOVERED THE FORMULA FOR--

BORED NOW. MOVING ON: YOU SAY THIS WAS A SETUP? WHY?

I'M NOT SURE. THEY SAID SOMETHING ABOUT PROTECTING THOR...

"PROTECTING"? I WAS PROTECTING THOR FROM SOMETHING--?

ACTUALLY, I THINK THEY WANTED TO PROTECT *HIM* FROM *YOU.*

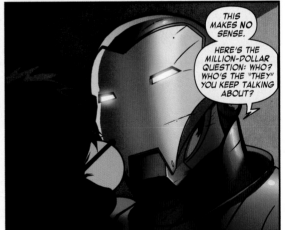

THIS MAKES NO SENSE.

HERE'S THE MILLION-DOLLAR QUESTION: WHO? WHO'S THE "THEY" YOU KEEP TALKING ABOUT?

TH-THEM!

OH.

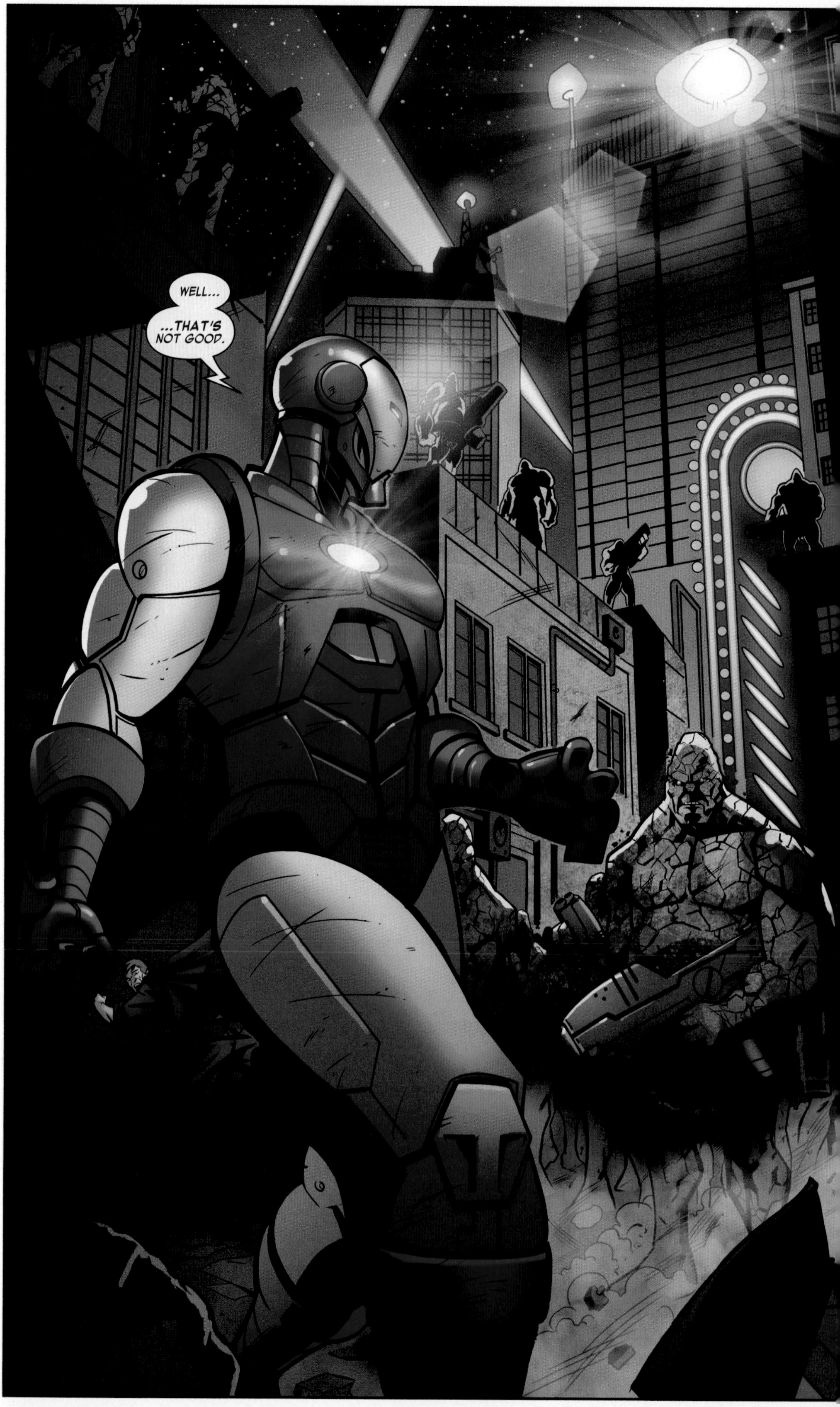
WELL...
...THAT'S NOT GOOD.

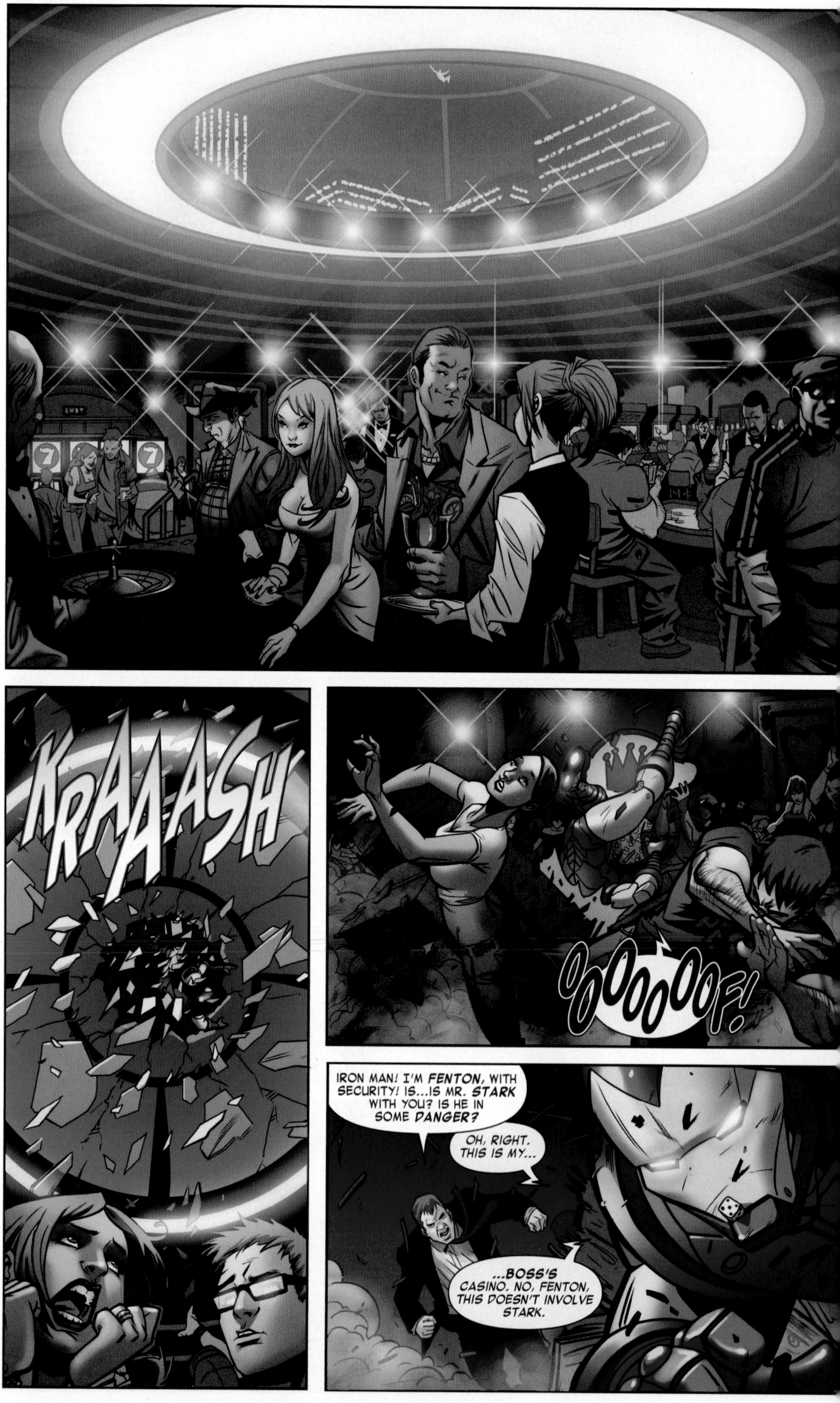
KRAAASH
OOOOOOF!
IRON MAN! I'M FENTON, WITH SECURITY! IS...IS MR. STARK WITH YOU? IS HE IN SOME DANGER?
OH, RIGHT. THIS IS MY...
...BOSS'S CASINO. NO, FENTON, THIS DOESN'T INVOLVE STARK.

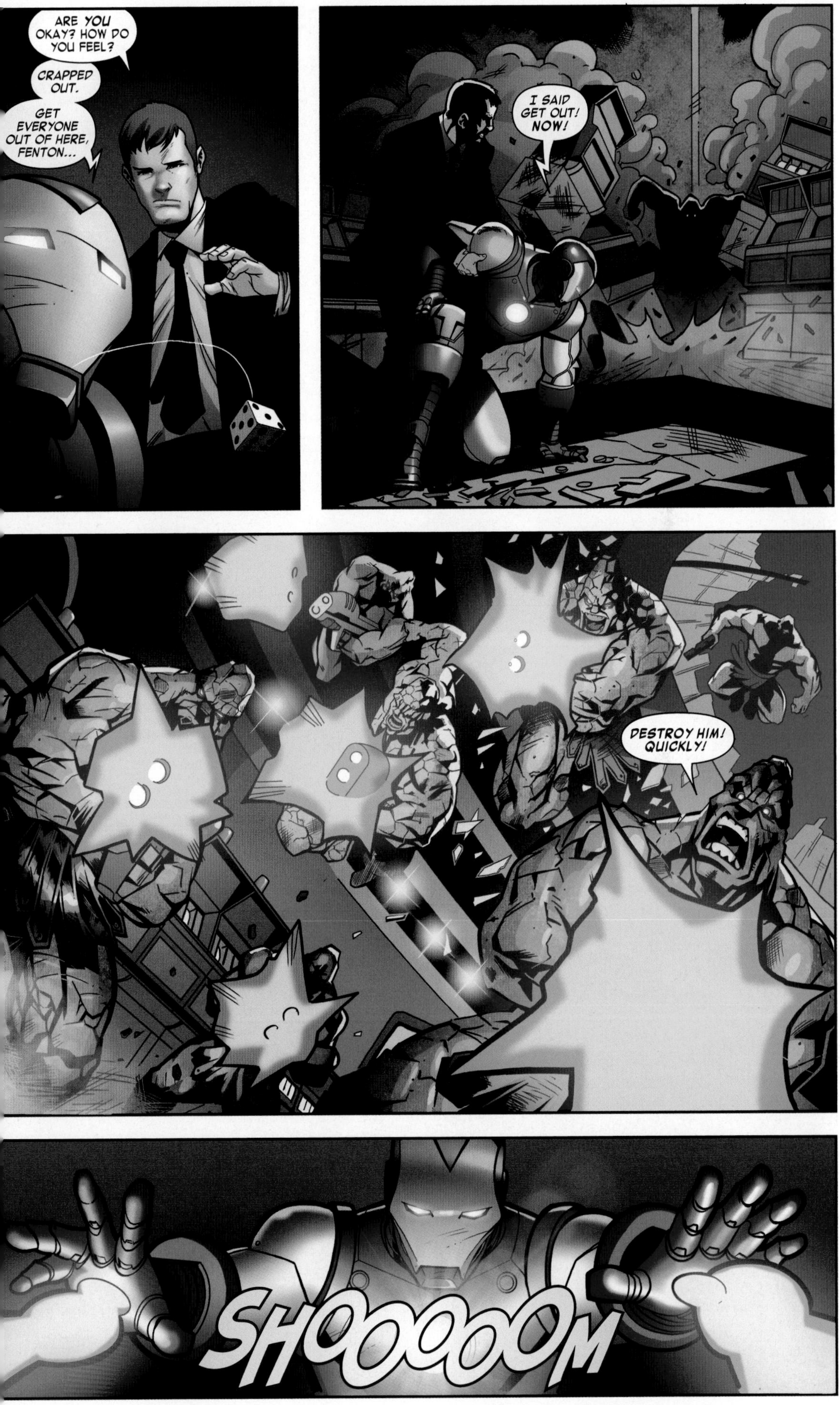
ARE YOU OKAY? HOW DO YOU FEEL?
CRAPPED OUT.
GET EVERYONE OUT OF HERE, FENTON...
I SAID GET OUT! NOW!
DESTROY HIM! QUICKLY!
SHOOOOOOM

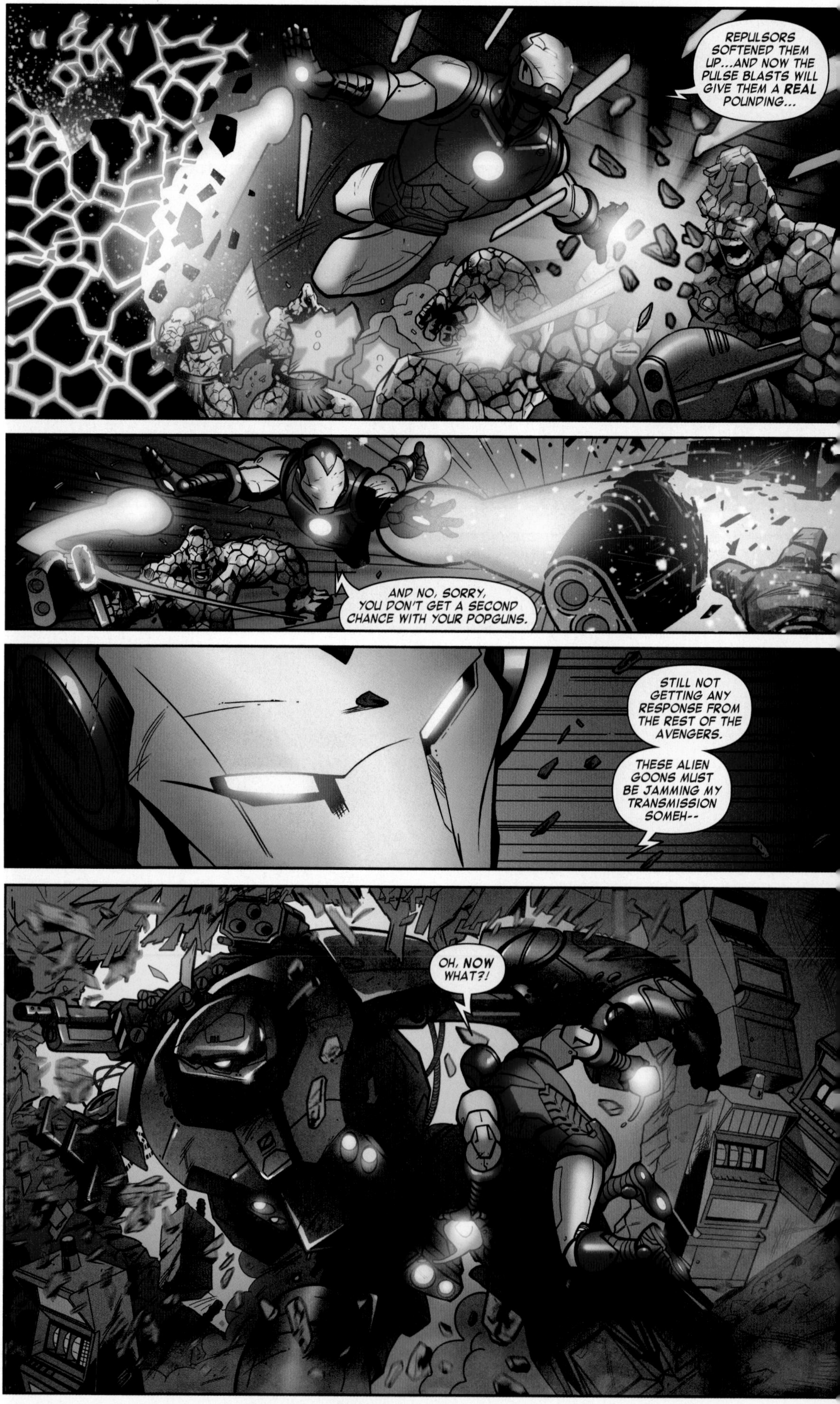
REPULSORS SOFTENED THEM UP...AND NOW THE PULSE BLASTS WILL GIVE THEM A REAL POUNDING...
AND NO, SORRY, YOU DON'T GET A SECOND CHANCE WITH YOUR POPGUNS.
STILL NOT GETTING ANY RESPONSE FROM THE REST OF THE AVENGERS.
THESE ALIEN GOONS MUST BE JAMMING MY TRANSMISSION SOMEH--
OH, NOW WHAT?!

KLAAAANG
RIGHT. THAT'S IT.
I'M ALREADY GOING TO HAVE TO WRITE THIS PLACE OFF AS A LOSS.
IF YOU THINK I'M GOING TO DAMAGE THE PROPERTY EVEN MORE BY GOING THREE ROUNDS WITH ROCK 'EM SOCK 'EM HERE...
YOU CAN FORGET IT.

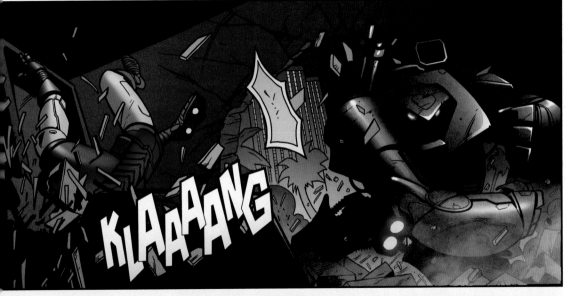

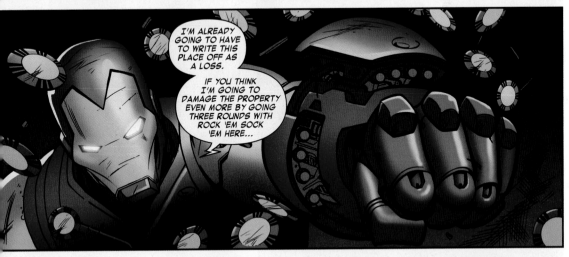

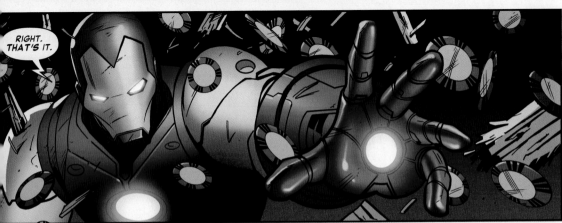

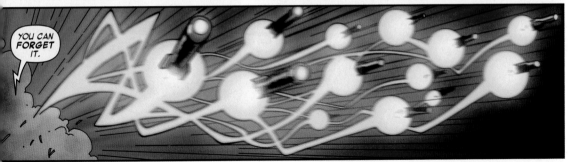

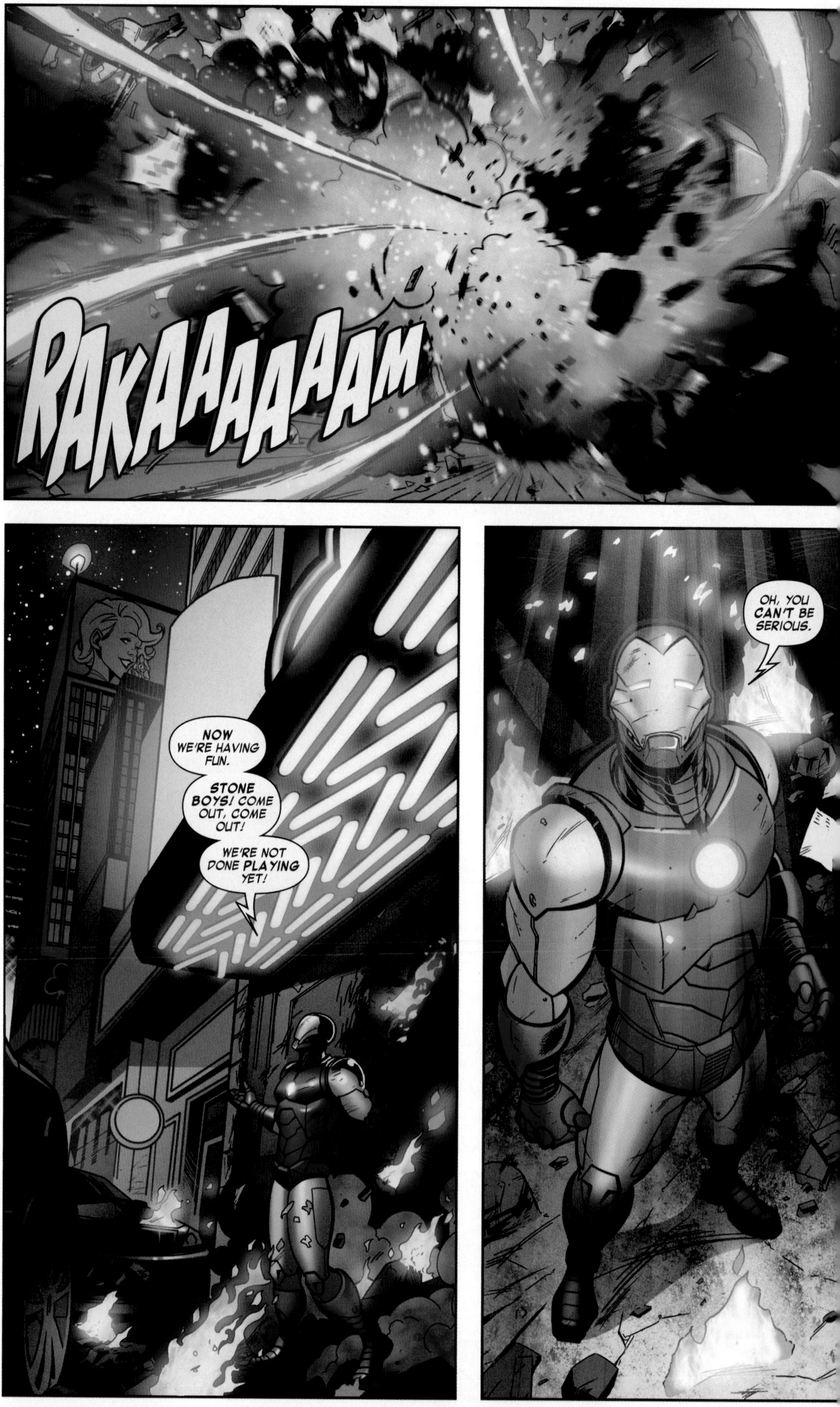
RAKAAAAAAAM
NOW WE'RE HAVING FUN.
STONE BOYS! COME OUT, COME OUT!
WE'RE NOT DONE PLAYING YET!
OH, YOU CAN'T BE SERIOUS.

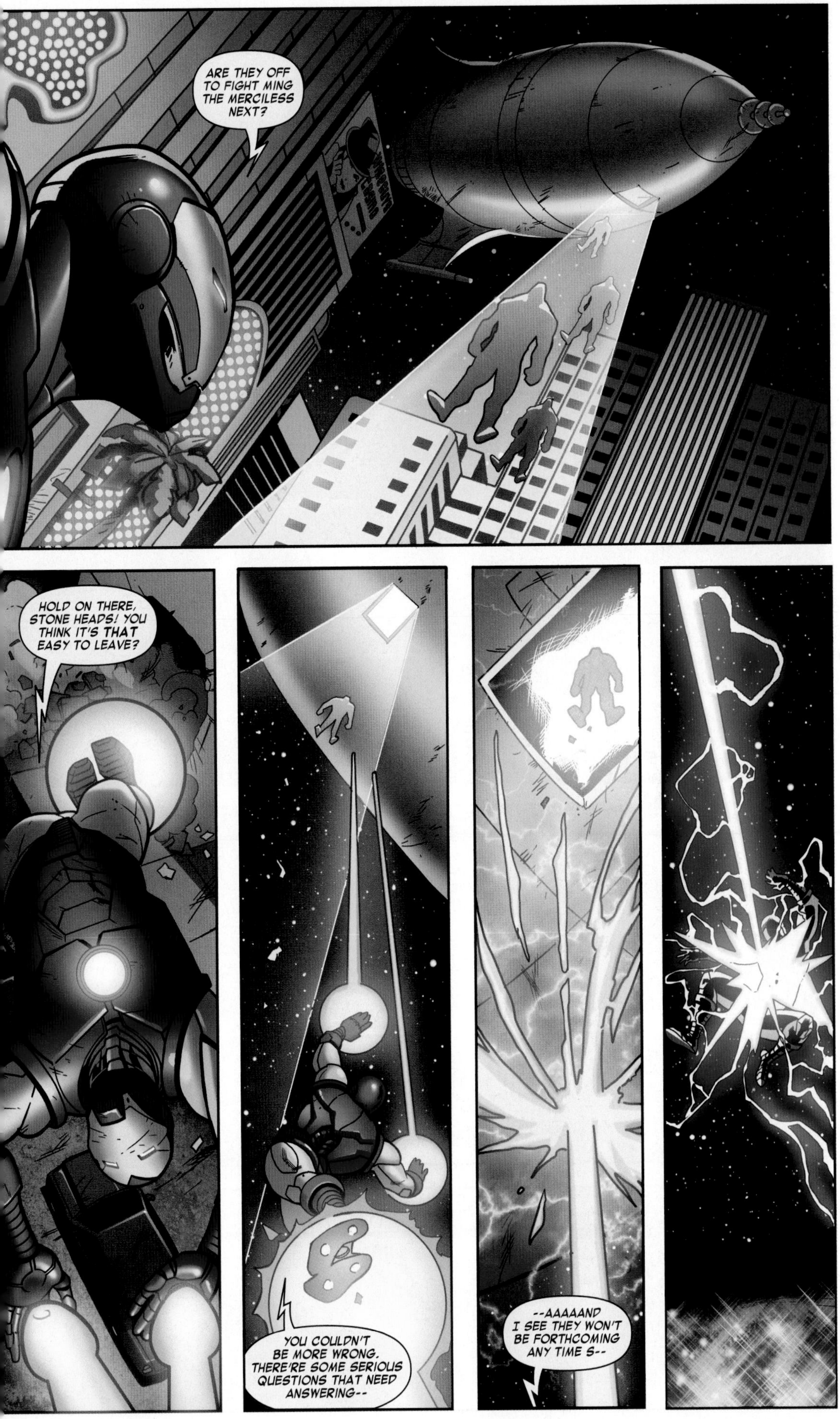
ARE THEY OFF TO FIGHT MING THE MERCILESS NEXT?
HOLD ON THERE, STONE HEADS! YOU THINK IT'S THAT EASY TO LEAVE?
YOU COULDN'T BE MORE WRONG. THERE'RE SOME SERIOUS QUESTIONS THAT NEED ANSWERING--
--AAAAAND I SEE THEY WON'T BE FORTHCOMING ANY TIME S--

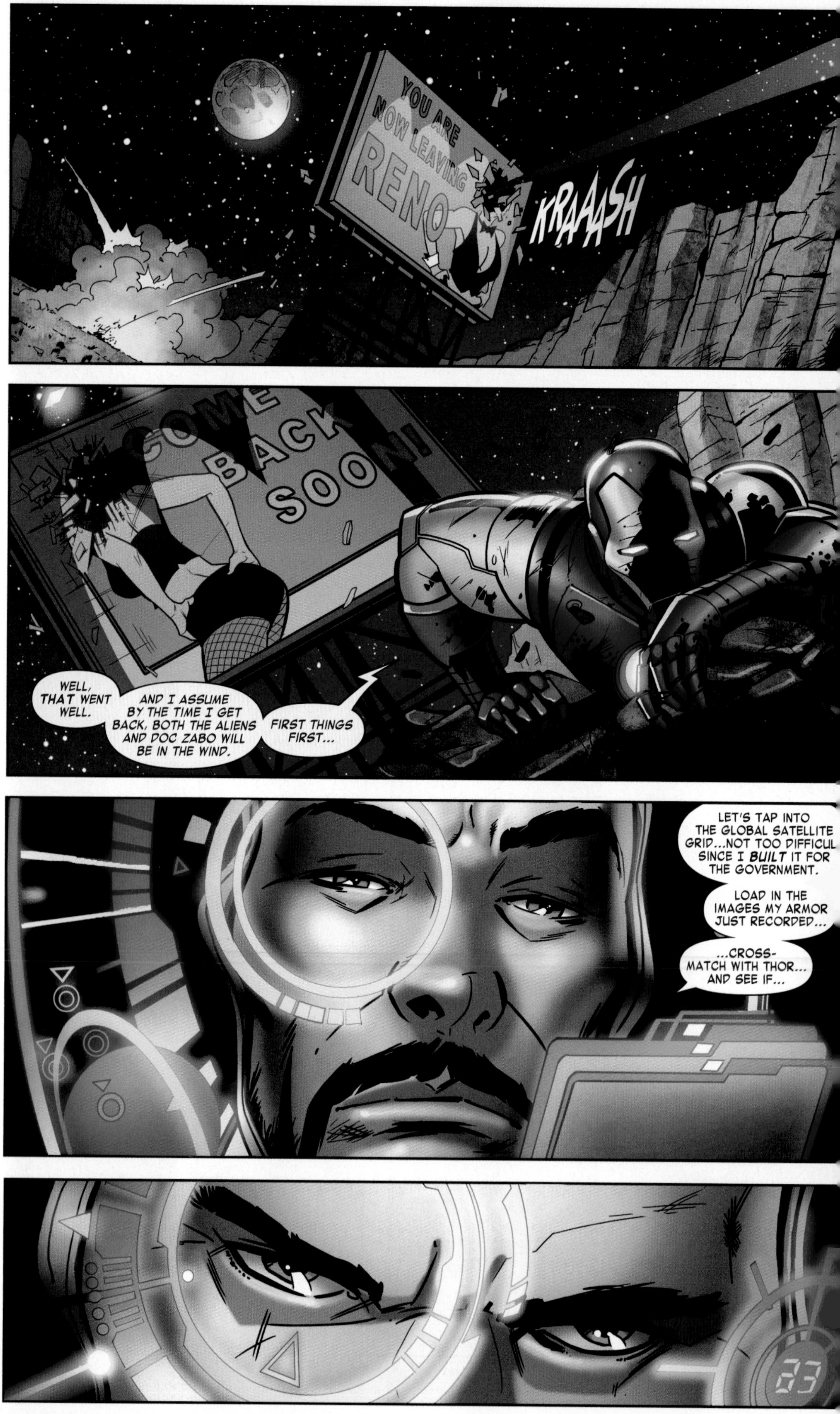
YOU ARE NOW LEAVING RENO
KRAAASH
COME BACK SOON!
WELL, THAT WENT WELL.
AND I ASSUME BY THE TIME I GET BACK, BOTH THE ALIENS AND DOC ZABO WILL BE IN THE WIND.
FIRST THINGS FIRST...
LET'S TAP INTO THE GLOBAL SATELLITE GRID...NOT TOO DIFFICUL SINCE I BUILT IT FOR THE GOVERNMENT.
LOAD IN THE IMAGES MY ARMOR JUST RECORDED...
...CROSS-MATCH WITH THOR... AND SEE IF...

...AT'S FROM A SATELLITE PICTURE IN NORWAY MONTHS AGO...NORAD ALERTED US TO THE DEPARTURE OF AN UNKNOWN SPACE VESSEL...

...AND IT'S THE *FIRST* RECORDED IMAGE OF THOR. ANYWHERE.

THOR'S INVOLVEMENT WAS AN OPEN QUESTION AT THE HIGHEST LEVELS OF GOVERNMENT, ACCORDING TO THESE REPORTS I'M ACCESSING...

BUT WHEN HE JOINED UP WITH THE AVENGERS, THE UPPER ECHELON OF THE AIR FORCE CONCLUDED HE MUST HAVE DRIVEN OFF AN ALIEN INVASION.

WHAT IF THEY WERE WRONG? WHAT IF THEY DROPPED HIM OFF?

WHAT IF HE'S AN ALLY OF THEIRS? SOME SORT OF INVADING ALIEN HIMSELF?

THAT WOULD EXPLAIN HIS POWERS... HIS RIDICULOUS STORIES ABOUT BEING A GOD... EVERYTHING!

AND THEY, OR HE, MUST HAVE FIGURED OUT SOMEHOW I WAS GETTING SUSPICIOUS...

AND DECIDED TO "PROTECT" HIM FROM BEING FOUND OUT.

I'LL MAKE A QUICK SWEEP OF RENO, MAKE SURE THEY'RE GONE, SEE IF I CAN FIND ZABO...

...AND THEN I'M GOING TO ASK SOME VERY HARD QUESTIONS...

...OF A CERTAIN "THUNDER GOD."

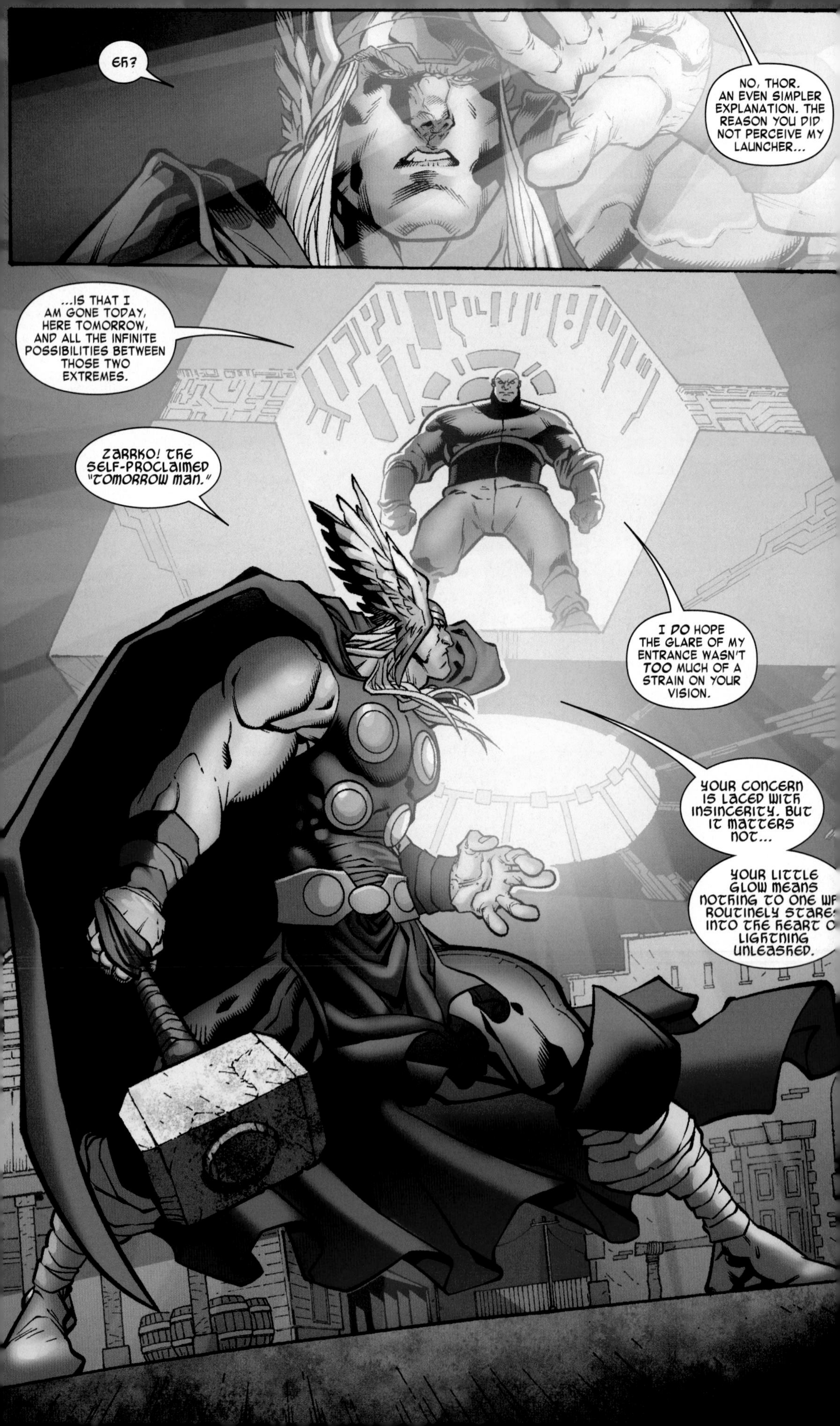
EH?
NO, THOR. AN EVEN SIMPLER EXPLANATION. THE REASON YOU DID NOT PERCEIVE MY LAUNCHER...
...IS THAT I AM GONE TODAY, HERE TOMORROW, AND ALL THE INFINITE POSSIBILITIES BETWEEN THOSE TWO EXTREMES.
ZARRKO! THE SELF-PROCLAIMED "TOMORROW MAN."
I DO HOPE THE GLARE OF MY ENTRANCE WASN'T TOO MUCH OF A STRAIN ON YOUR VISION.
YOUR CONCERN IS LACED WITH INSINCERITY. BUT IT MATTERS NOT...
YOUR LITTLE GLOW MEANS NOTHING TO ONE WH ROUTINELY STARE INTO THE HEART O LIGHTNING UNLEASHED.

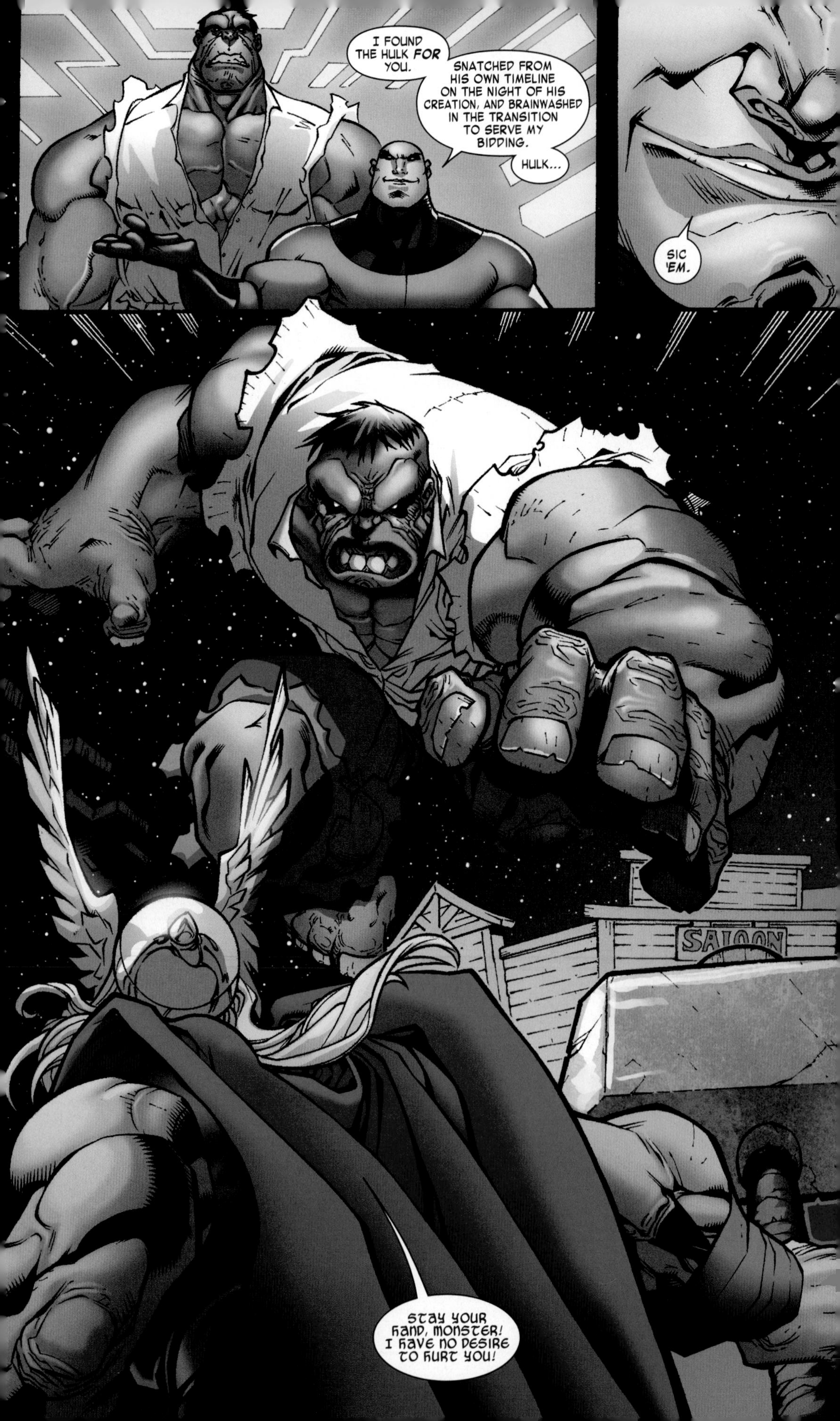
I FOUND THE HULK *FOR* YOU.
SNATCHED FROM HIS OWN TIMELINE ON THE NIGHT OF HIS CREATION, AND BRAINWASHED IN THE TRANSITION TO SERVE MY BIDDING.
HULK...
SIC 'EM.
SALOON
STAY YOUR HAND, MONSTER! I HAVE NO DESIRE TO HURT YOU!

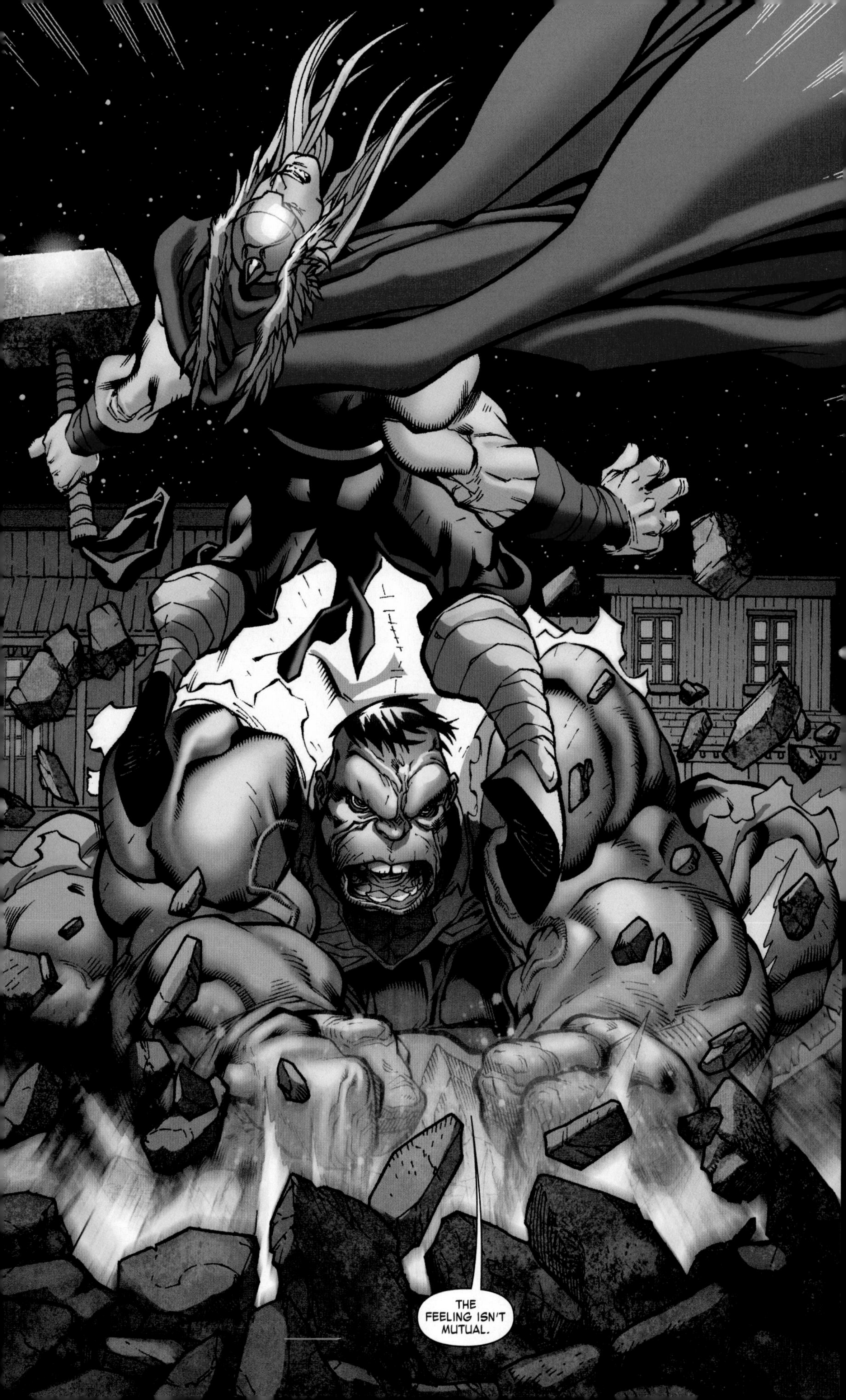
THE FEELING ISN'T MUTUAL.

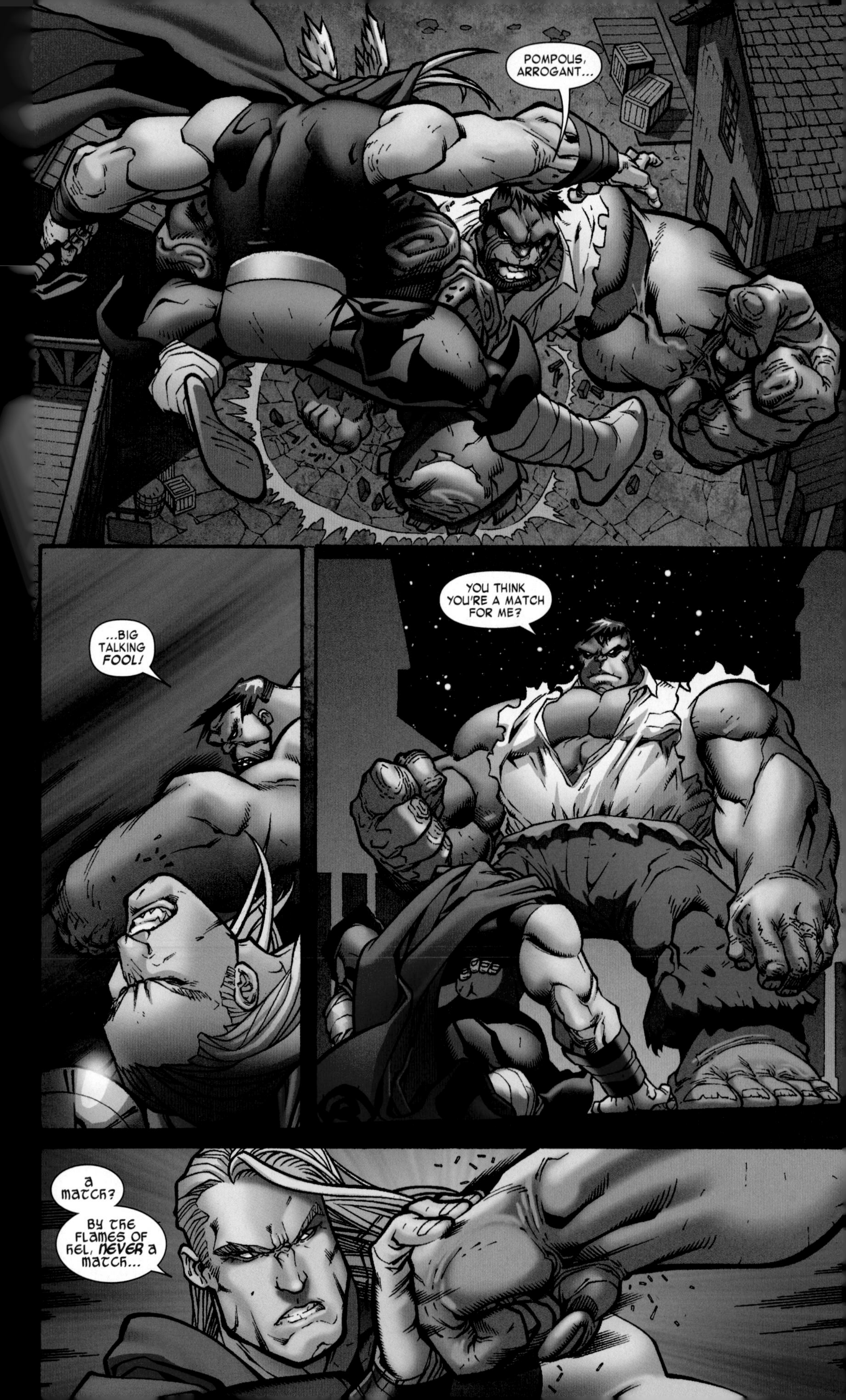
POMPOUS, ARROGANT...
...BIG TALKING FOOL!
YOU THINK YOU'RE A MATCH FOR ME?
A MATCH?
BY THE FLAMES OF HEL, NEVER A MATCH...

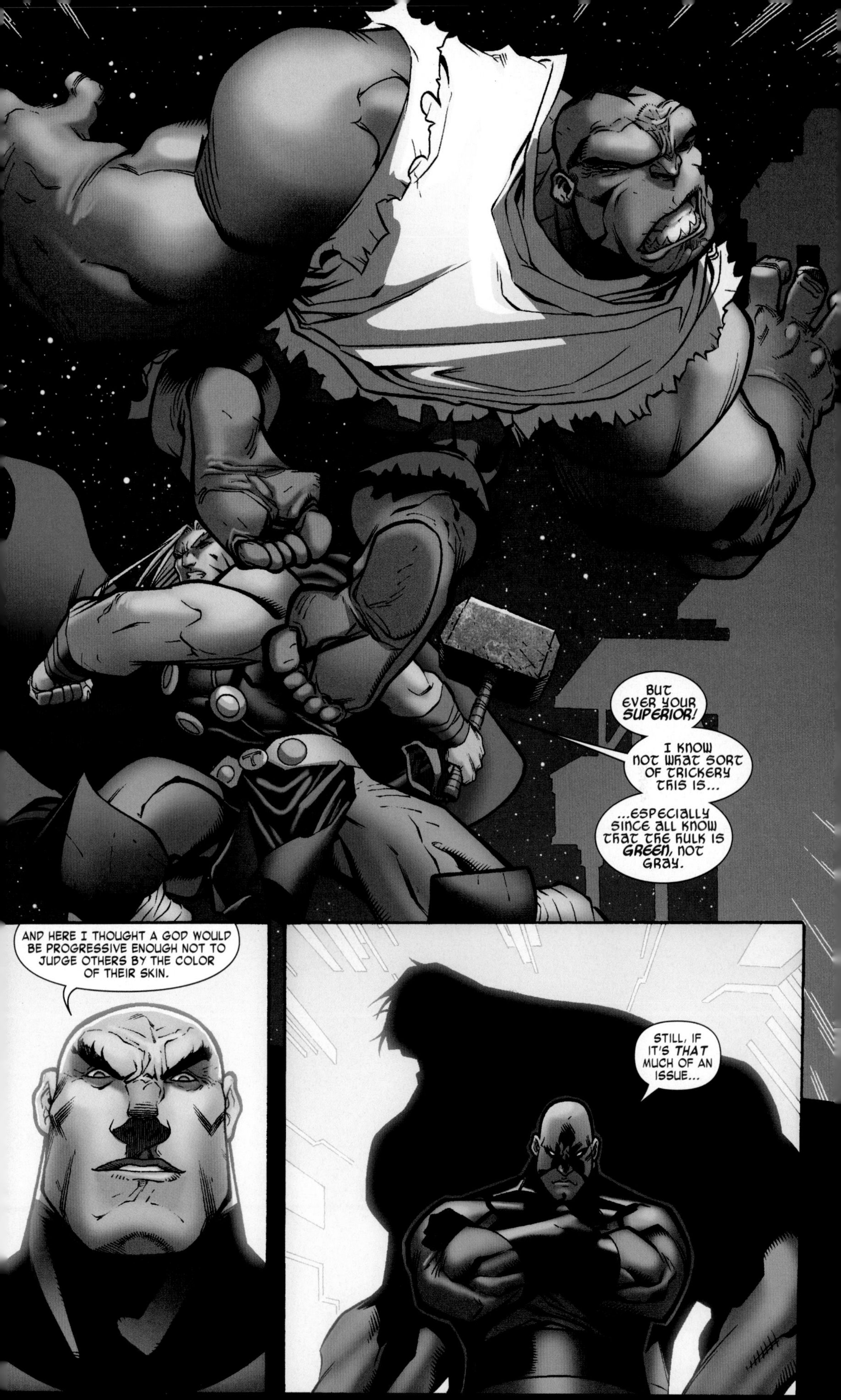
BUT EVER YOUR SUPERIOR!
I KNOW NOT WHAT SORT OF TRICKERY THIS IS...
...ESPECIALLY SINCE ALL KNOW THAT THE HULK IS GREEN, NOT GRAY.
AND HERE I THOUGHT A GOD WOULD BE PROGRESSIVE ENOUGH NOT TO JUDGE OTHERS BY THE COLOR OF THEIR SKIN.
STILL, IF IT'S THAT MUCH OF AN ISSUE...

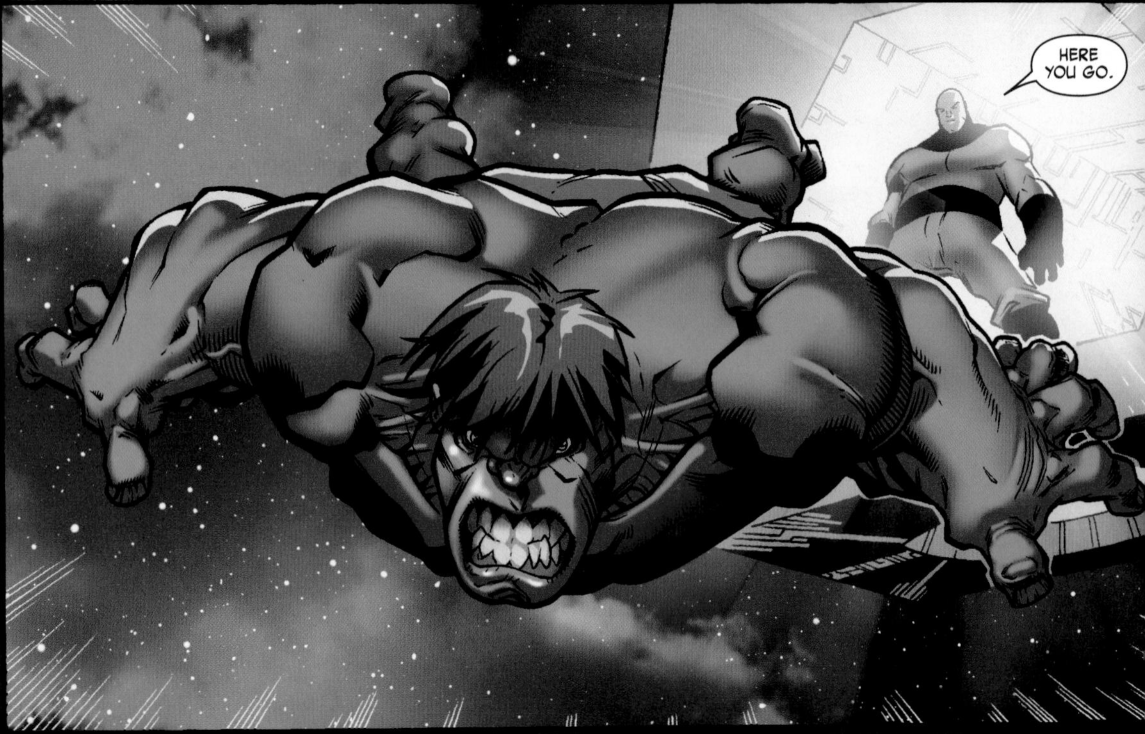
HERE YOU GO.

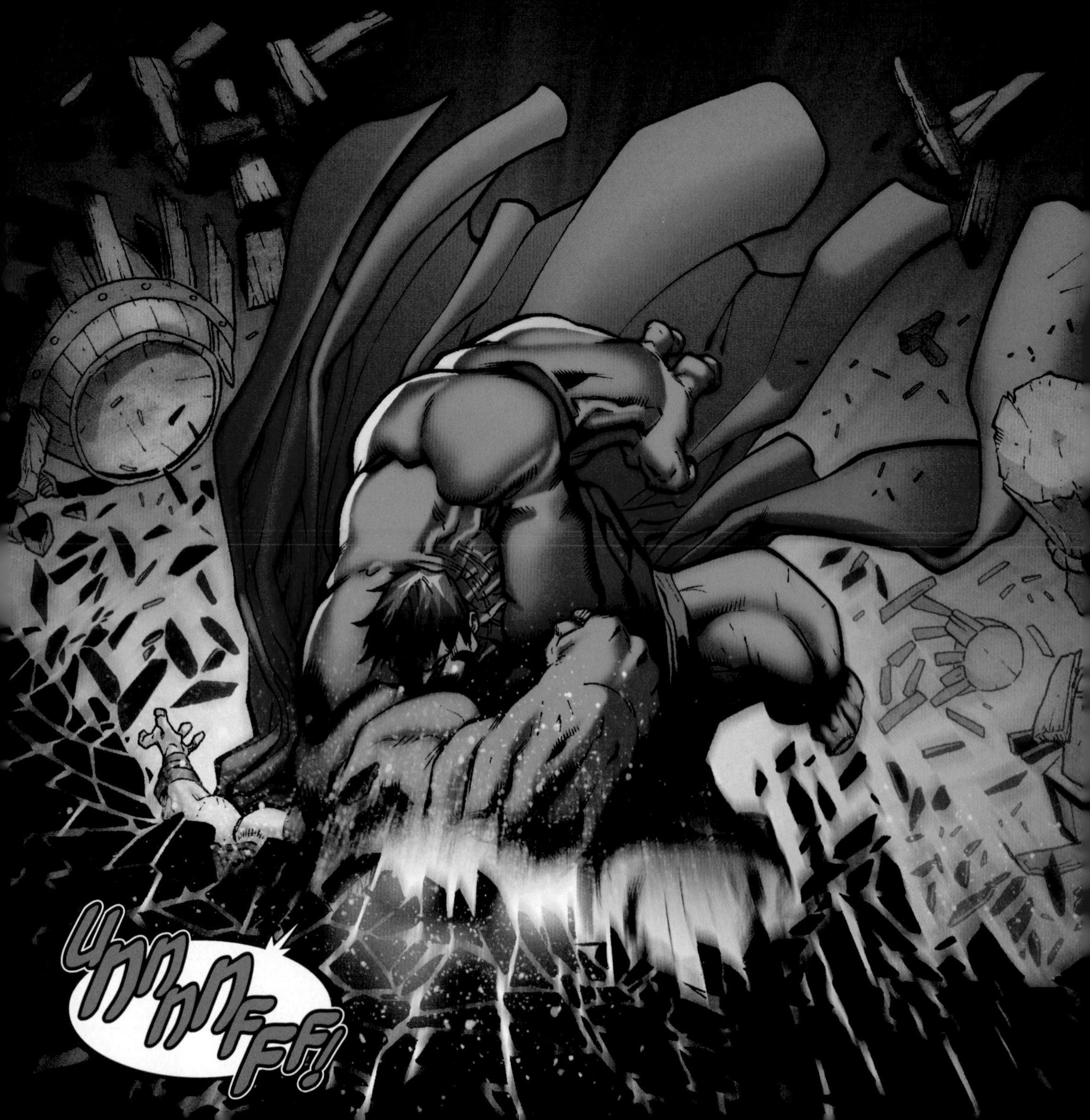
UNNNNFFF!

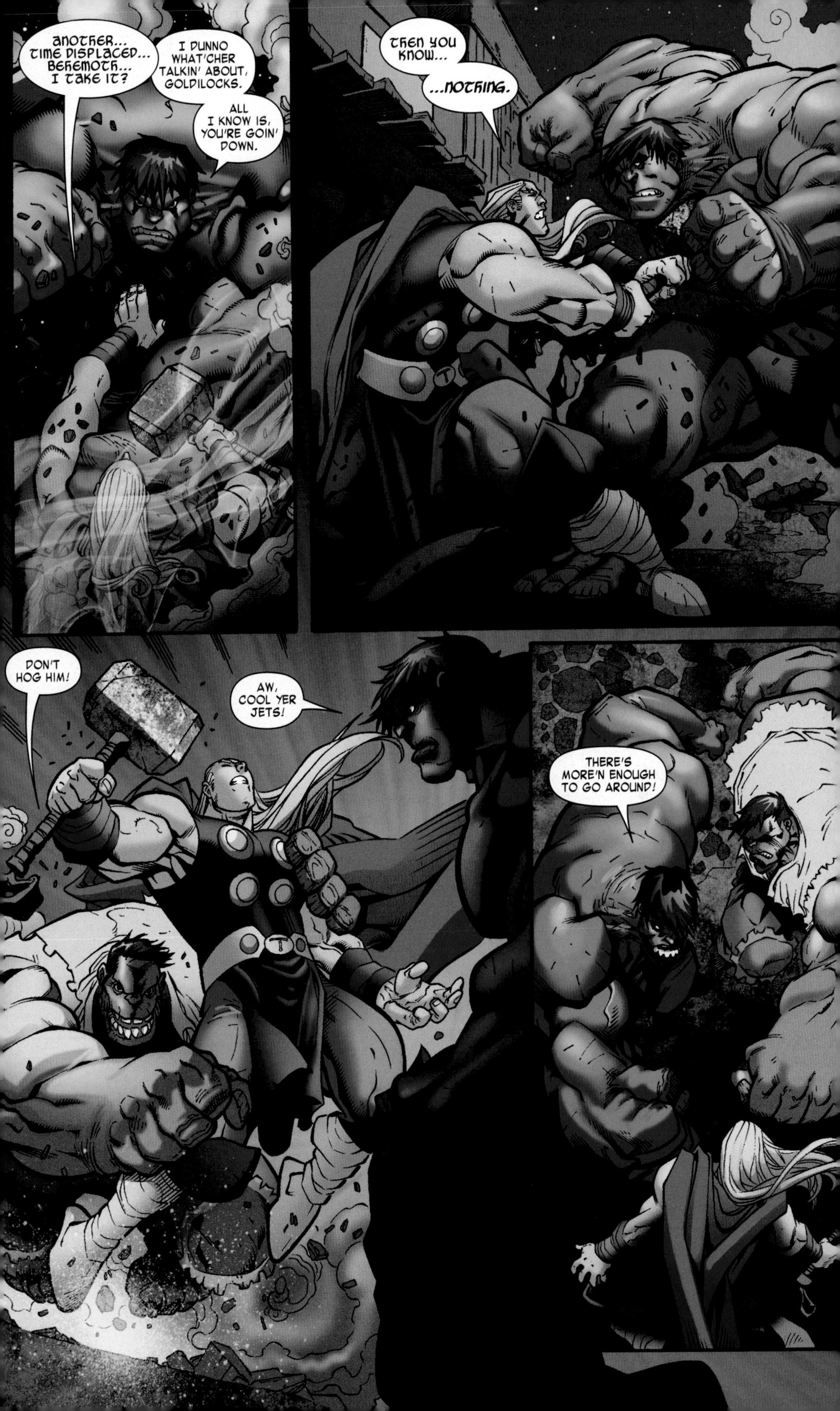
ANOTHER... TIME DISPLACED... BEHEMOTH... I TAKE IT?
I DUNNO WHAT'CHER TALKIN' ABOUT, GOLDILOCKS.
ALL I KNOW IS, YOU'RE GOIN' DOWN.
THEN YOU KNOW...
...NOTHING.
DON'T HOG HIM!
AW, COOL YER JETS!
THERE'S MORE'N ENOUGH TO GO AROUND!

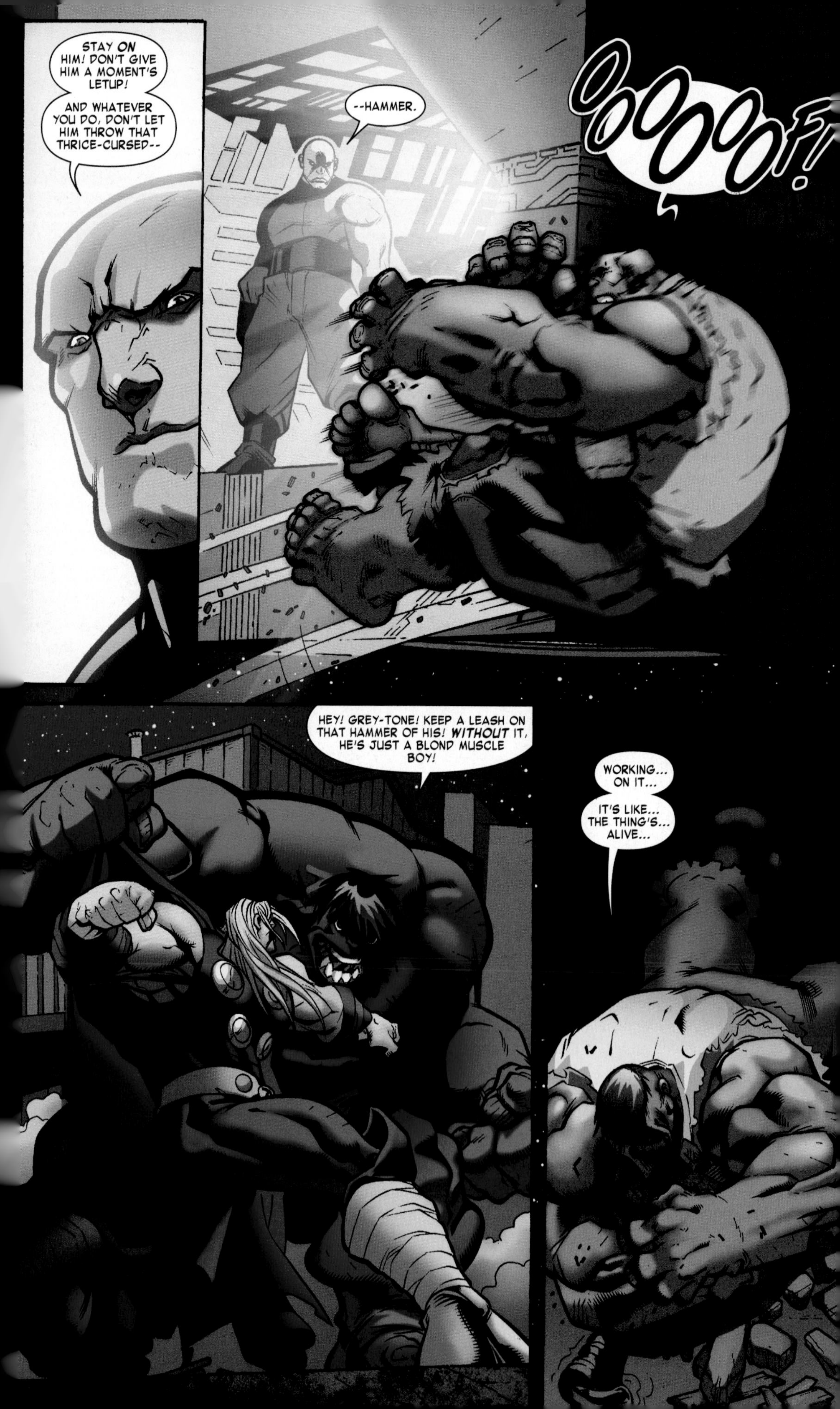
STAY ON HIM! DON'T GIVE HIM A MOMENT'S LETUP!
AND WHATEVER YOU DO, DON'T LET HIM THROW THAT THRICE-CURSED--
--HAMMER.
OOOOOOF!
HEY! GREY-TONE! KEEP A LEASH ON THAT HAMMER OF HIS! WITHOUT IT, HE'S JUST A BLOND MUSCLE BOY!
WORKING... ON IT...
IT'S LIKE... THE THING'S... ALIVE...

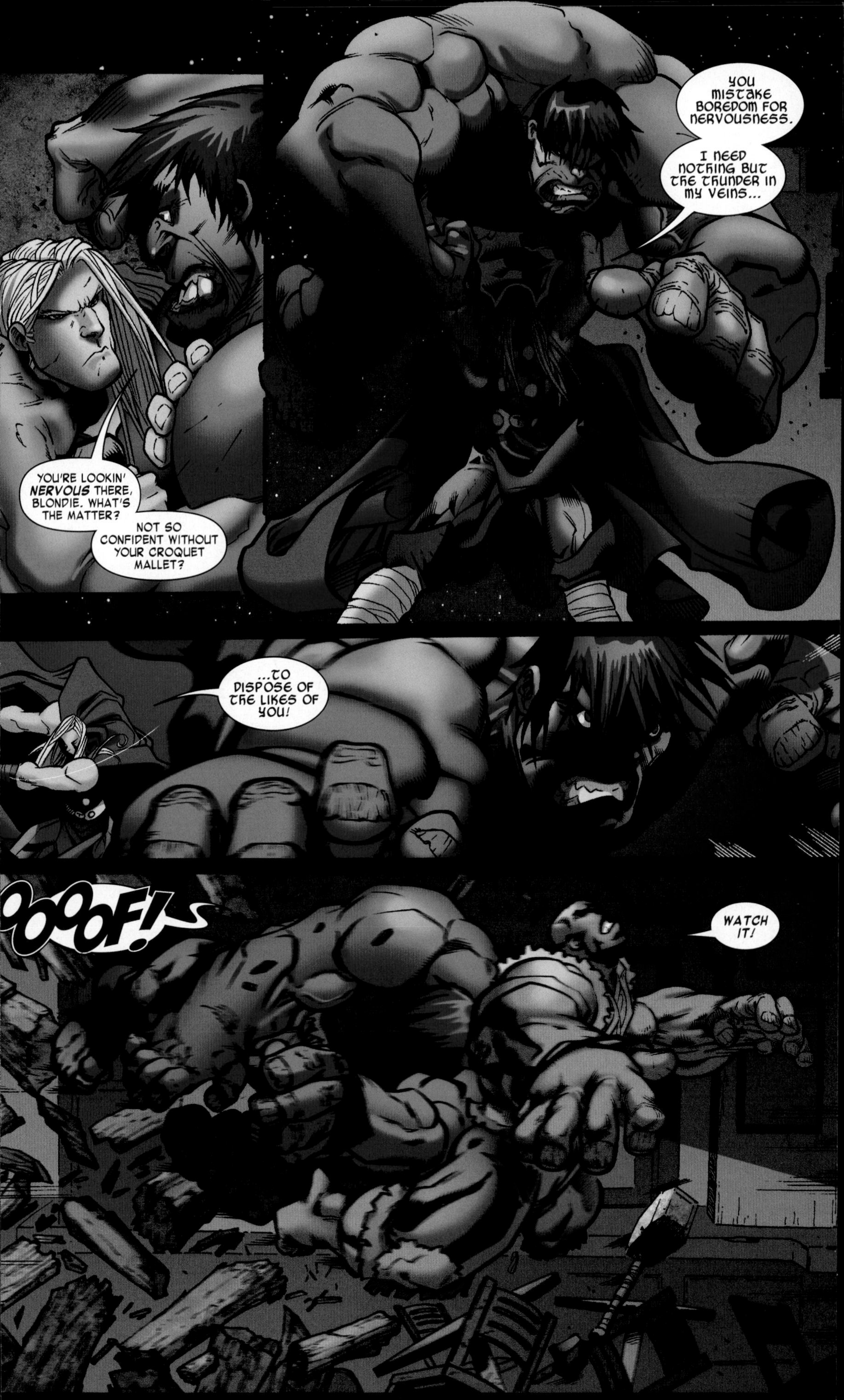

YOU'RE LOOKIN' *NERVOUS* THERE, BLONDIE. WHAT'S THE MATTER?
NOT SO CONFIDENT WITHOUT YOUR CROQUET MALLET?
YOU MISTAKE BOREDOM FOR NERVOUSNESS.
I NEED NOTHING BUT THE THUNDER IN MY VEINS...
...TO DISPOSE OF THE LIKES OF YOU!
OOOOF!
WATCH IT!

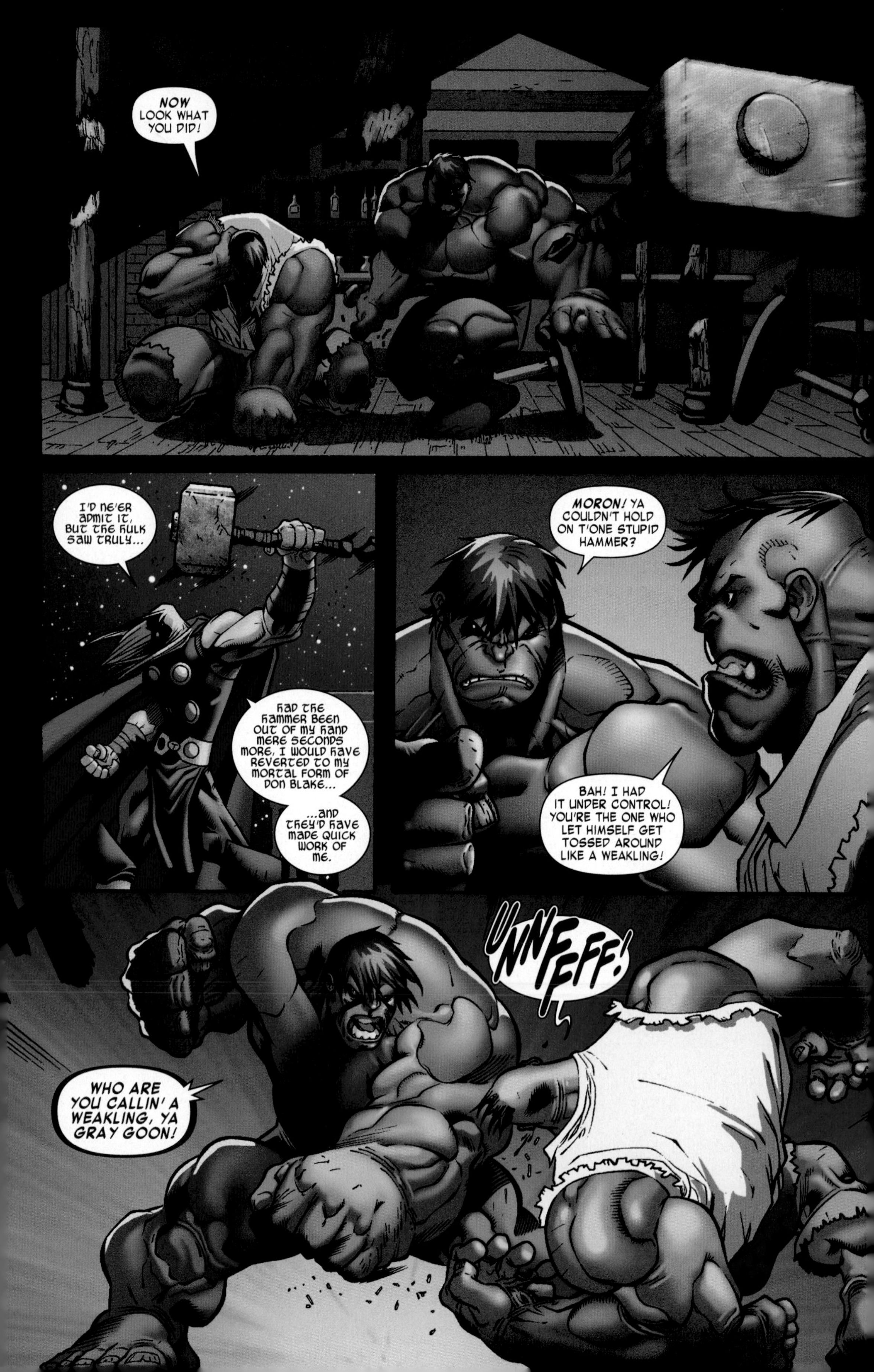
NOW LOOK WHAT YOU DID!
I'D NE'ER ADMIT IT, BUT THE HULK SAW TRULY...
HAD THE HAMMER BEEN OUT OF MY HAND MERE SECONDS MORE, I WOULD HAVE REVERTED TO MY MORTAL FORM OF DON BLAKE...
...AND THEY'D HAVE MADE QUICK WORK OF ME.
MORON! YA COULDN'T HOLD ON T'ONE STUPID HAMMER?
BAH! I HAD IT UNDER CONTROL! YOU'RE THE ONE WHO LET HIMSELF GET TOSSED AROUND LIKE A WEAKLING!
UNNFFFF!
WHO ARE YOU CALLIN' A WEAKLING, YA GRAY GOON!

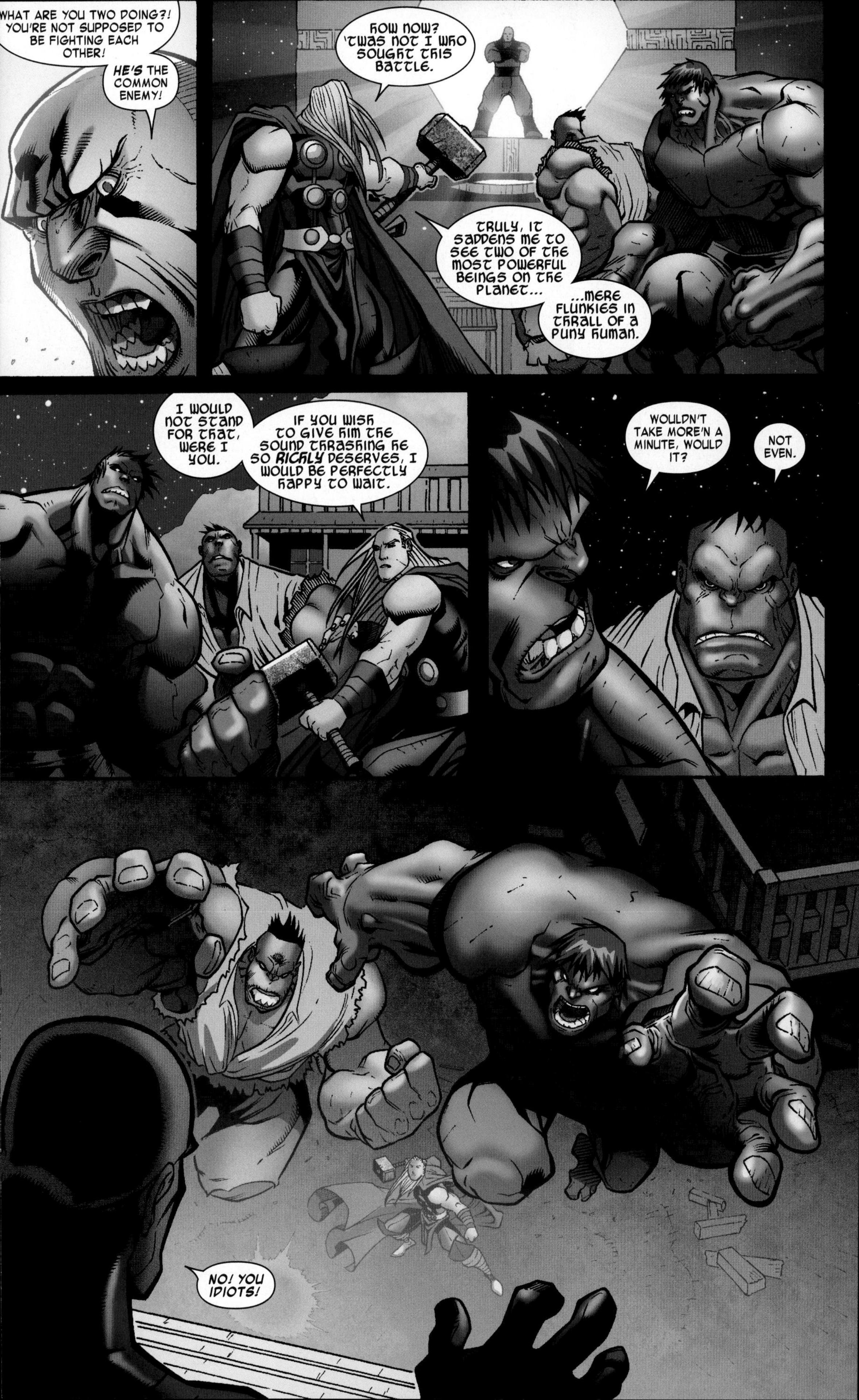

WHAT ARE YOU TWO DOING?! YOU'RE NOT SUPPOSED TO BE FIGHTING EACH OTHER!
HE'S THE COMMON ENEMY!
HOW NOW? 'TWAS NOT I WHO SOUGHT THIS BATTLE.
TRULY, IT SADDENS ME TO SEE TWO OF THE MOST POWERFUL BEINGS ON THE PLANET...
...MERE FLUNKIES IN THRALL OF A PUNY HUMAN.
I WOULD NOT STAND FOR THAT, WERE I YOU.
IF YOU WISH TO GIVE HIM THE SOUND THRASHING HE SO RICHLY DESERVES, I WOULD BE PERFECTLY HAPPY TO WAIT.
WOULDN'T TAKE MORE'N A MINUTE, WOULD IT?
NOT EVEN.
NO! YOU IDIOTS!

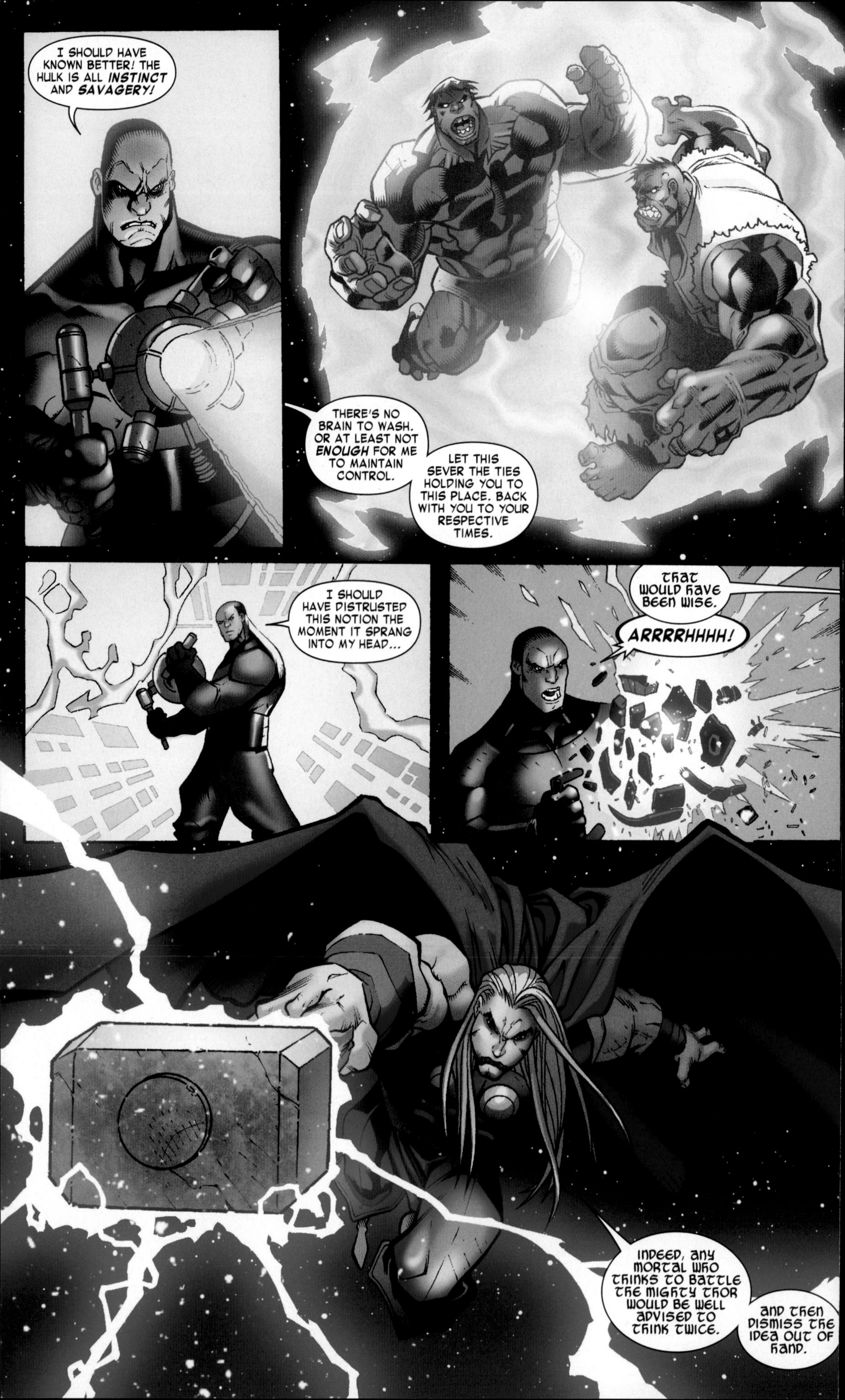
I SHOULD HAVE KNOWN BETTER! THE HULK IS ALL *INSTINCT* AND *SAVAGERY!*
THERE'S NO BRAIN TO WASH. OR AT LEAST NOT *ENOUGH* FOR ME TO MAINTAIN CONTROL.
LET THIS SEVER THE TIES HOLDING YOU TO THIS PLACE. BACK WITH YOU TO YOUR RESPECTIVE TIMES.
I SHOULD HAVE DISTRUSTED THIS NOTION THE MOMENT IT SPRANG INTO MY HEAD...
THAT WOULD HAVE BEEN WISE.
ARRRRHHHH!
INDEED, ANY MORTAL WHO THINKS TO BATTLE THE MIGHTY THOR WOULD BE WELL ADVISED TO THINK TWICE.
AND THEN DISMISS THE IDEA OUT OF HAND.

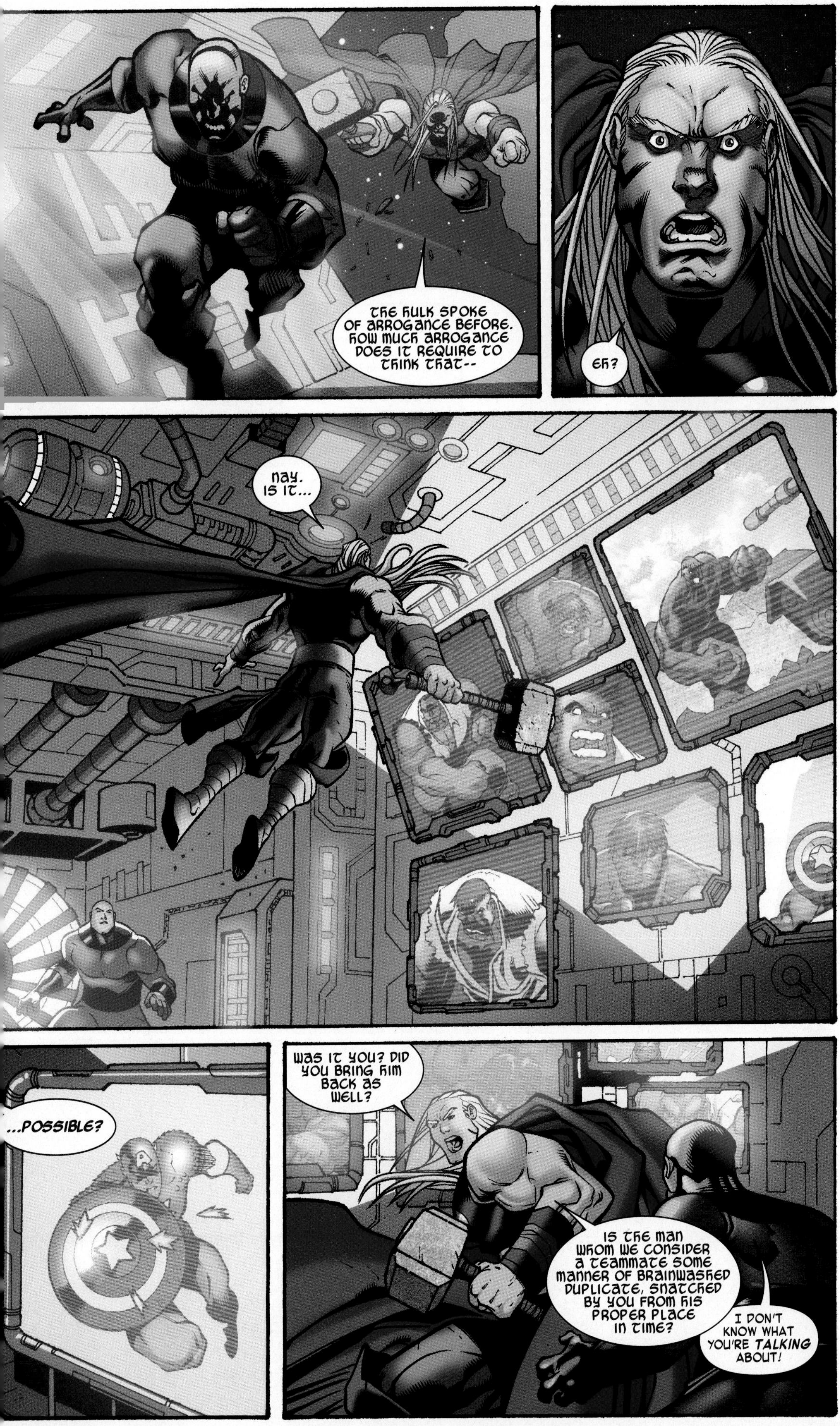
THE HULK SPOKE OF ARROGANCE BEFORE. HOW MUCH ARROGANCE DOES IT REQUIRE TO THINK THAT--
EH?
NAY. IS IT...
...POSSIBLE?
WAS IT YOU? DID YOU BRING HIM BACK AS WELL?
IS THE MAN WHOM WE CONSIDER A TEAMMATE SOME MANNER OF BRAINWASHED DUPLICATE, SNATCHED BY YOU FROM HIS PROPER PLACE IN TIME?
I DON'T KNOW WHAT YOU'RE *TALKING* ABOUT!

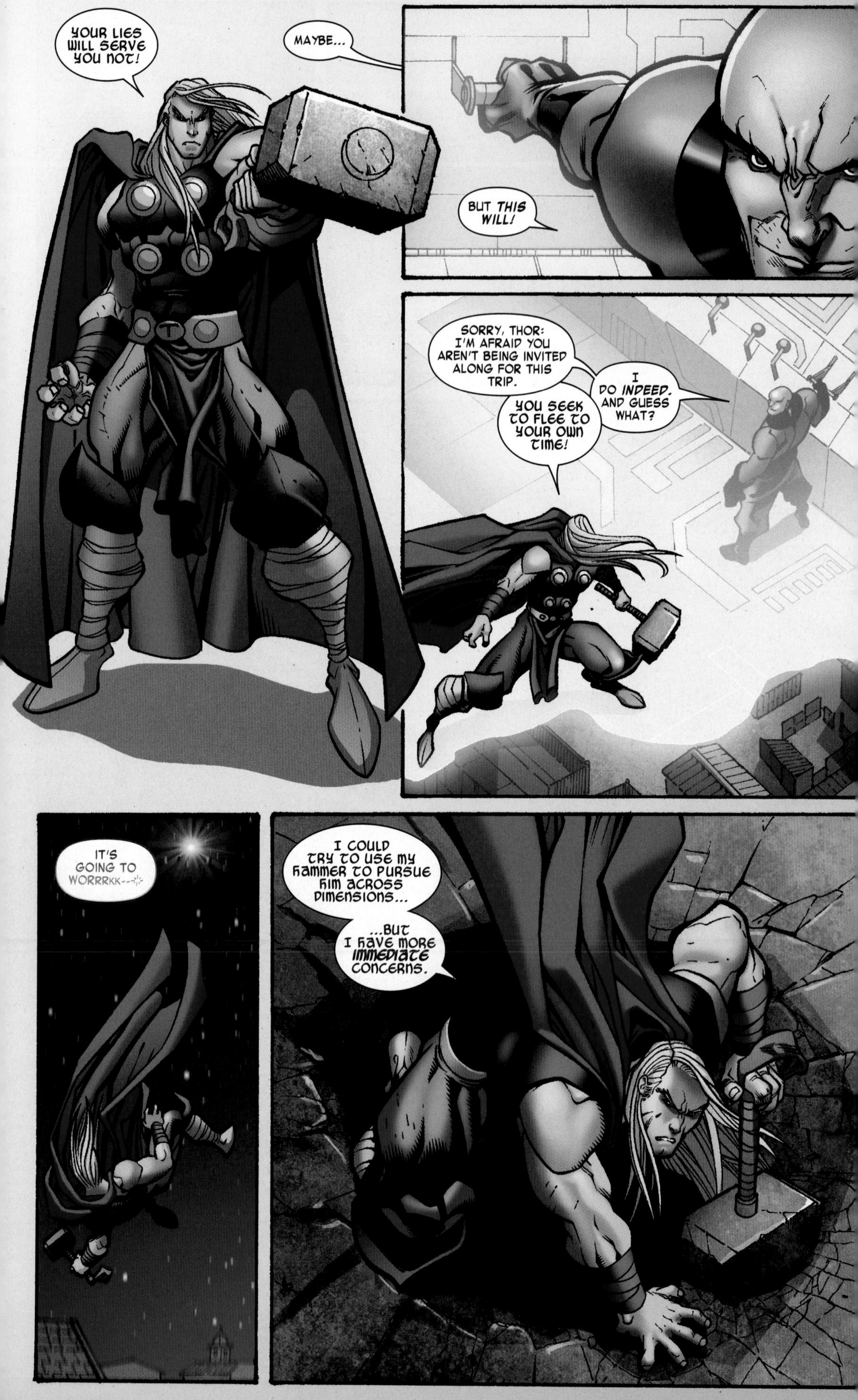

YOUR LIES WILL SERVE YOU NOT!
MAYBE...
BUT THIS WILL!
SORRY, THOR: I'M AFRAID YOU AREN'T BEING INVITED ALONG FOR THIS TRIP.
YOU SEEK TO FLEE TO YOUR OWN TIME!
I DO INDEED. AND GUESS WHAT?
IT'S GOING TO WORRRKK--
I COULD TRY TO USE MY HAMMER TO PURSUE HIM ACROSS DIMENSIONS...
...BUT I HAVE MORE IMMEDIATE CONCERNS.

I WAS CONCERNED THAT IF I EMPLOYED MAGICKS WITH THOR TO THE DEGREE I DID WITH HIS ALLIES, HE WOULD PERCEIVE MY HAND.

SO ZARRKO AND HIS MACHINATIONS WITH THE HULKS WERE GENUINE ENOUGH...

...WHILE A SIMPLE ILLUSION PROVIDED THOR HIS GLIMPSE OF CAPTAIN AMERICA ON THE SCREEN, TO ZARRKO'S GENUINE CONFUSION.

AS FOR THOR'S ASSOCIATES, ALLIES OF MINE WERE HAPPY TO DO MY BIDDING, AIDED BY SIMPLE GLAMOURS AND ILLUSIONS.

THE ENCHANTRESS ATTENDED TO CAPTAIN AMERICA, IN A WORLD THAT AT NO TIME WAS EVER WHAT HE PERCEIVED IT TO BE...

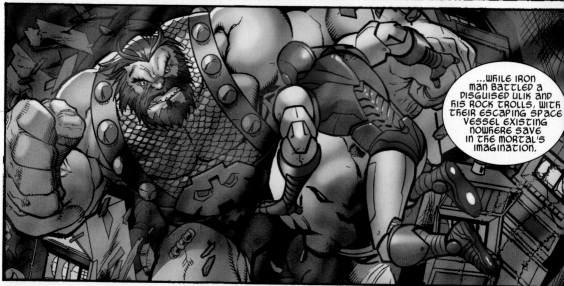

...WHILE IRON MAN BATTLED A DISGUISED ULIK AND HIS ROCK TROLLS, WITH THEIR ESCAPING SPACE VESSEL EXISTING NOWHERE SAVE IN THE MORTAL'S IMAGINATION.

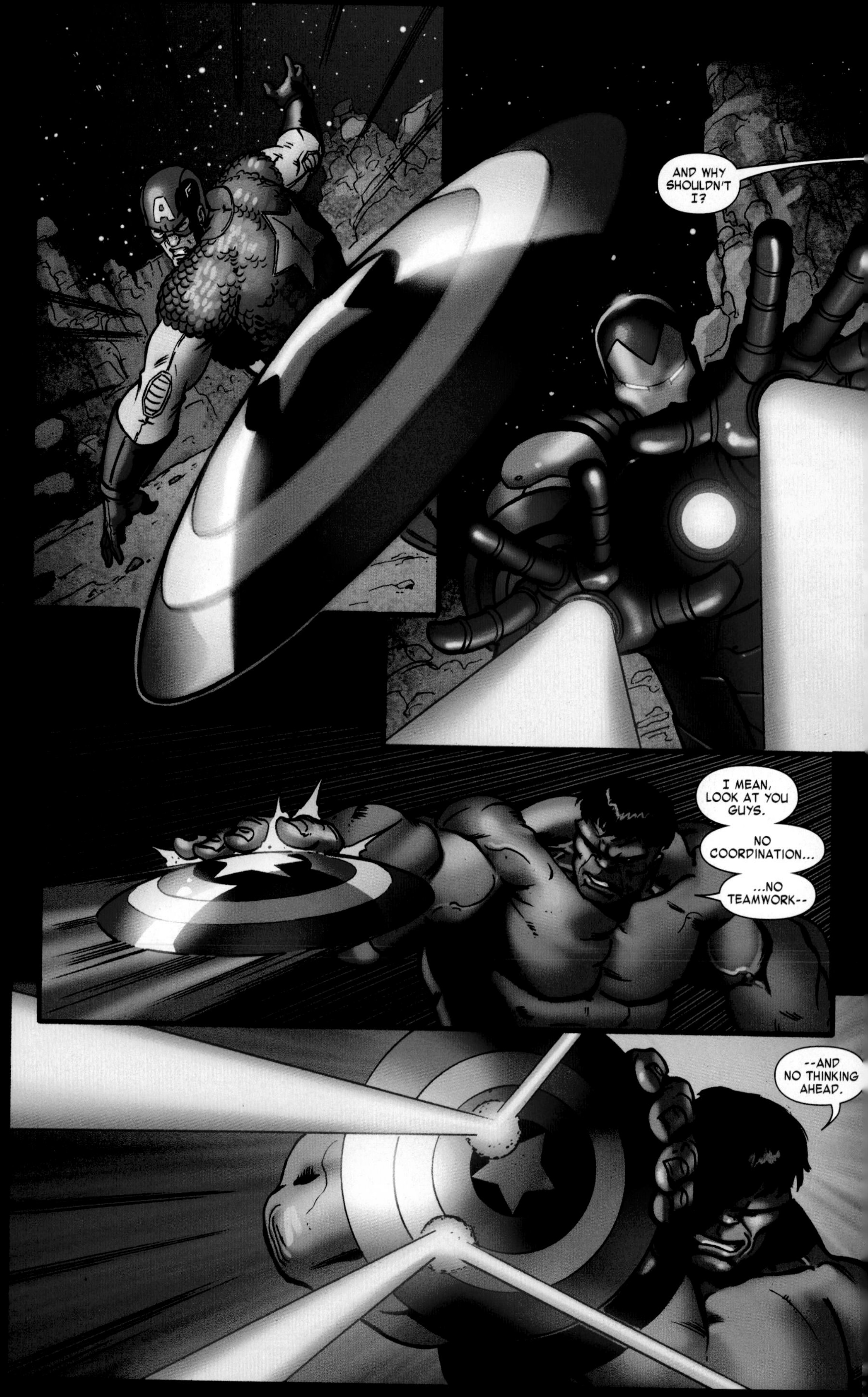
AND WHY SHOULDN'T I?
I MEAN, LOOK AT YOU GUYS.
NO COORDINATION...
...NO TEAMWORK--
--AND NO THINKING AHEAD.

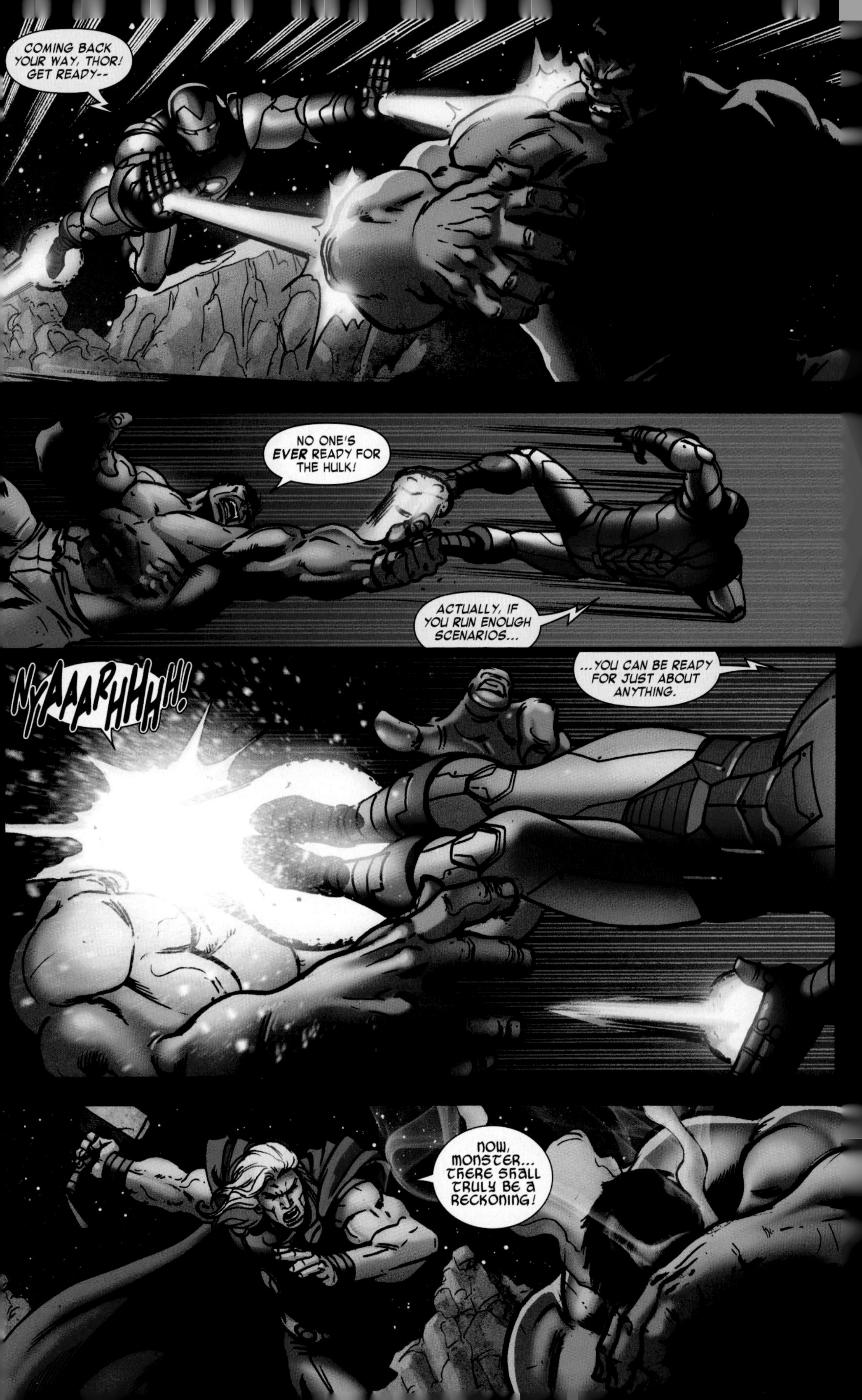
COMING BACK YOUR WAY, THOR! GET READY--
NO ONE'S EVER READY FOR THE HULK!
ACTUALLY, IF YOU RUN ENOUGH SCENARIOS...
...YOU CAN BE READY FOR JUST ABOUT ANYTHING.
NYAAARHHHH!
NOW, MONSTER... THERE SHALL TRULY BE A RECKONING!

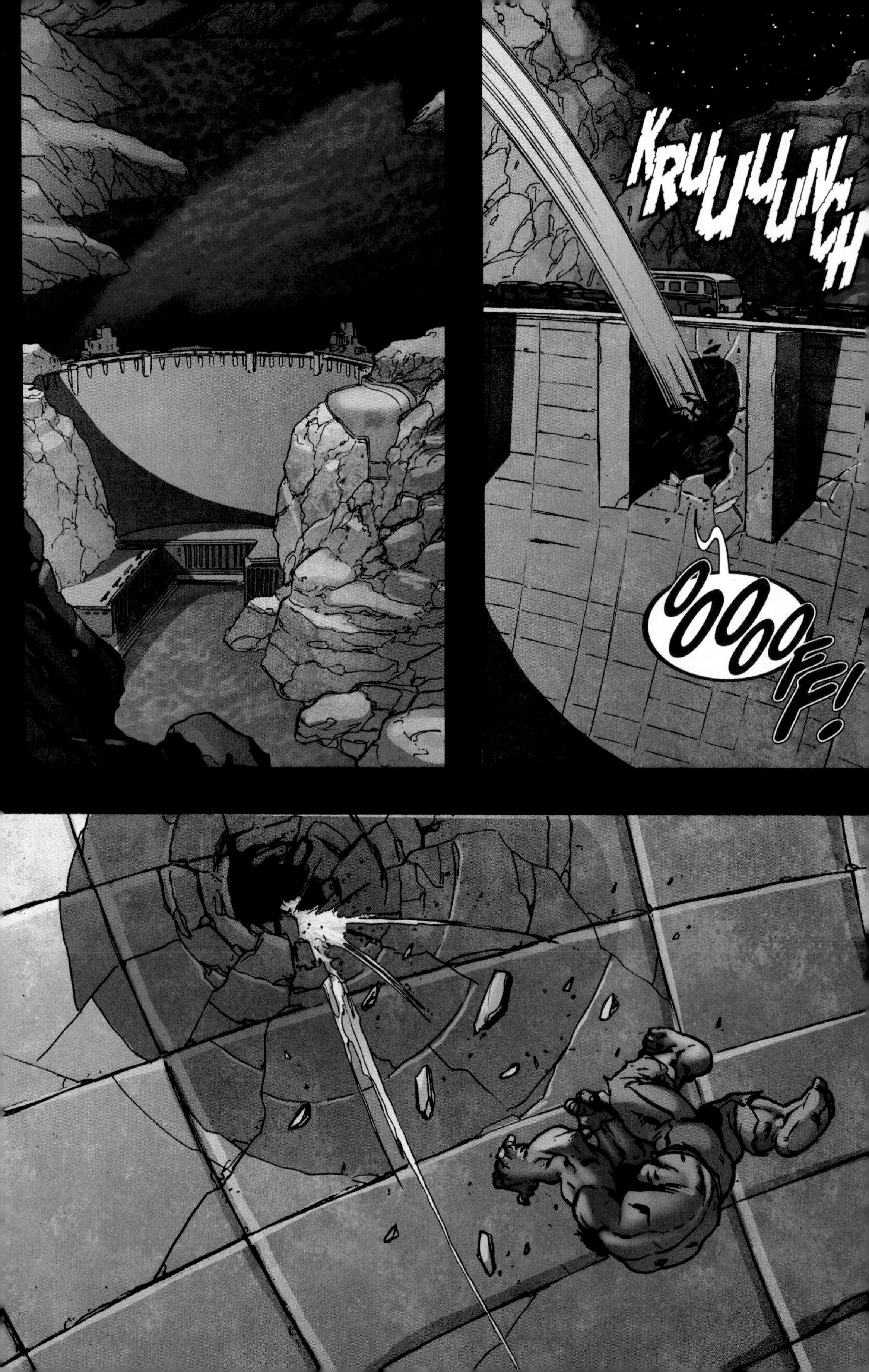
KRUUUUNCH
OOOOOFF!

THOR, WAIT!

ONE SIDE! MAYHAP HE IS STILL NOT--

THOR, SOMETHING'S GOING ON! MY WEAPONS WENT OFF BY THEMSELVES, AND YOU LOOK CRAZED!

--ABOUT?

HOW... ODD... I... WHY DID I--?

WHAT ARE YOU BABBLING--?

THE THINGS HE WAS SAYING... ABOUT HOW WE WERE FALLING FOR THE SAME THING...

I KNOW I WASN'T HERE FOR IT, BUT THE WASP TOLD ME YOU CAME TOGETHER BECAUSE OF MISUNDERSTANDINGS GENERATED BY--

LOKI.

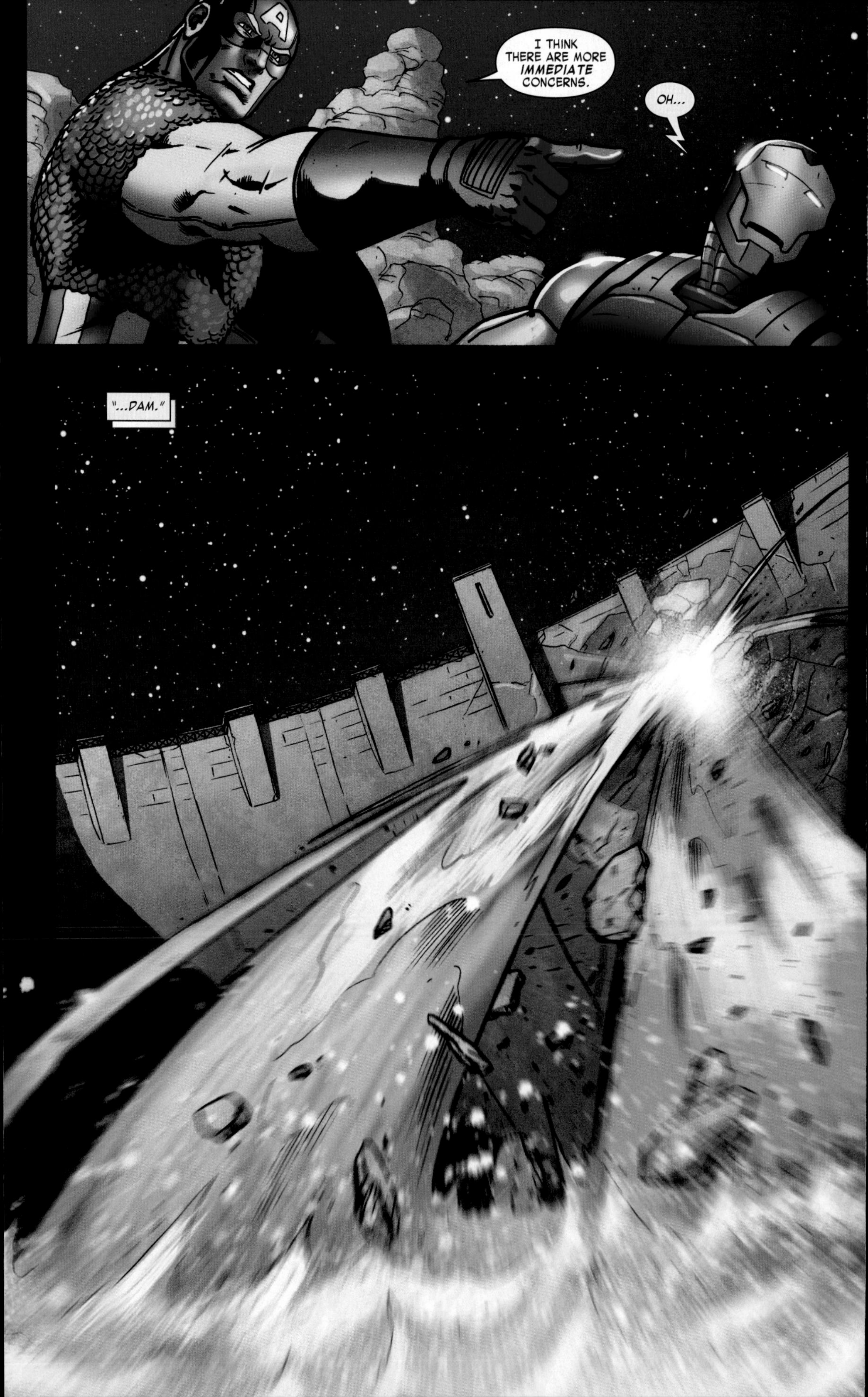
I THINK THERE ARE MORE *IMMEDIATE* CONCERNS.
OH...
"...DAM."

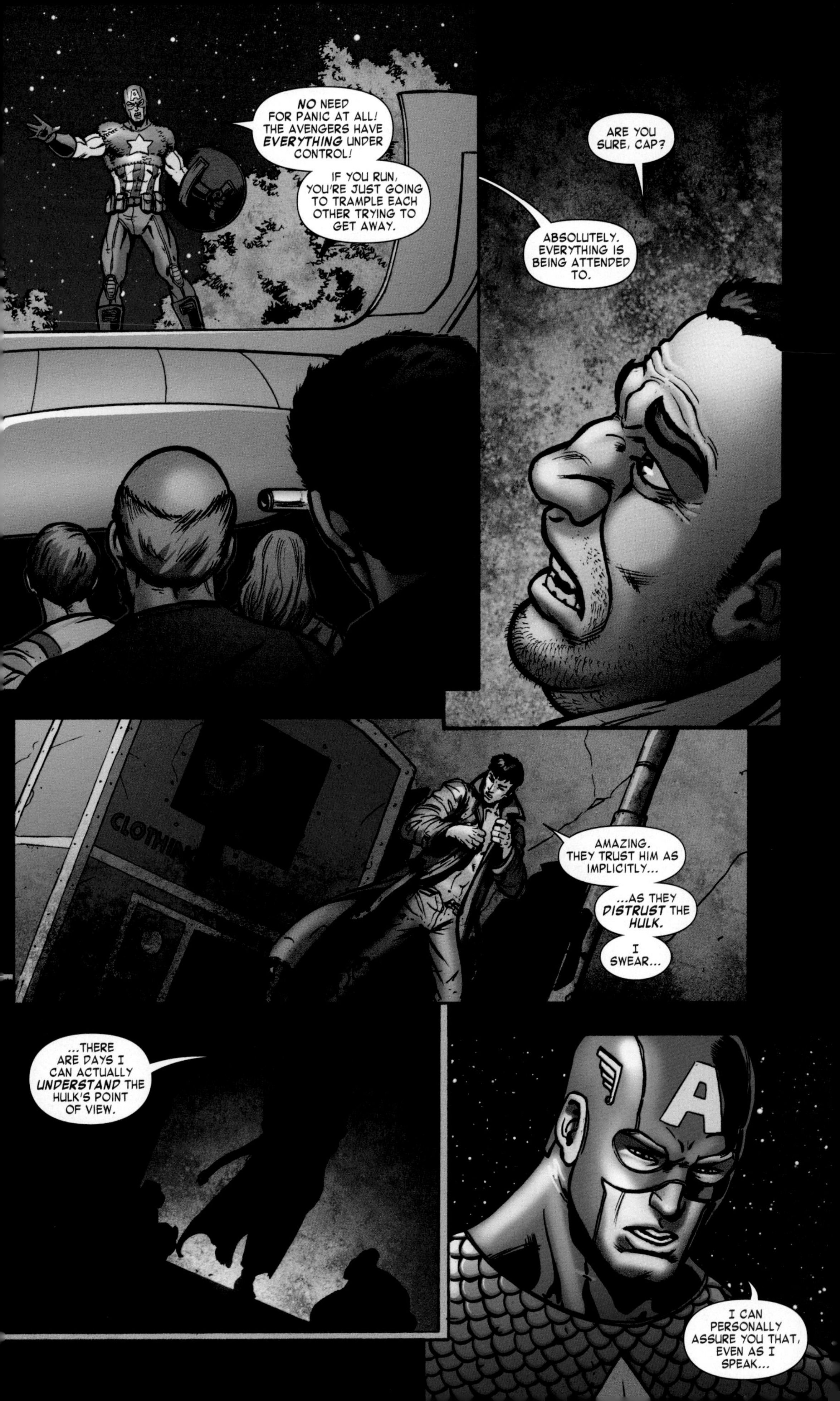

NO NEED FOR PANIC AT ALL! THE AVENGERS HAVE EVERYTHING UNDER CONTROL!
IF YOU RUN, YOU'RE JUST GOING TO TRAMPLE EACH OTHER TRYING TO GET AWAY.
ARE YOU SURE, CAP?
ABSOLUTELY. EVERYTHING IS BEING ATTENDED TO.
CLOTHIN
AMAZING. THEY TRUST HIM AS IMPLICITLY...
...AS THEY DISTRUST THE HULK.
I SWEAR...
...THERE ARE DAYS I CAN ACTUALLY UNDERSTAND THE HULK'S POINT OF VIEW.
I CAN PERSONALLY ASSURE YOU THAT, EVEN AS I SPEAK...

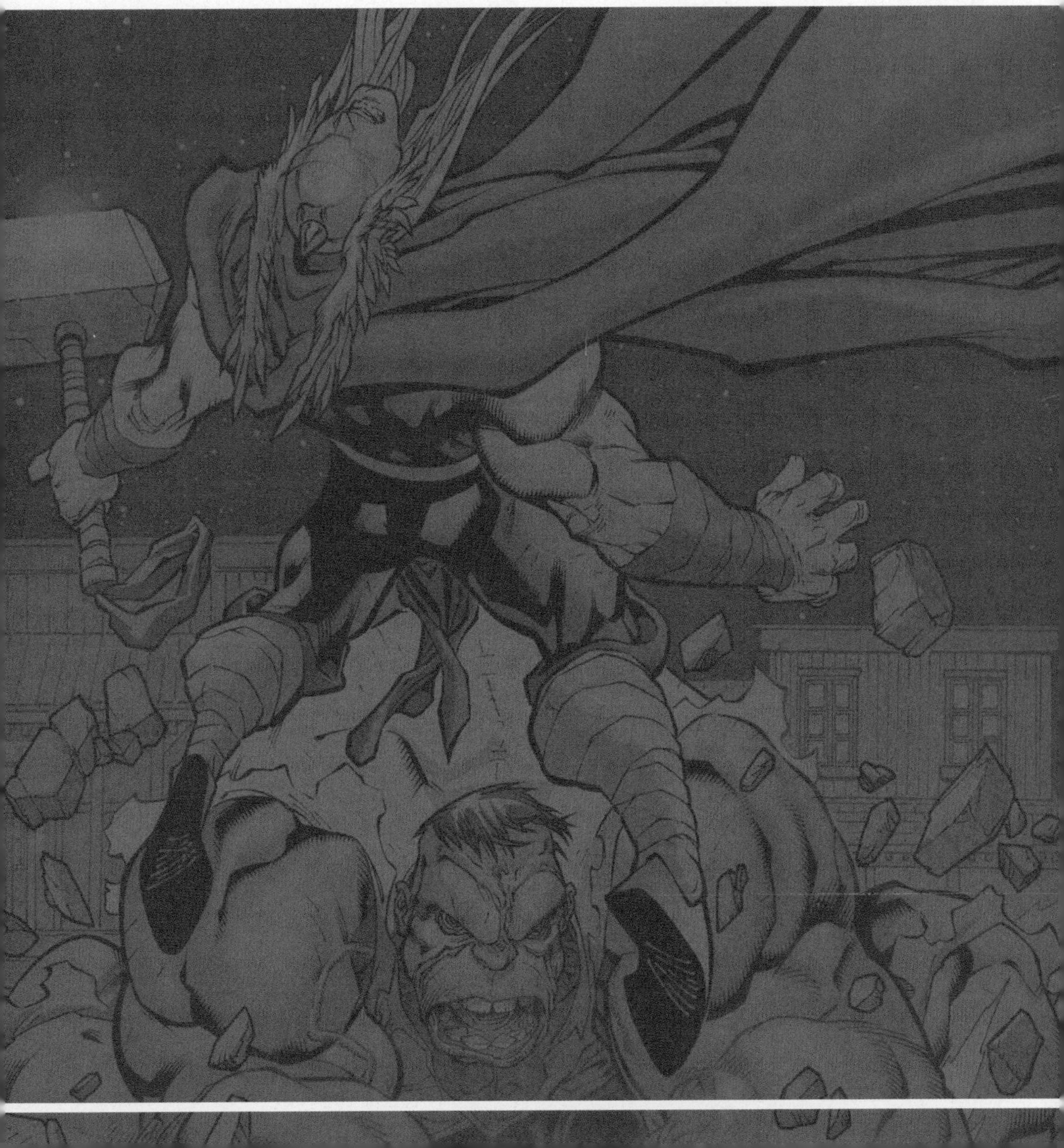

AVENGERS (2016) #1 THEIR RANKS SHATTERED BY *CIVIL WAR II*, EARTH'S MIGHTIEST HEROES MUST FIND THE RESOLVE TO STAND UNITED ONE FINAL TIME AGAINST THEIR GREATEST FOE: KANG THE CONQUERER!

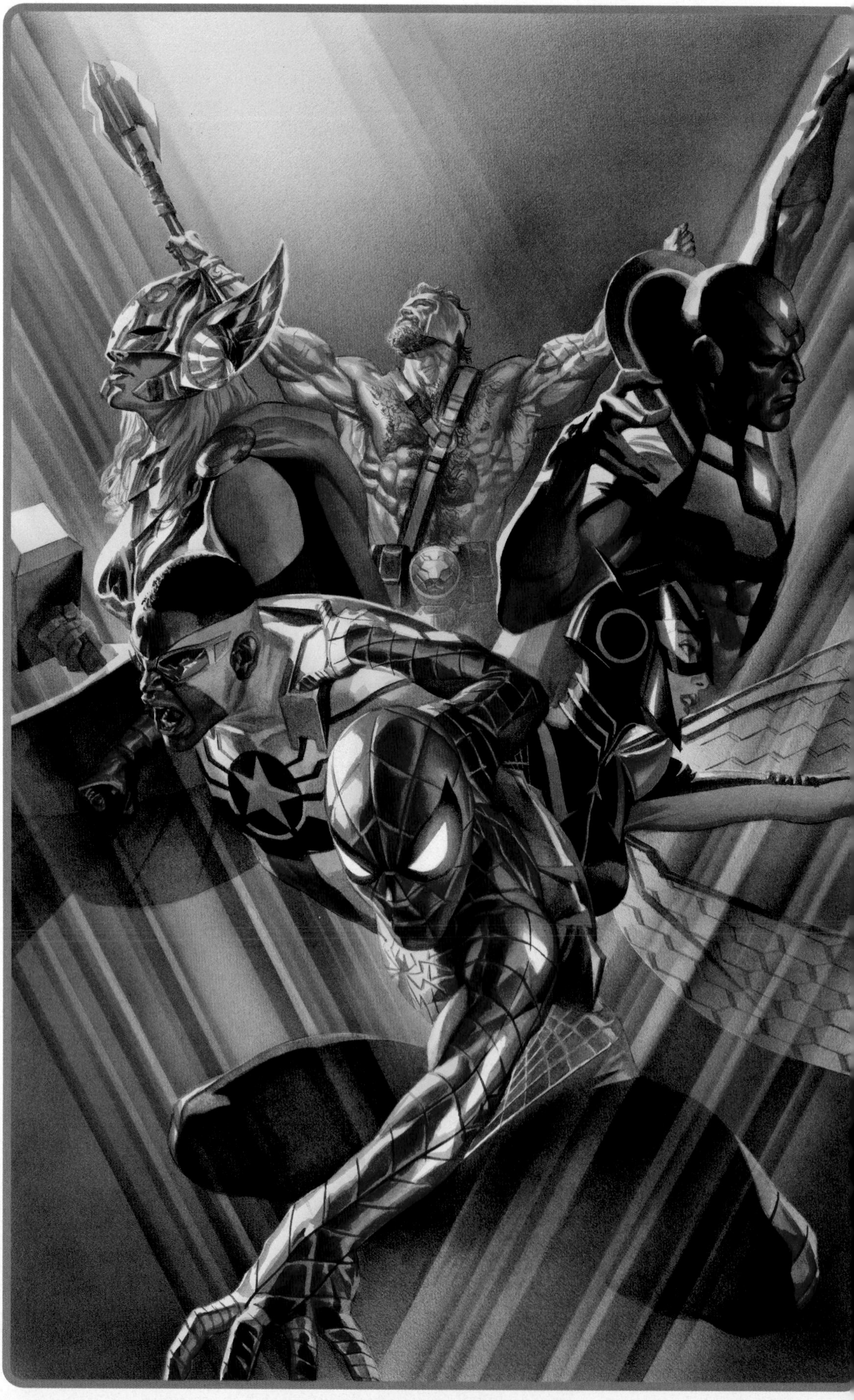

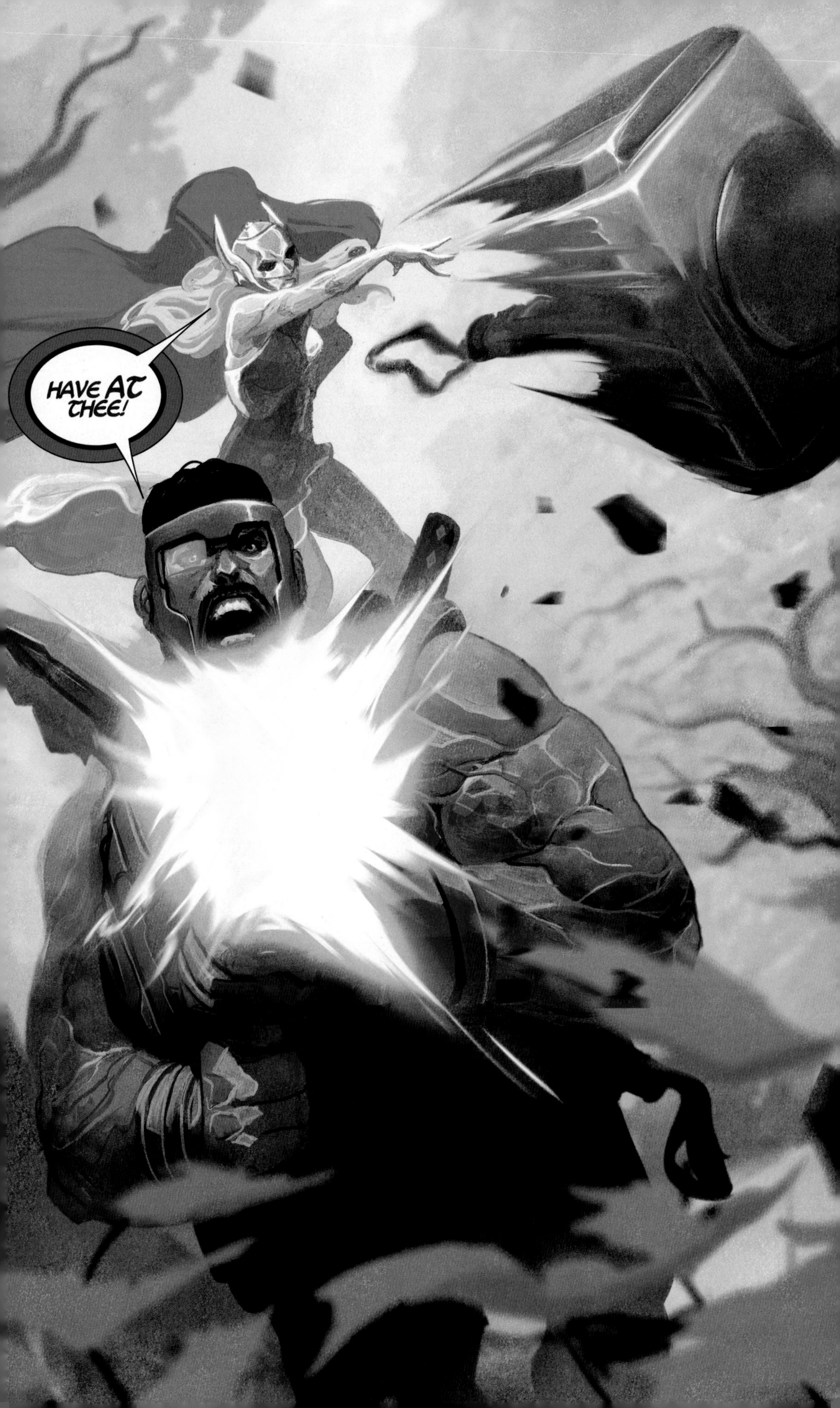
HAVE AT THEE!

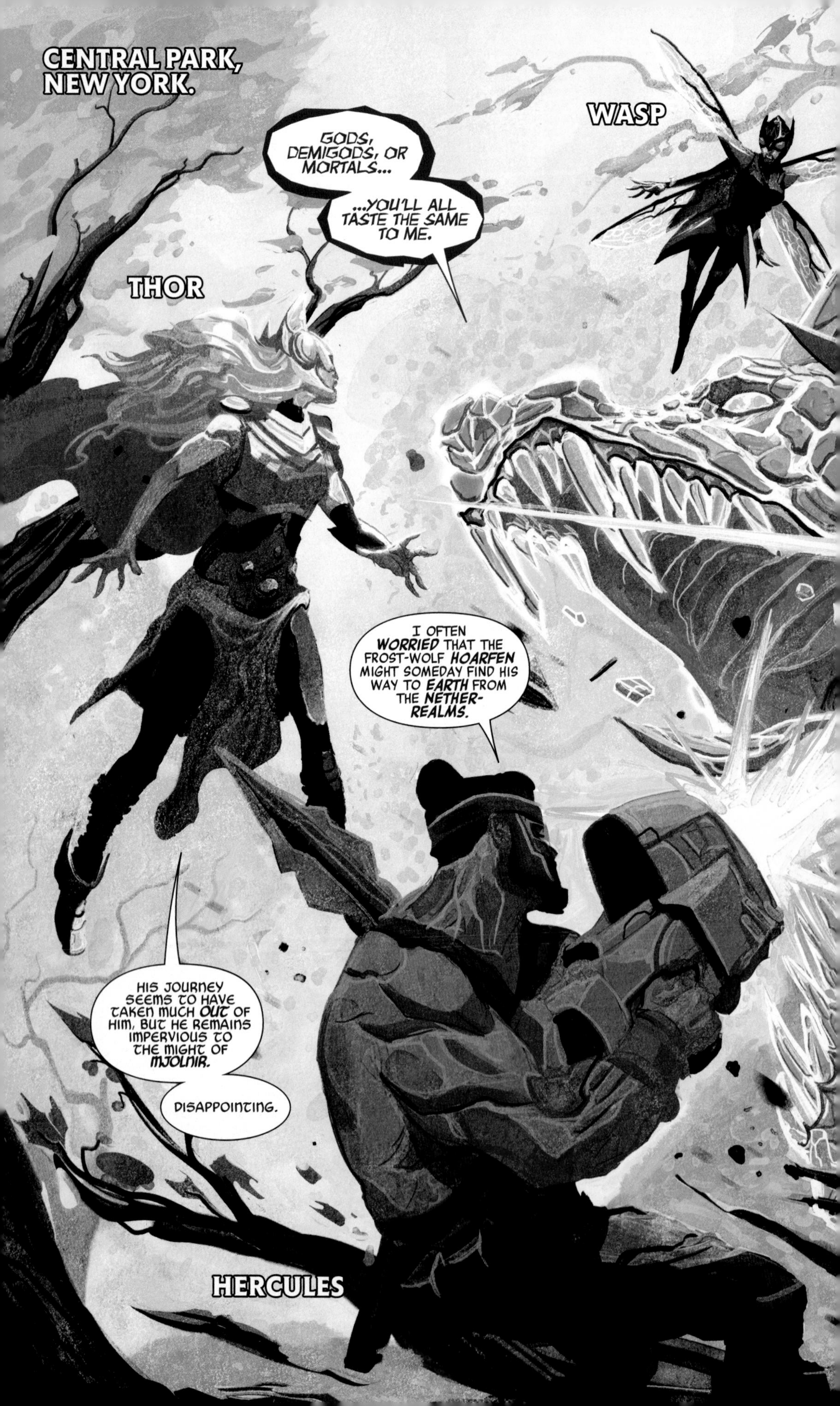
CENTRAL PARK, NEW YORK.
WASP
GODS, DEMIGODS, OR MORTALS...
...YOU'LL ALL TASTE THE SAME TO ME.
THOR
I OFTEN WORRIED THAT THE FROST-WOLF HOARFEN MIGHT SOMEDAY FIND HIS WAY TO EARTH FROM THE NETHER-REALMS.
HIS JOURNEY SEEMS TO HAVE TAKEN MUCH OUT OF HIM, BUT HE REMAINS IMPERVIOUS TO THE MIGHT OF MJOLNIR.
DISAPPOINTING.
HERCULES

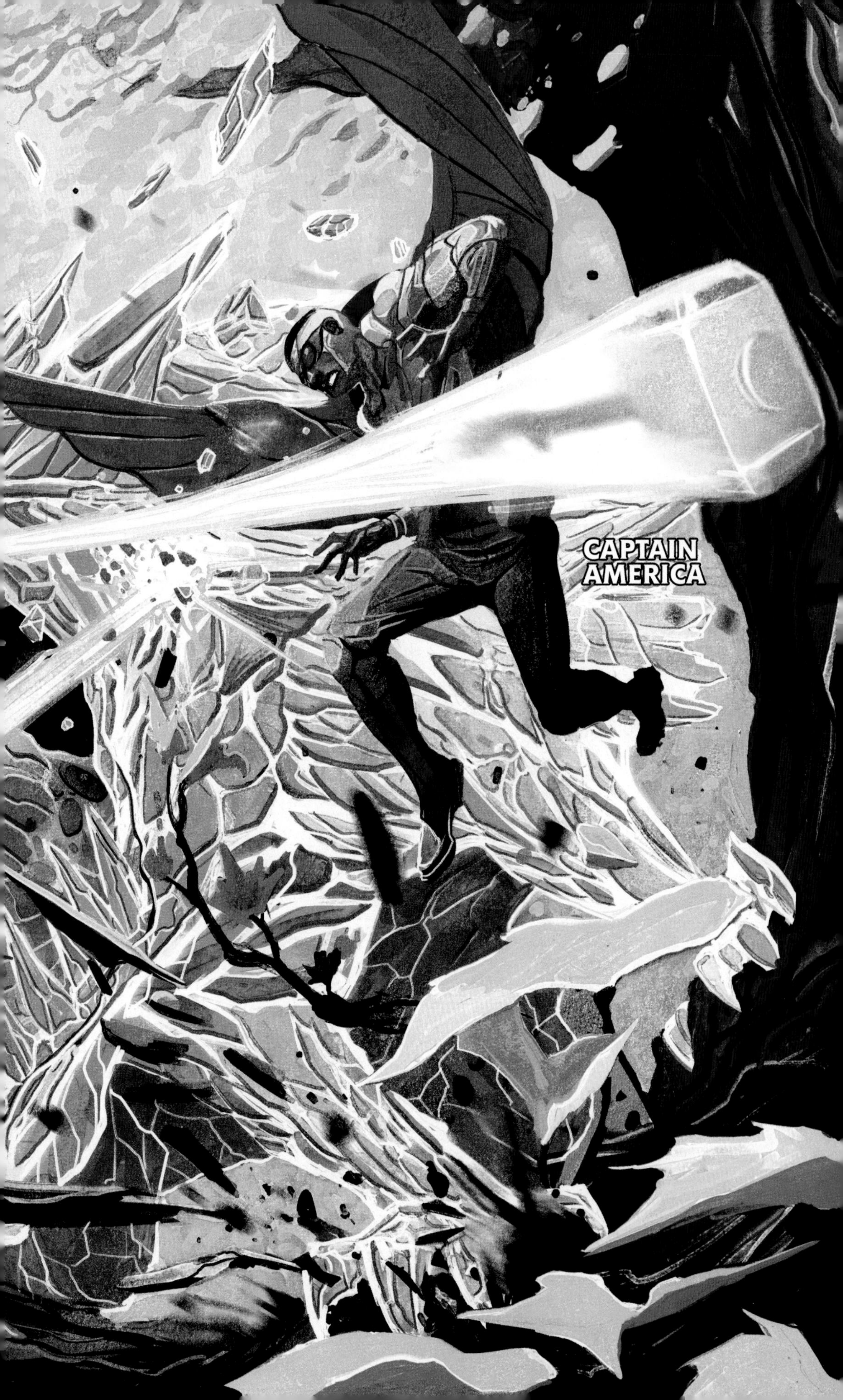
CAPTAIN
AMERICA

THE AVENGERS

WASP
Nadia Pym

THOR
Jane Foster

CAPTAIN AMERICA
Sam Wilson

VISION

SPIDER-MAN
Peter Parker

HERCULES

Writer	**Mark Waid**
Artist	**Mike del Mundo**
Color Artists	**Mike del Mundo with Marco D'alfonso**
Letterer	**VC's Cory Petit**
Cover	**Alex Ross**
Variant Covers	**Adam Kubert & Sonia Oback; John Tyler Christopher; Alex Maleev; Butch Guice & Rachelle Rosenberg; Daniel Acuña**
Assistant Editor	**Alanna Smith**
Editor	**Tom Brevoort**
Editor in Chief	**Axel Alonso**
Chief Creative Officer	**Joe Quesada**
Publisher	**Dan Buckley**
Executive Producer	**Alan Fine**

The Avengers created by **Stan Lee & Jack Kirby**

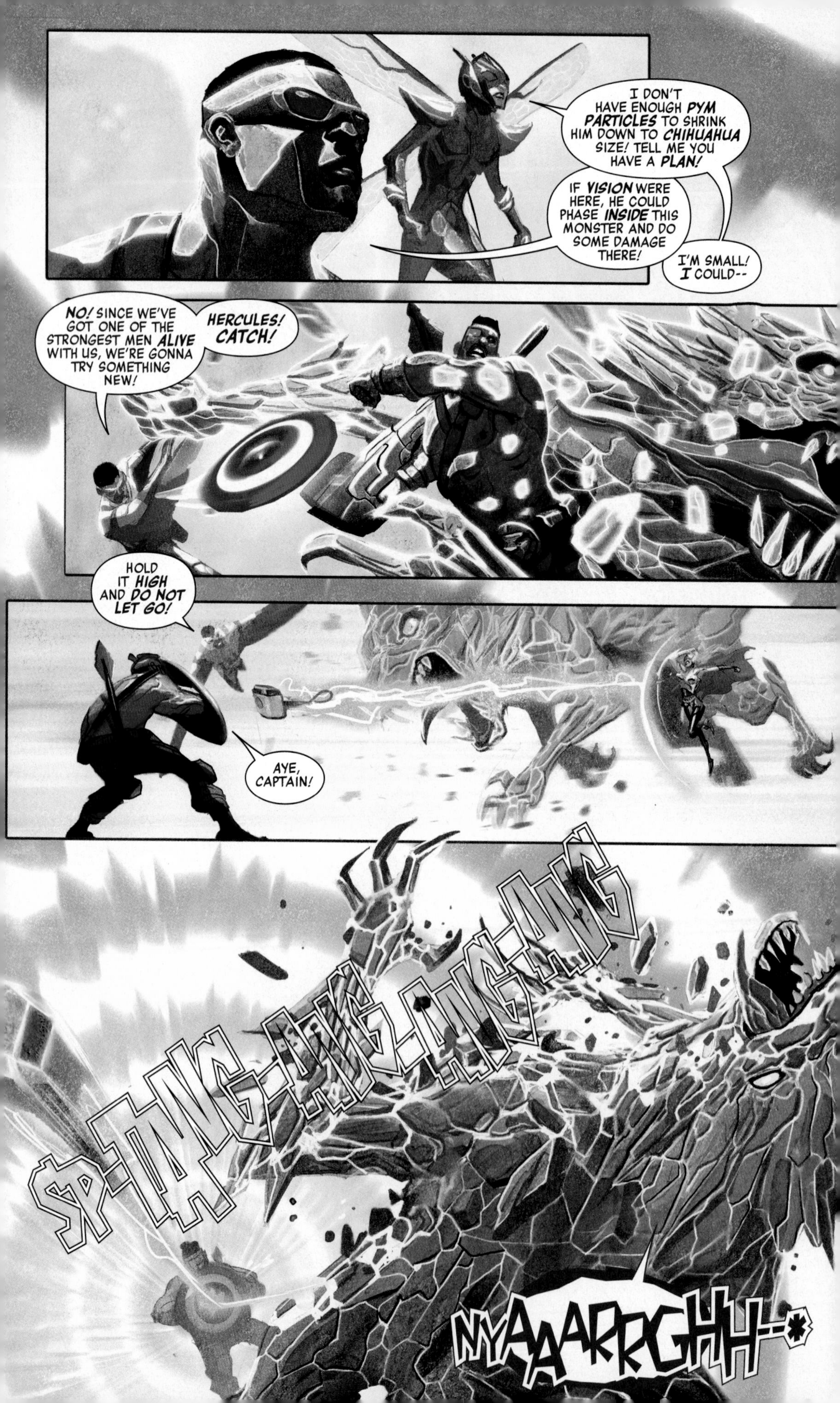
I DON'T HAVE ENOUGH PYM PARTICLES TO SHRINK HIM DOWN TO CHIHUAHUA SIZE! TELL ME YOU HAVE A PLAN!
IF VISION WERE HERE, HE COULD PHASE INSIDE THIS MONSTER AND DO SOME DAMAGE THERE!
I'M SMALL! I COULD--
NO! SINCE WE'VE GOT ONE OF THE STRONGEST MEN ALIVE WITH US, WE'RE GONNA TRY SOMETHING NEW!
HERCULES! CATCH!
HOLD IT HIGH AND DO NOT LET GO!
AYE, CAPTAIN!
SP-TANG-ANG-ANG-ANG
NYAAARRGHH--*

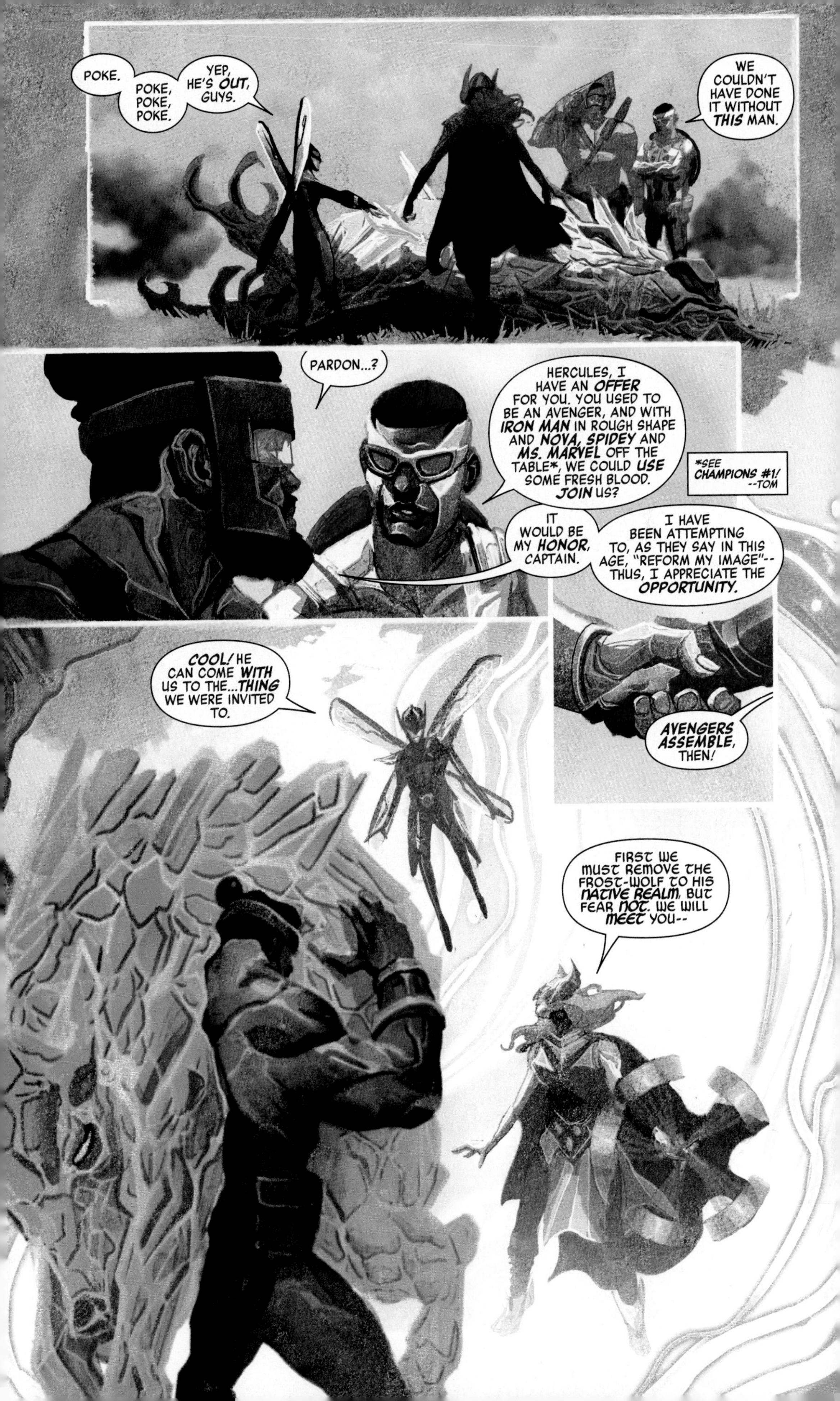
POKE.
POKE, POKE, POKE.
YEP, HE'S OUT, GUYS.
WE COULDN'T HAVE DONE IT WITHOUT THIS MAN.
PARDON...?
HERCULES, I HAVE AN OFFER FOR YOU. YOU USED TO BE AN AVENGER, AND WITH IRON MAN IN ROUGH SHAPE AND NOVA, SPIDEY AND MS. MARVEL OFF THE TABLE*, WE COULD USE SOME FRESH BLOOD. JOIN US?
*SEE CHAMPIONS #1! --TOM
IT WOULD BE MY HONOR, CAPTAIN.
I HAVE BEEN ATTEMPTING TO, AS THEY SAY IN THIS AGE, "REFORM MY IMAGE"-- THUS, I APPRECIATE THE OPPORTUNITY.
AVENGERS ASSEMBLE, THEN!
COOL! HE CAN COME WITH US TO THE...THING WE WERE INVITED TO.
FIRST WE MUST REMOVE THE FROST-WOLF TO HIS NATIVE REALM, BUT FEAR NOT. WE WILL MEET YOU--

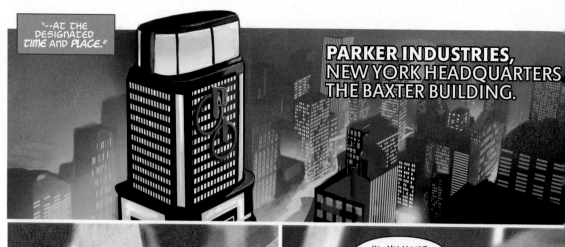

"--AT THE DESIGNATED *TIME* AND *PLACE*."

PARKER INDUSTRIES,
NEW YORK HEADQUARTERS
THE BAXTER BUILDING.

HI. MY NAME IS *PETER PARKER*, VERY LUCKY *TECH* GAZILLIONAIRE WHO CRAWLED HIS WAY LIKE A...

...*SNAIL*... LET'S SAY *SNAIL*... FROM PHOTOJOURNALISM TO *HERE*--TO A POSITION WHERE I CAN GIVE *BACK* BETTER THAN I *GOT*.

AND DO *I* HAVE AN OFFER FOR *YOU*.

MS. BEACHUM, GIVE THESE FOLKS A PLACE TO *SIT DOWN* AND BE *COMFORTABLE*.

YOU BET, BOSS. ONE *RISING TABLE*, LITERALLY COMING *UP*.

KLIK

HUH.

WELL, IT'S NOT AN *AMBUSH*.

I WAS IN THE MOOD FOR AN AMBUSH.

YOU GUYS KNOW WHO *OWNS* THIS BUILDING, RIGHT?

ME.

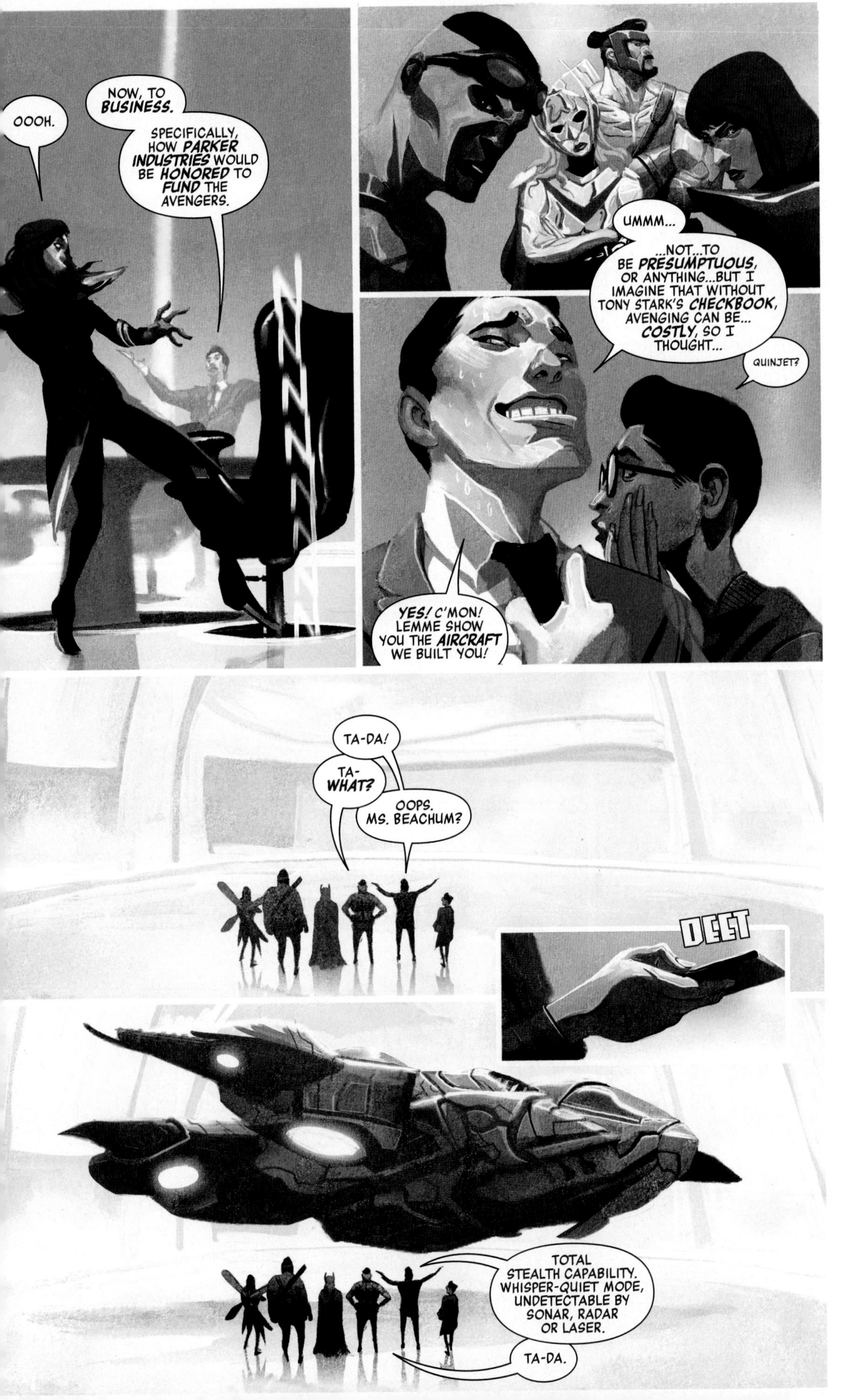
OOOH.
NOW, TO BUSINESS.
SPECIFICALLY, HOW PARKER INDUSTRIES WOULD BE HONORED TO FUND THE AVENGERS.
UMMM...
...NOT...TO BE PRESUMPTUOUS, OR ANYTHING...BUT I IMAGINE THAT WITHOUT TONY STARK'S CHECKBOOK, AVENGING CAN BE... COSTLY, SO I THOUGHT...
QUINJET?
YES! C'MON! LEMME SHOW YOU THE AIRCRAFT WE BUILT YOU!
TA-DA!
TA-WHAT?
OOPS. MS. BEACHUM?
BEET
TOTAL STEALTH CAPABILITY. WHISPER-QUIET MODE, UNDETECTABLE BY SONAR, RADAR OR LASER.
TA-DA.

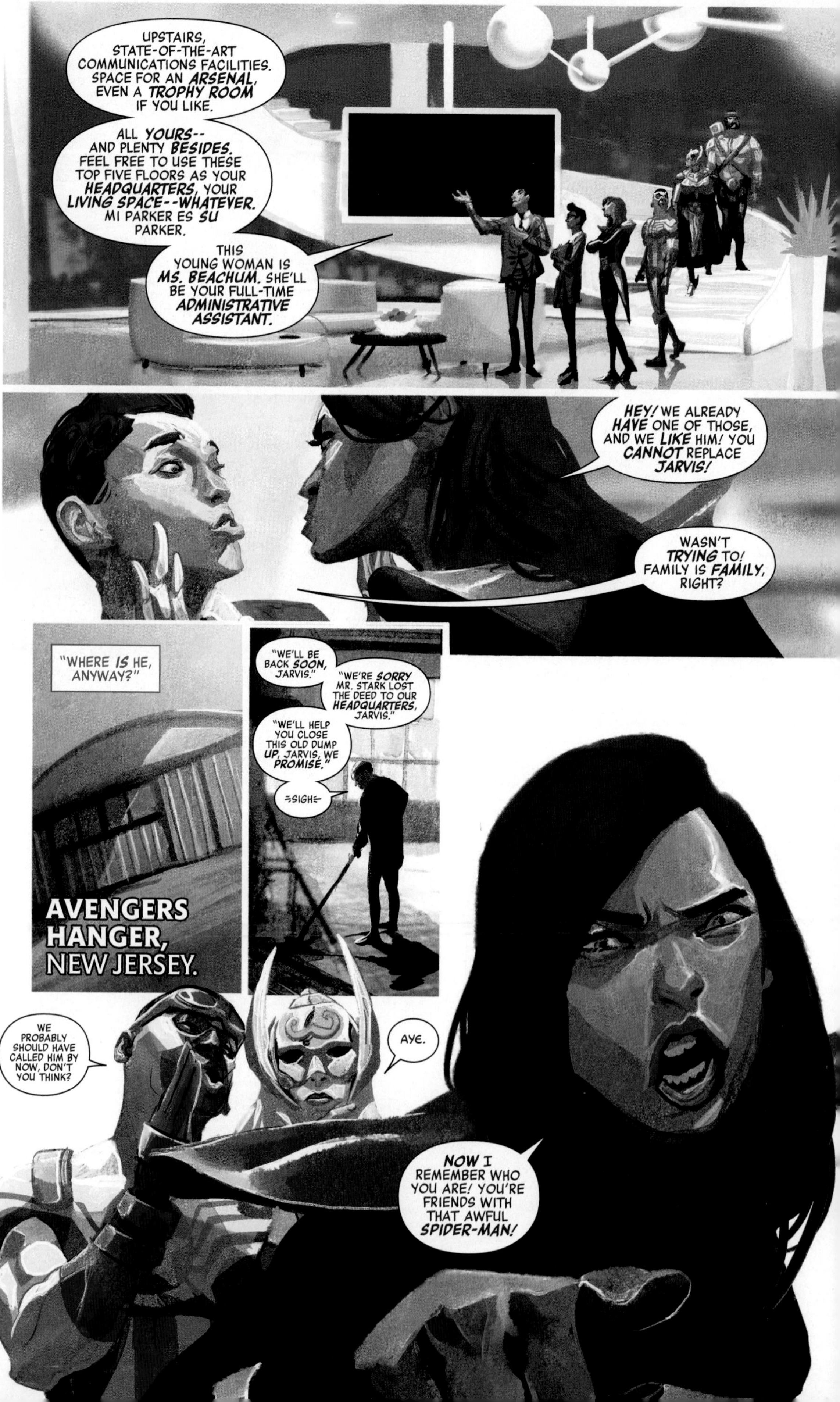
UPSTAIRS, STATE-OF-THE-ART COMMUNICATIONS FACILITIES. SPACE FOR AN ARSENAL, EVEN A TROPHY ROOM IF YOU LIKE.
ALL YOURS-- AND PLENTY BESIDES. FEEL FREE TO USE THESE TOP FIVE FLOORS AS YOUR HEADQUARTERS, YOUR LIVING SPACE--WHATEVER. MI PARKER ES SU PARKER.
THIS YOUNG WOMAN IS MS. BEACHUM. SHE'LL BE YOUR FULL-TIME ADMINISTRATIVE ASSISTANT.
HEY! WE ALREADY HAVE ONE OF THOSE, AND WE LIKE HIM! YOU CANNOT REPLACE JARVIS!
WASN'T TRYING TO! FAMILY IS FAMILY, RIGHT?
"WHERE IS HE, ANYWAY?"
AVENGERS HANGER, NEW JERSEY.
"WE'LL BE BACK SOON, JARVIS."
"WE'RE SORRY MR. STARK LOST THE DEED TO OUR HEADQUARTERS, JARVIS."
"WE'LL HELP YOU CLOSE THIS OLD DUMP UP, JARVIS, WE PROMISE."
=SIGH=
WE PROBABLY SHOULD HAVE CALLED HIM BY NOW, DON'T YOU THINK?
AYE.
NOW I REMEMBER WHO YOU ARE! YOU'RE FRIENDS WITH THAT AWFUL SPIDER-MAN!

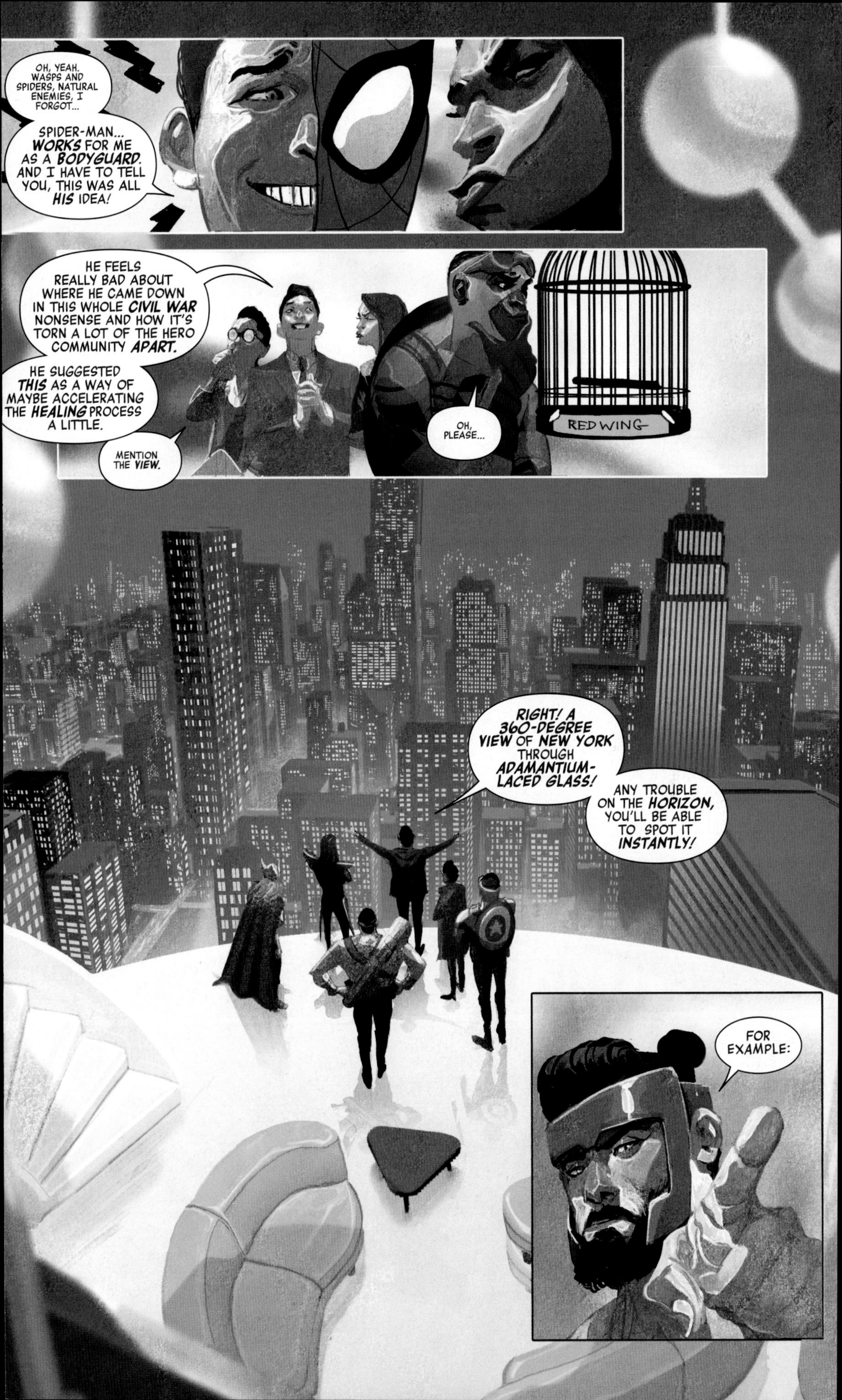
OH, YEAH. WASPS AND SPIDERS, NATURAL ENEMIES, I FORGOT...
SPIDER-MAN... WORKS FOR ME AS A BODYGUARD. AND I HAVE TO TELL YOU, THIS WAS ALL HIS IDEA!
HE FEELS REALLY BAD ABOUT WHERE HE CAME DOWN IN THIS WHOLE CIVIL WAR NONSENSE AND HOW IT'S TORN A LOT OF THE HERO COMMUNITY APART.
HE SUGGESTED THIS AS A WAY OF MAYBE ACCELERATING THE HEALING PROCESS A LITTLE.
MENTION THE VIEW.
OH, PLEASE...
REDWING
RIGHT! A 360-DEGREE VIEW OF NEW YORK THROUGH ADAMANTIUM-LACED GLASS!
ANY TROUBLE ON THE HORIZON, YOU'LL BE ABLE TO SPOT IT INSTANTLY!
FOR EXAMPLE:

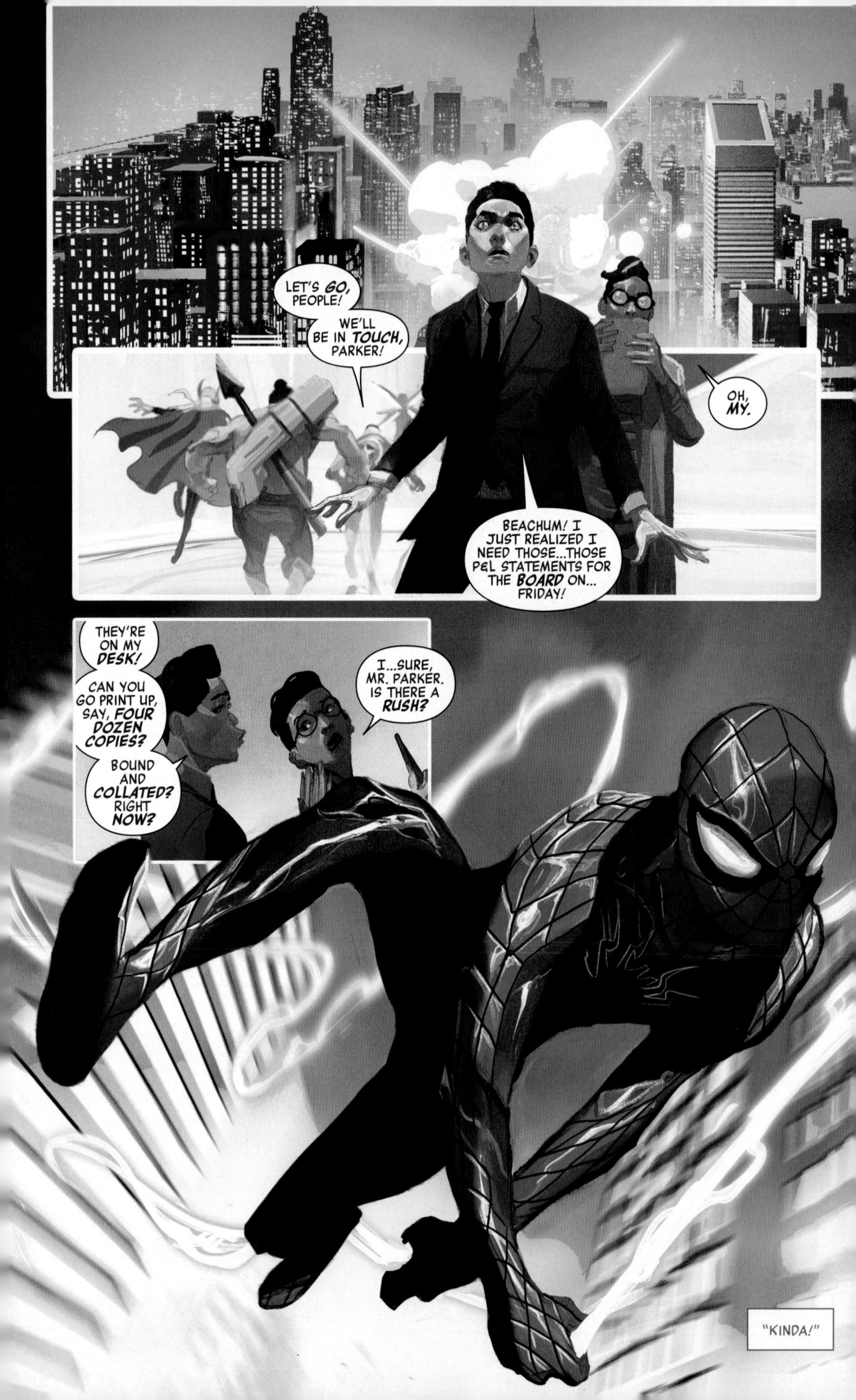
LET'S GO, PEOPLE!
WE'LL BE IN TOUCH, PARKER!
OH, MY.
BEACHUM! I JUST REALIZED I NEED THOSE...THOSE P&L STATEMENTS FOR THE BOARD ON... FRIDAY!
THEY'RE ON MY DESK!
CAN YOU GO PRINT UP, SAY, FOUR DOZEN COPIES?
BOUND AND COLLATED? RIGHT NOW?
I...SURE, MR. PARKER. IS THERE A RUSH?
"KINDA!"

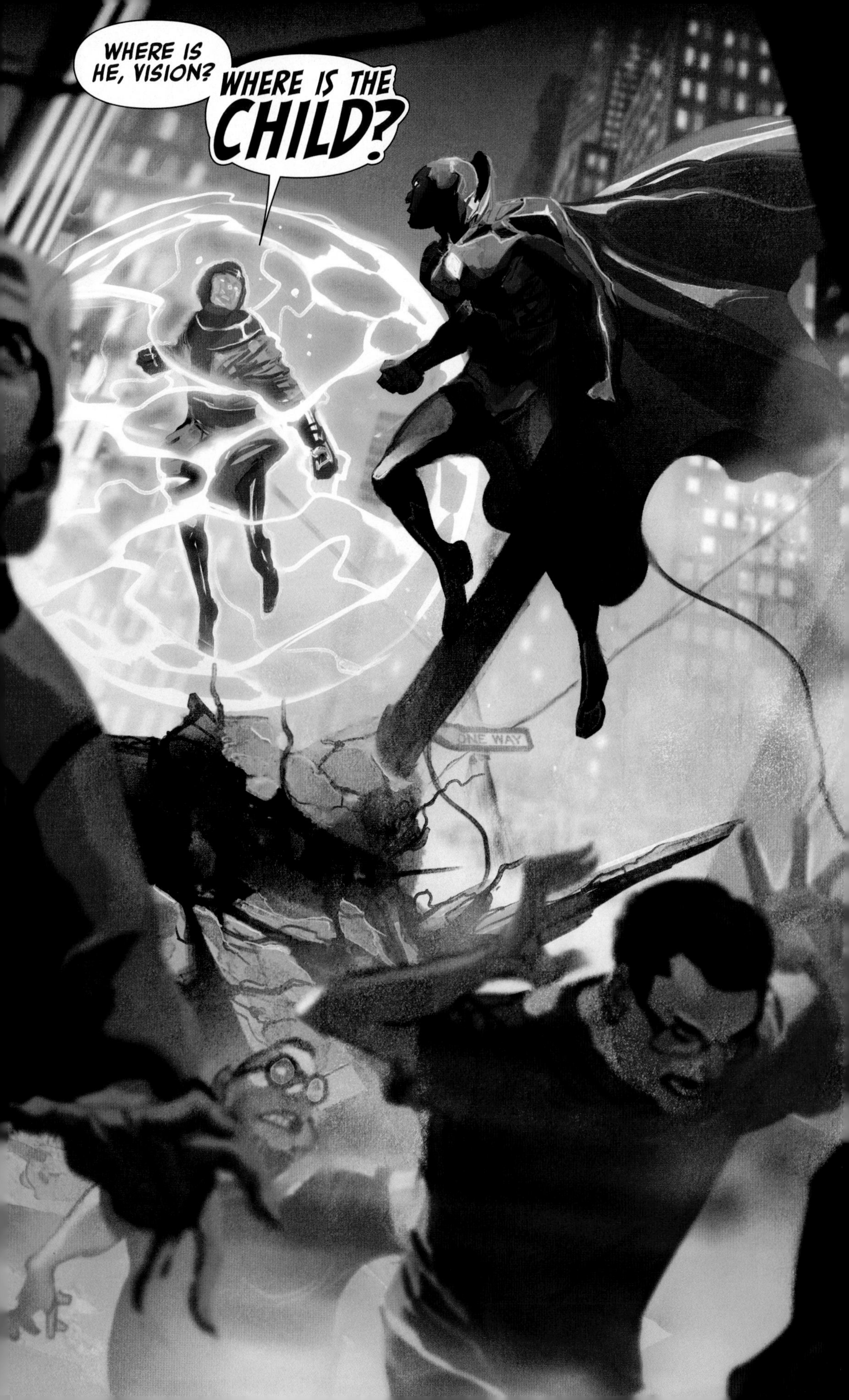
WHERE IS HE, VISION?
WHERE IS THE CHILD?
ONE WAY

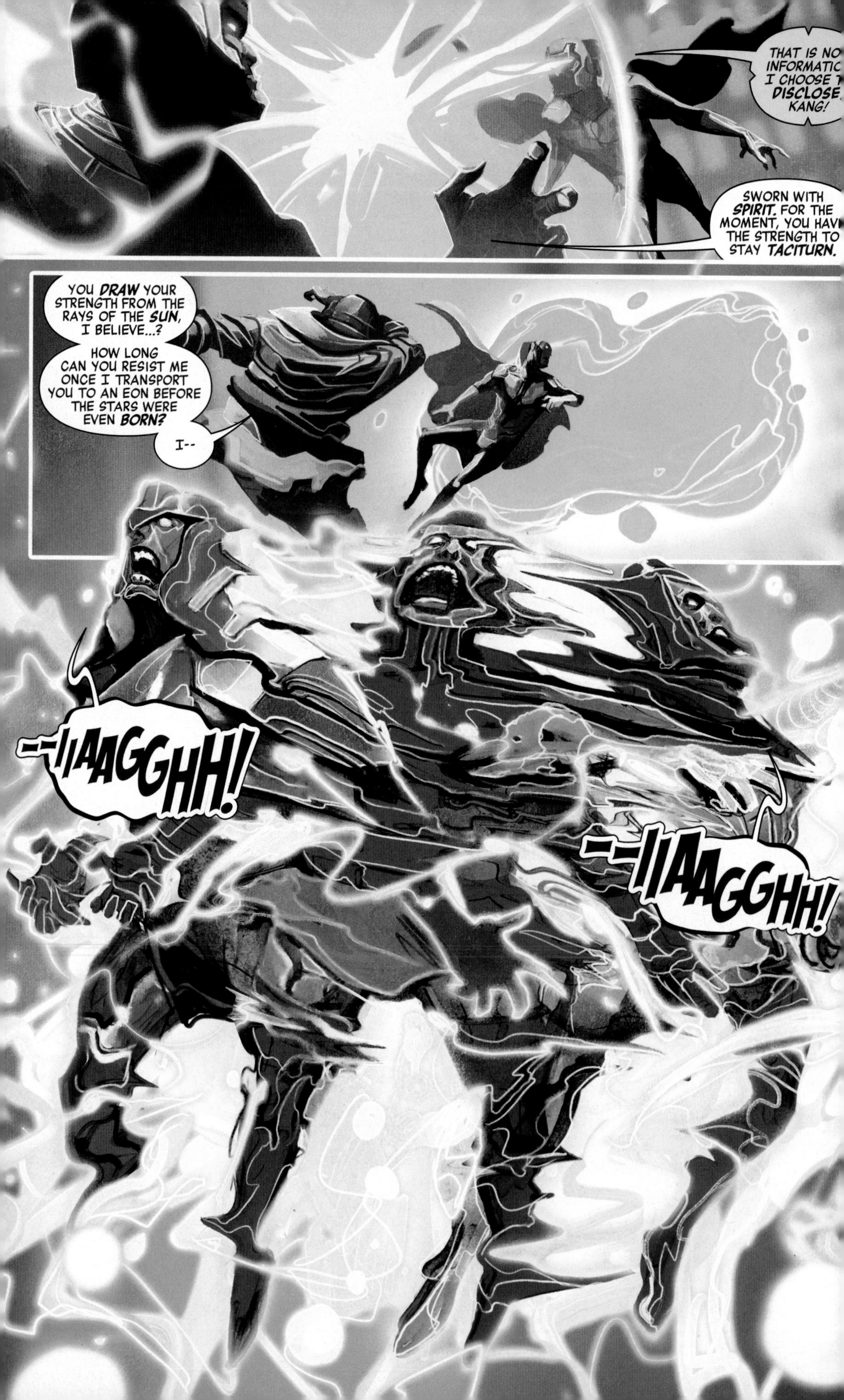
THAT IS NO INFORMATIC I CHOOSE T DISCLOSE, KANG!
SWORN WITH SPIRIT. FOR THE MOMENT, YOU HAV THE STRENGTH TO STAY TACITURN.
YOU DRAW YOUR STRENGTH FROM THE RAYS OF THE SUN, I BELIEVE...?
HOW LONG CAN YOU RESIST ME ONCE I TRANSPORT YOU TO AN EON BEFORE THE STARS WERE EVEN BORN?
I--
--IIAAGGHH!
--IIAAGGHH!

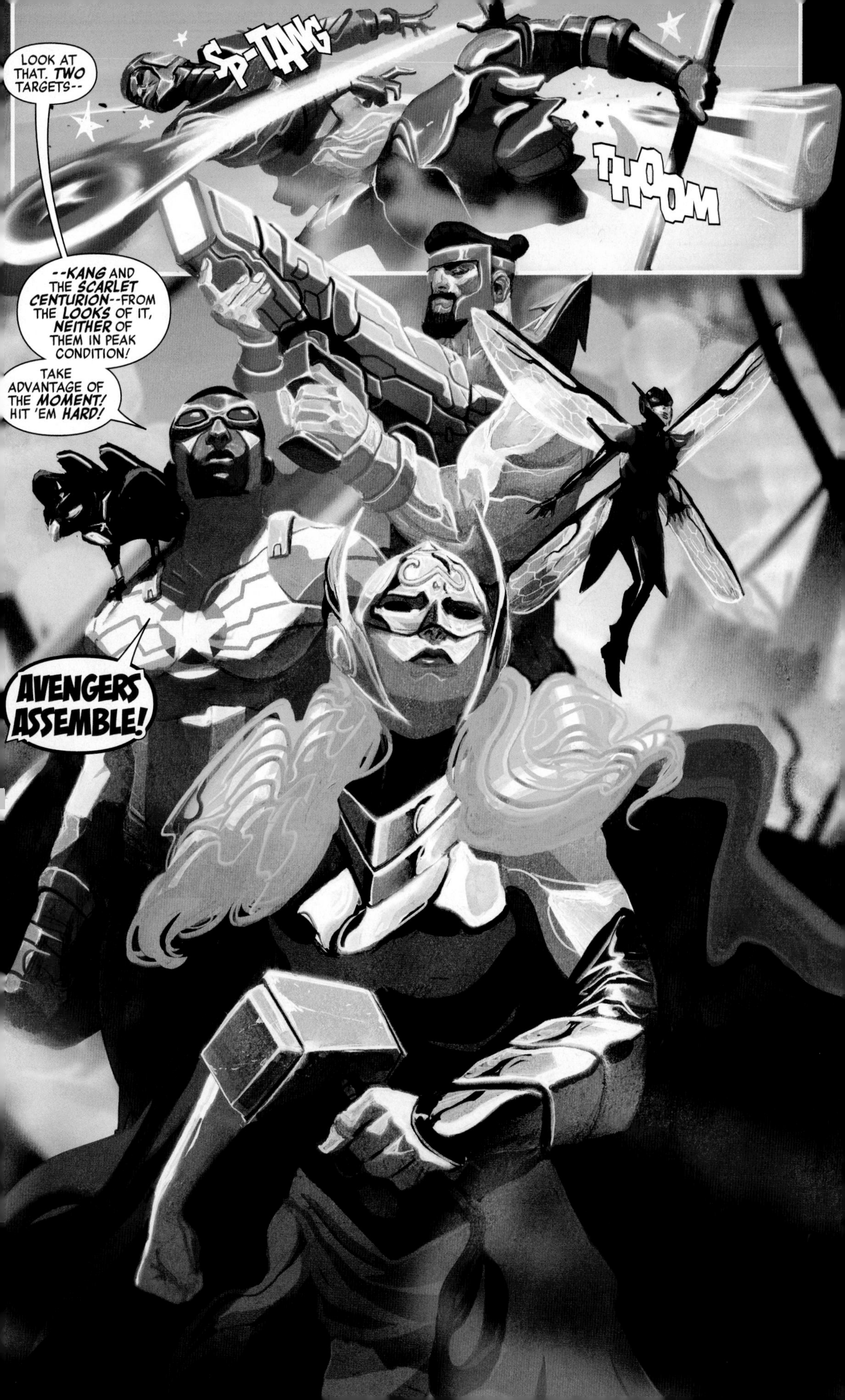
LOOK AT THAT. TWO TARGETS--
SP-TANG
THOOM
--KANG AND THE SCARLET CENTURION--FROM THE LOOKS OF IT, NEITHER OF THEM IN PEAK CONDITION!
TAKE ADVANTAGE OF THE MOMENT! HIT 'EM HARD!
AVENGERS ASSEMBLE!

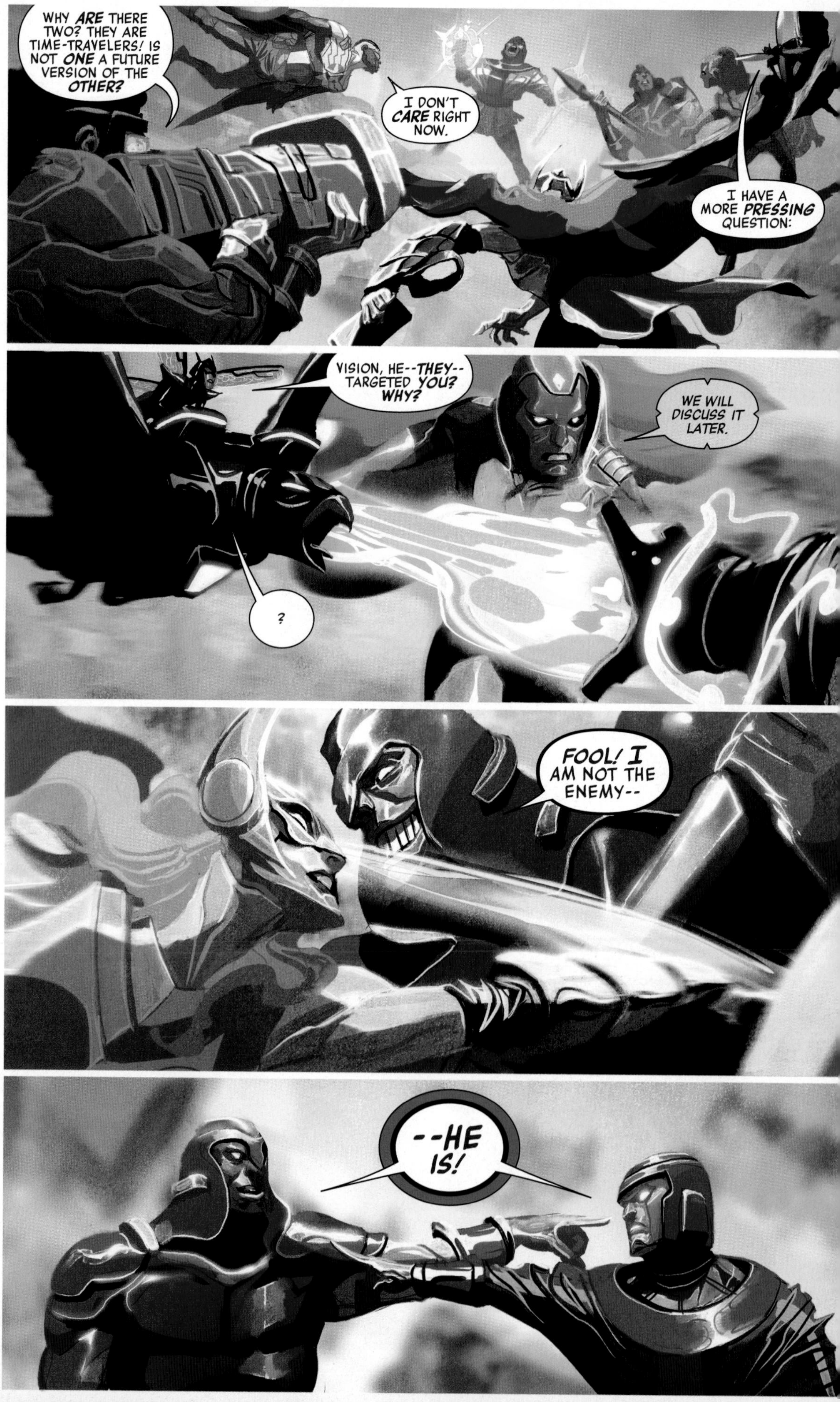
WHY ARE THERE TWO? THEY ARE TIME-TRAVELERS! IS NOT ONE A FUTURE VERSION OF THE OTHER?
I DON'T CARE RIGHT NOW.
I HAVE A MORE PRESSING QUESTION:
VISION, HE--THEY--TARGETED YOU? WHY?
WE WILL DISCUSS IT LATER.
?
FOOL! I AM NOT THE ENEMY--
--HE IS!

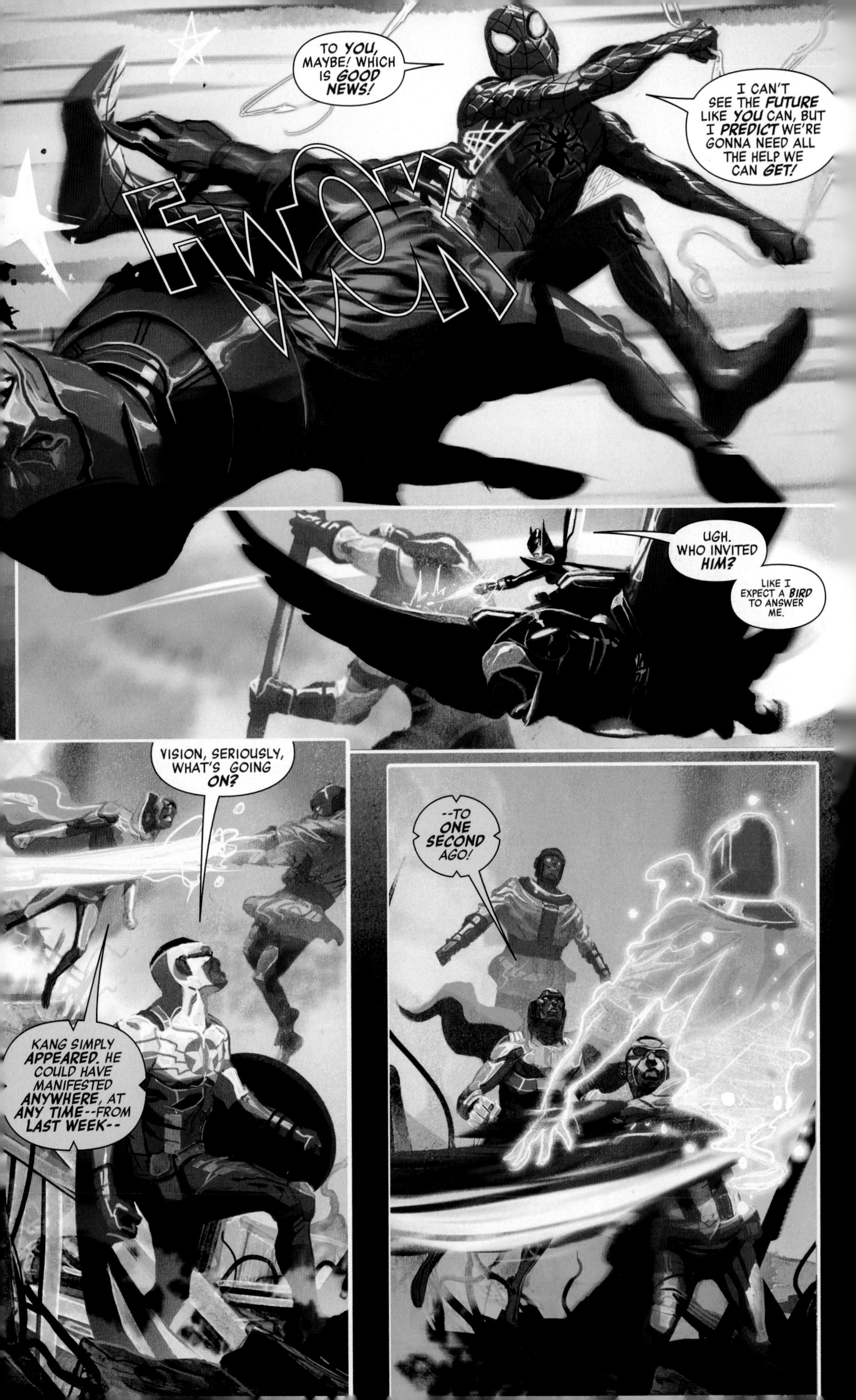
TO YOU, MAYBE! WHICH IS GOOD NEWS!
I CAN'T SEE THE FUTURE LIKE YOU CAN, BUT I PREDICT WE'RE GONNA NEED ALL THE HELP WE CAN GET!
FWOM
UGH. WHO INVITED HIM?
LIKE I EXPECT A BIRD TO ANSWER ME.
VISION, SERIOUSLY, WHAT'S GOING ON?
KANG SIMPLY APPEARED. HE COULD HAVE MANIFESTED ANYWHERE, AT ANY TIME--FROM LAST WEEK--
--TO ONE SECOND AGO!

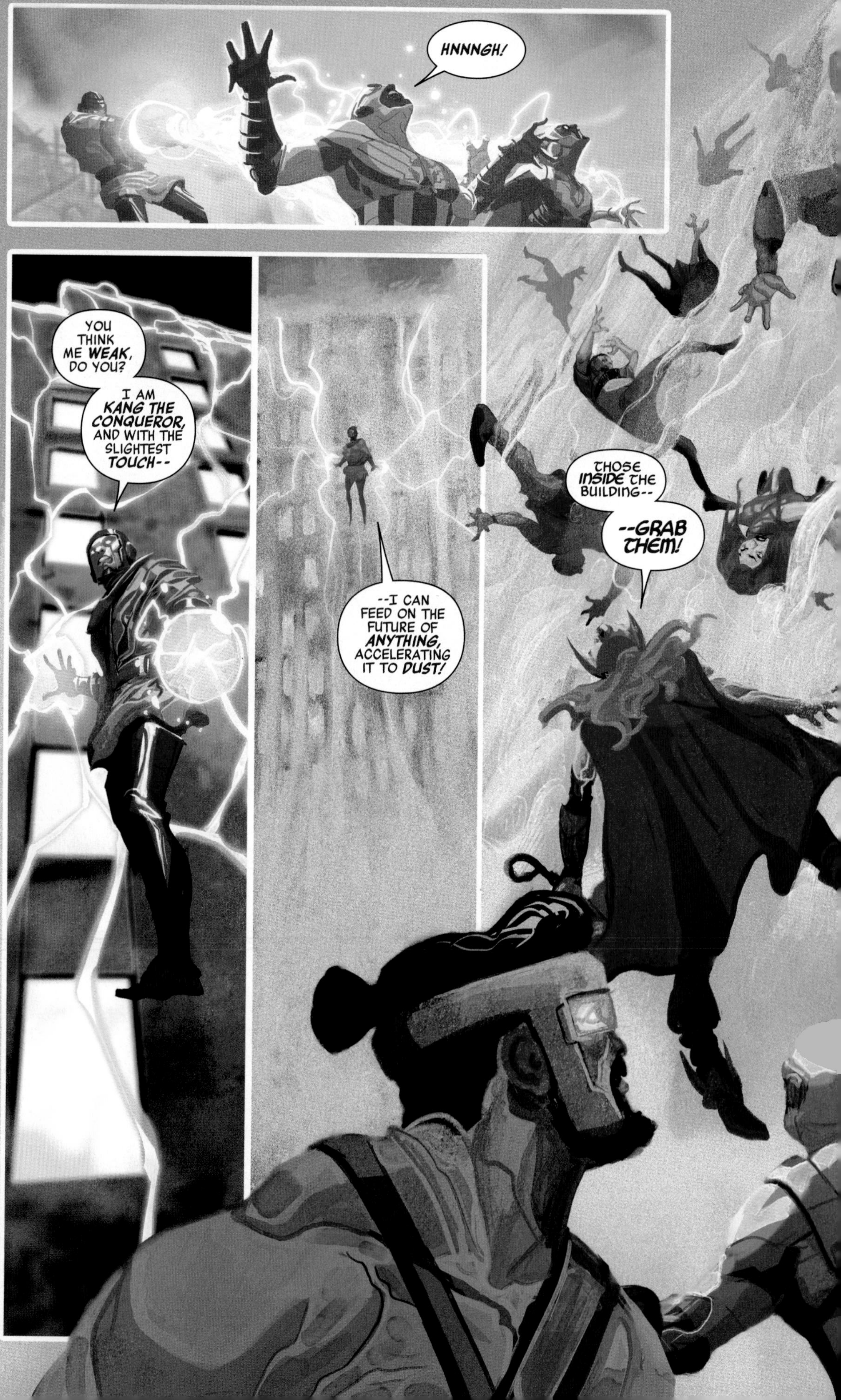
HNNNGH!
YOU THINK ME WEAK, DO YOU?
I AM KANG THE CONQUEROR, AND WITH THE SLIGHTEST TOUCH--
--I CAN FEED ON THE FUTURE OF ANYTHING, ACCELERATING IT TO DUST!
THOSE INSIDE THE BUILDING--
--GRAB THEM!

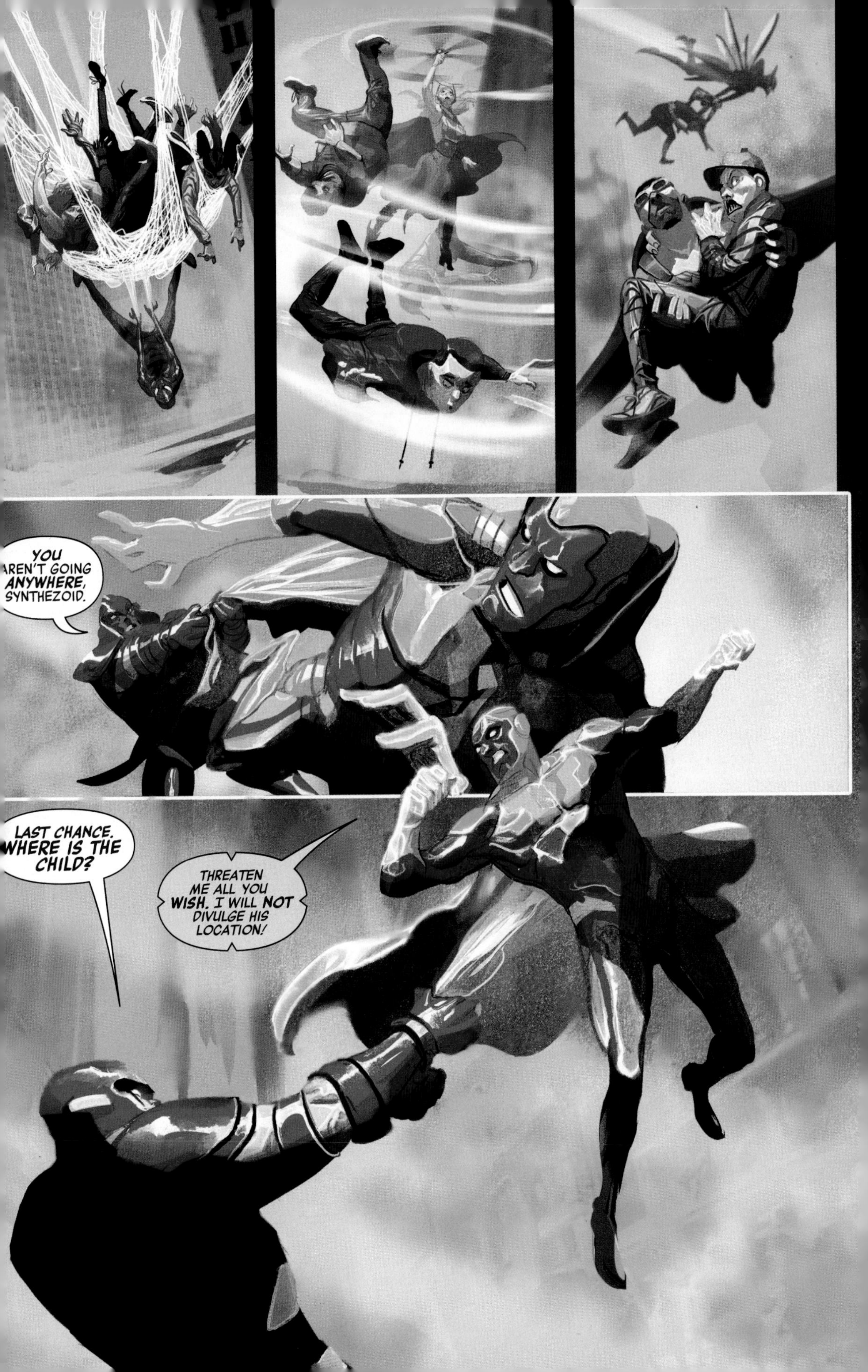
YOU AREN'T GOING ANYWHERE, SYNTHEZOID.
LAST CHANCE. WHERE IS THE CHILD?
THREATEN ME ALL YOU WISH. I WILL NOT DIVULGE HIS LOCATION!

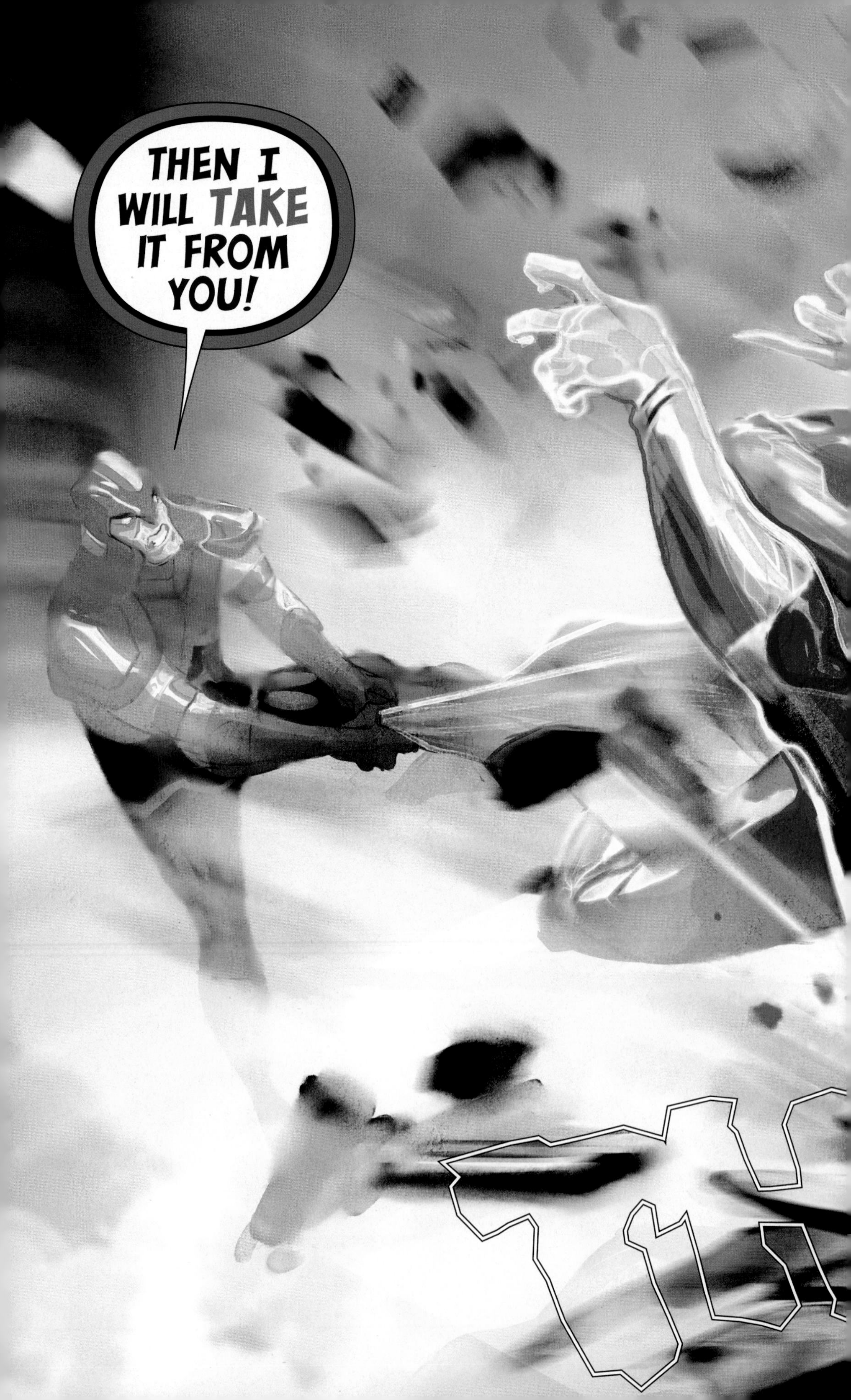
THEN I WILL TAKE IT FROM YOU!

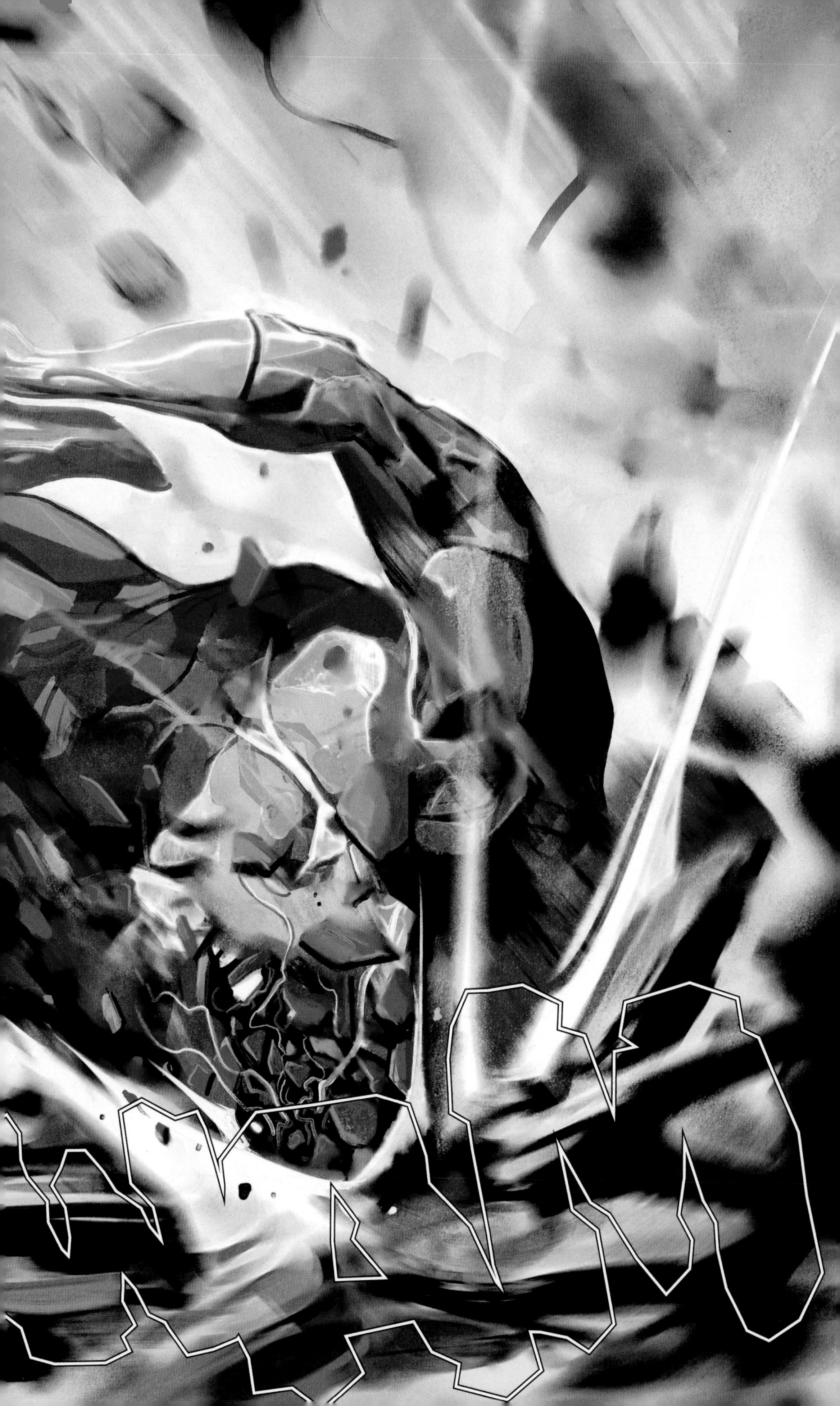

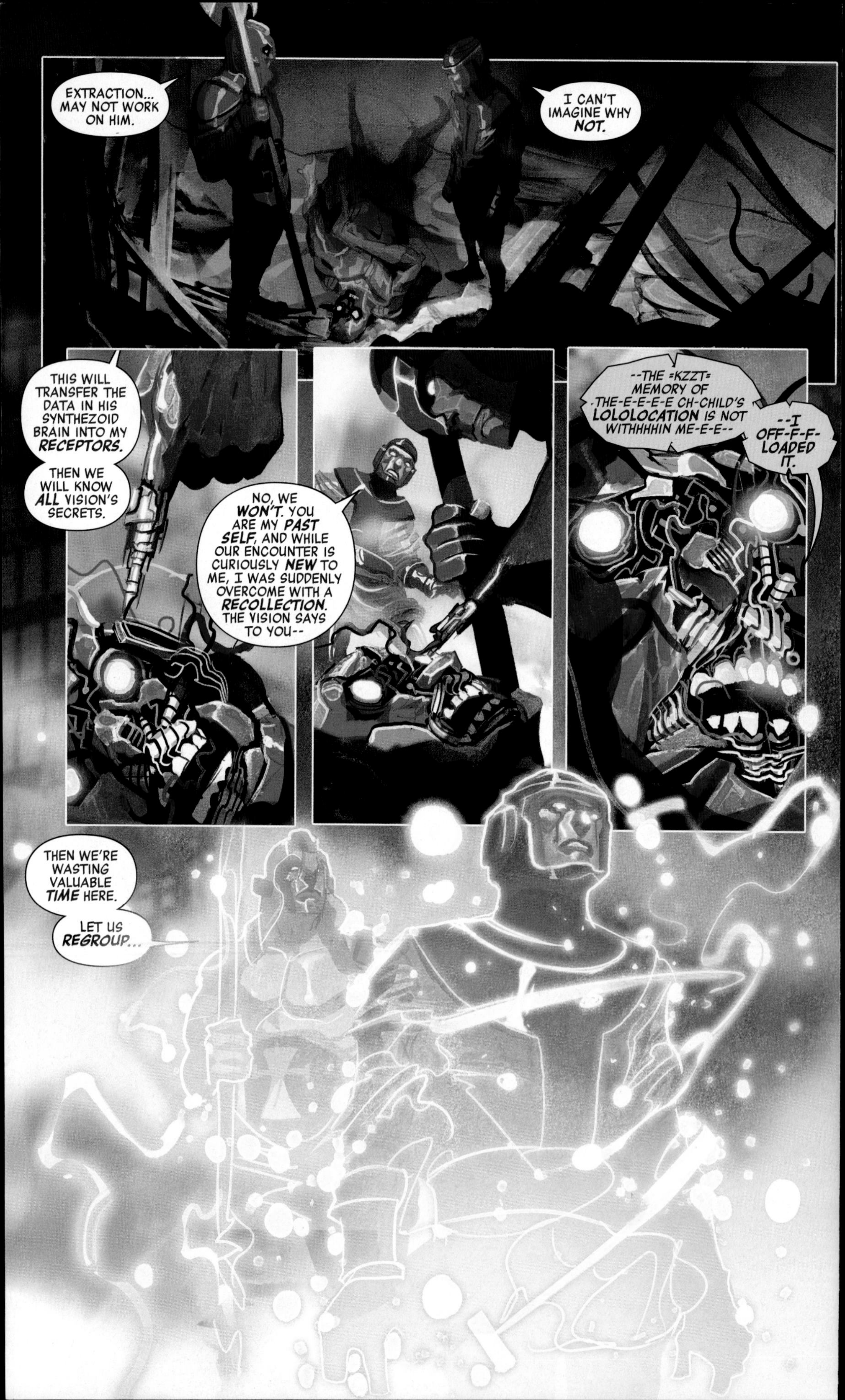
EXTRACTION... MAY NOT WORK ON HIM.
I CAN'T IMAGINE WHY NOT.
THIS WILL TRANSFER THE DATA IN HIS SYNTHEZOID BRAIN INTO MY RECEPTORS.
THEN WE WILL KNOW ALL VISION'S SECRETS.
NO, WE WON'T. YOU ARE MY PAST SELF, AND WHILE OUR ENCOUNTER IS CURIOUSLY NEW TO ME, I WAS SUDDENLY OVERCOME WITH A RECOLLECTION. THE VISION SAYS TO YOU--
--THE =KZZT= MEMORY OF THE-E-E-E CH-CHILD'S LOLOLOCATION IS NOT WITHHHHIN ME-E-E--
--I OFF-F-F-LOADED IT.
THEN WE'RE WASTING VALUABLE TIME HERE.
LET US REGROUP...

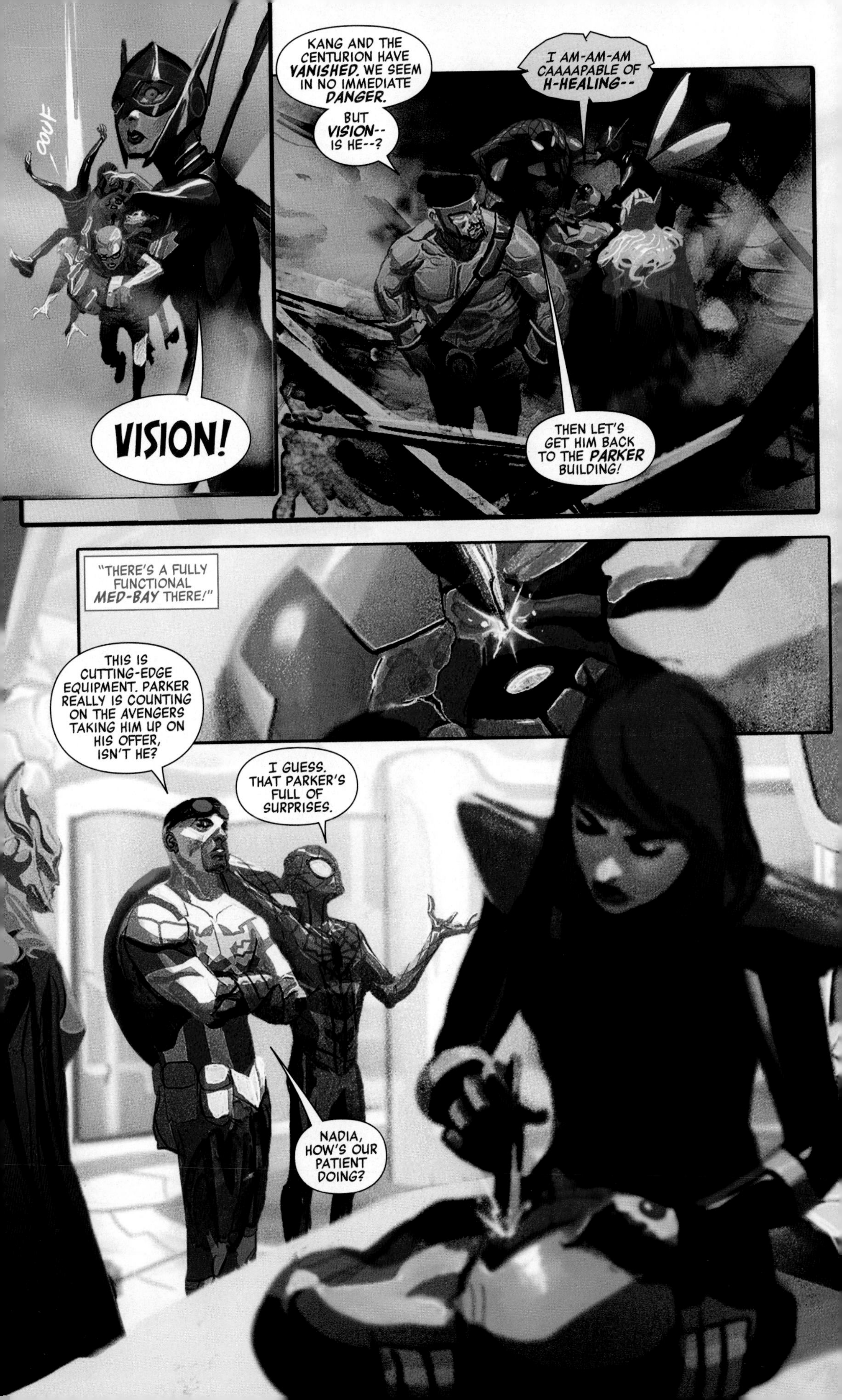
OOUF
VISION!
KANG AND THE CENTURION HAVE VANISHED. WE SEEM IN NO IMMEDIATE DANGER.
BUT VISION-- IS HE--?
I AM-AM-AM CAAAAPABLE OF H-HEALING--
THEN LET'S GET HIM BACK TO THE PARKER BUILDING!
"THERE'S A FULLY FUNCTIONAL MED-BAY THERE!"
THIS IS CUTTING-EDGE EQUIPMENT. PARKER REALLY IS COUNTING ON THE AVENGERS TAKING HIM UP ON HIS OFFER, ISN'T HE?
I GUESS. THAT PARKER'S FULL OF SURPRISES.
NADIA, HOW'S OUR PATIENT DOING?

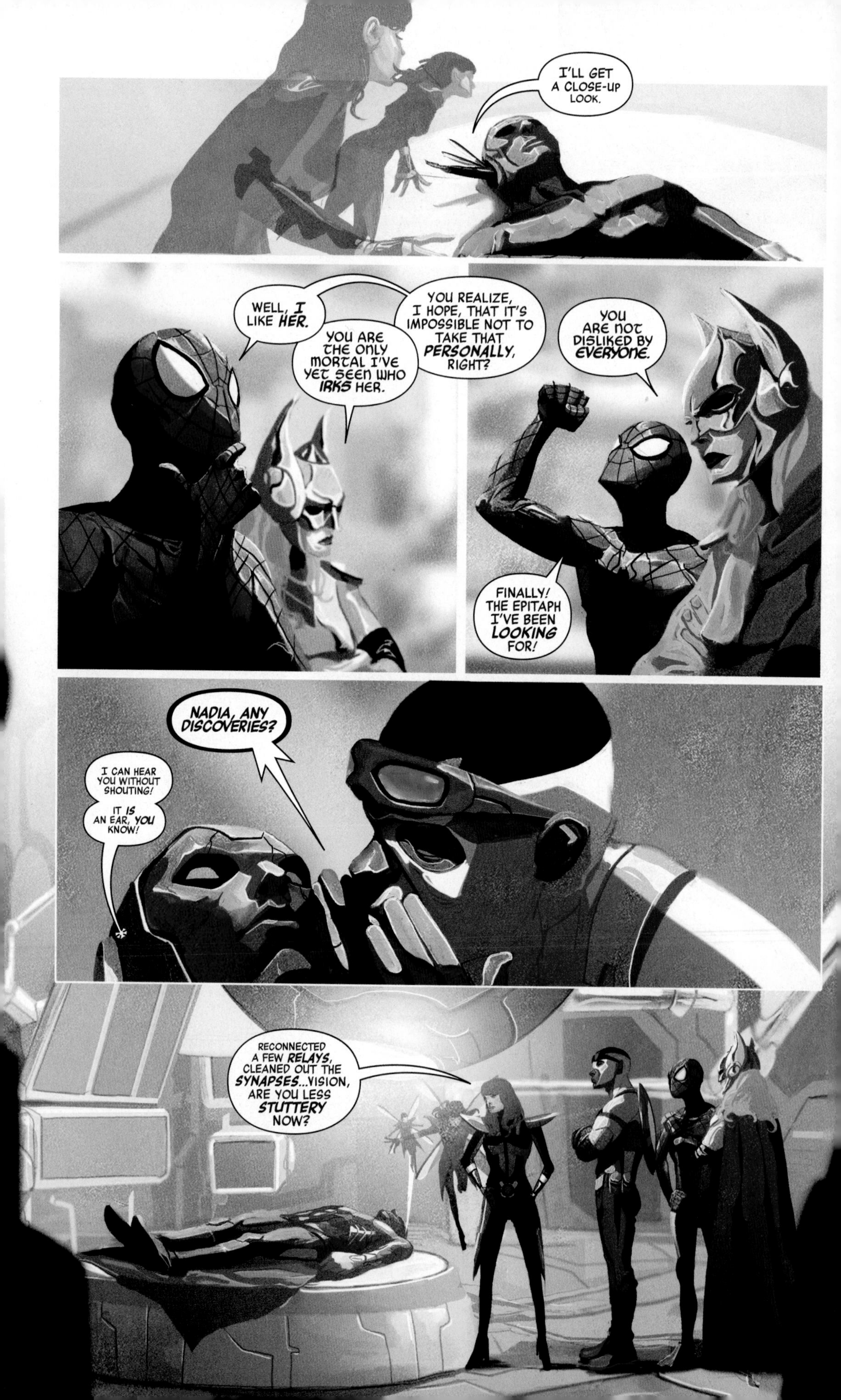
I'LL GET A CLOSE-UP LOOK.
WELL, I LIKE HER.
YOU REALIZE, I HOPE, THAT IT'S IMPOSSIBLE NOT TO TAKE THAT PERSONALLY, RIGHT?
YOU ARE THE ONLY MORTAL I'VE YET SEEN WHO IRKS HER.
YOU ARE NOT DISLIKED BY EVERYONE.
FINALLY! THE EPITAPH I'VE BEEN LOOKING FOR!
NADIA, ANY DISCOVERIES?
I CAN HEAR YOU WITHOUT SHOUTING!
IT IS AN EAR, YOU KNOW!
RECONNECTED A FEW RELAYS, CLEANED OUT THE SYNAPSES...VISION, ARE YOU LESS STUTTERY NOW?

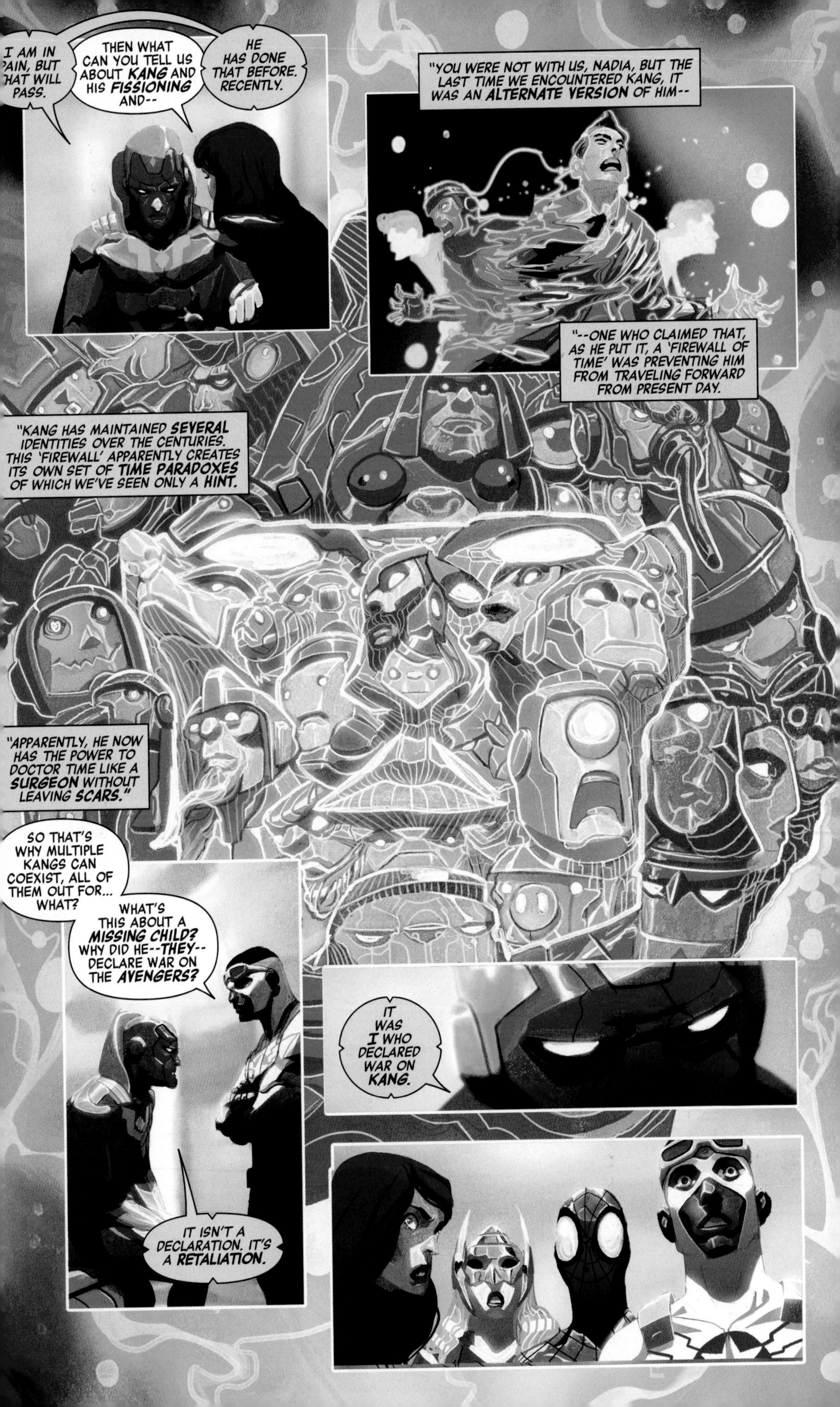

I AM IN PAIN, BUT THAT WILL PASS.
THEN WHAT CAN YOU TELL US ABOUT KANG AND HIS FISSIONING AND--
HE HAS DONE THAT BEFORE. RECENTLY.
"YOU WERE NOT WITH US, NADIA, BUT THE LAST TIME WE ENCOUNTERED KANG, IT WAS AN ALTERNATE VERSION OF HIM--
"--ONE WHO CLAIMED THAT, AS HE PUT IT, A 'FIREWALL OF TIME' WAS PREVENTING HIM FROM TRAVELING FORWARD FROM PRESENT DAY.
"KANG HAS MAINTAINED SEVERAL IDENTITIES OVER THE CENTURIES. THIS 'FIREWALL' APPARENTLY CREATES ITS OWN SET OF TIME PARADOXES OF WHICH WE'VE SEEN ONLY A HINT.
"APPARENTLY, HE NOW HAS THE POWER TO DOCTOR TIME LIKE A SURGEON WITHOUT LEAVING SCARS."
SO THAT'S WHY MULTIPLE KANGS CAN COEXIST, ALL OF THEM OUT FOR... WHAT?
WHAT'S THIS ABOUT A MISSING CHILD? WHY DID HE--THEY--DECLARE WAR ON THE AVENGERS?
IT ISN'T A DECLARATION. IT'S A RETALIATION.
IT WAS I WHO DECLARED WAR ON KANG.

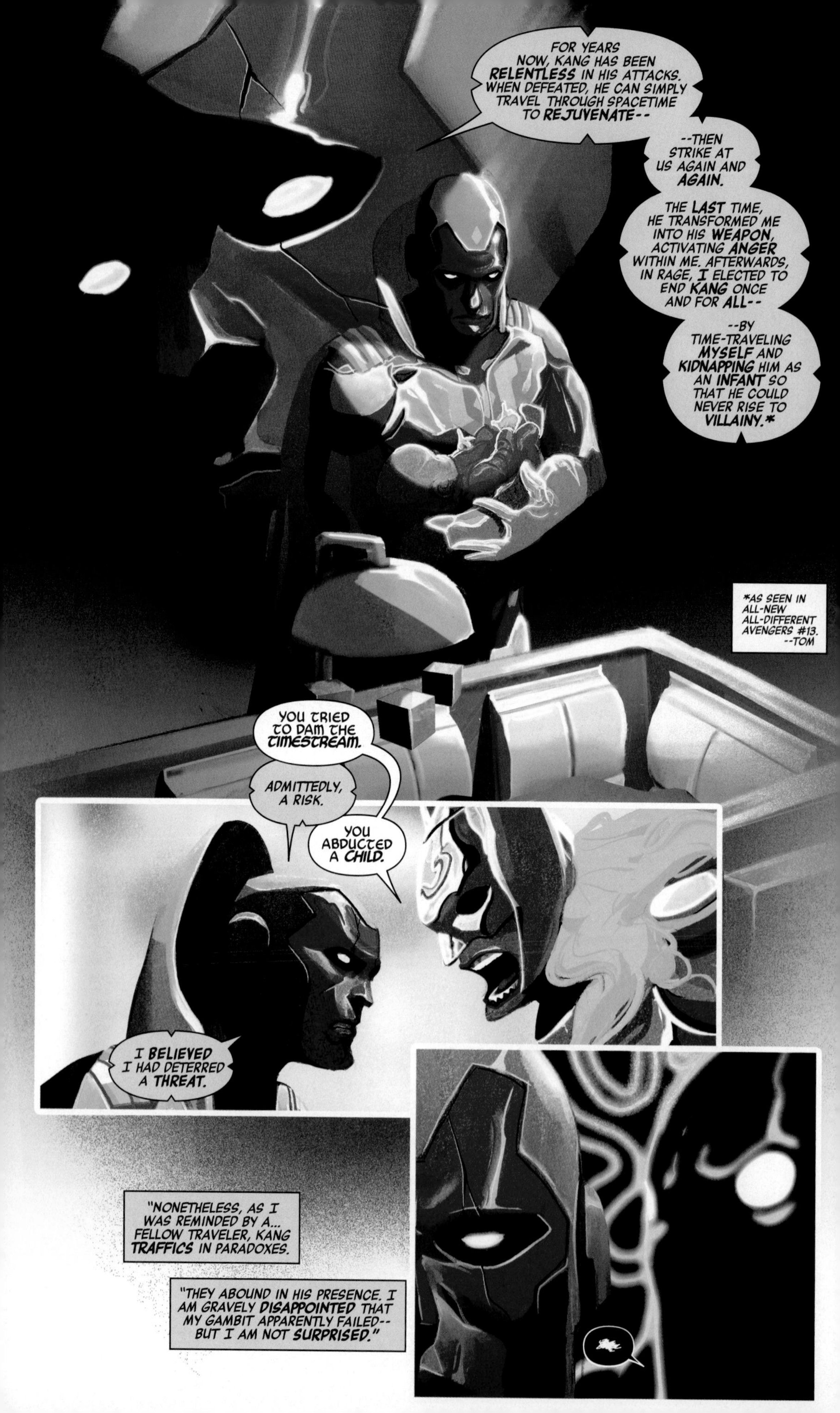
FOR YEARS NOW, KANG HAS BEEN RELENTLESS IN HIS ATTACKS. WHEN DEFEATED, HE CAN SIMPLY TRAVEL THROUGH SPACETIME TO REJUVENATE--
--THEN STRIKE AT US AGAIN AND AGAIN.
THE LAST TIME, HE TRANSFORMED ME INTO HIS WEAPON, ACTIVATING ANGER WITHIN ME. AFTERWARDS, IN RAGE, I ELECTED TO END KANG ONCE AND FOR ALL--
--BY TIME-TRAVELING MYSELF AND KIDNAPPING HIM AS AN INFANT SO THAT HE COULD NEVER RISE TO VILLAINY.*
*AS SEEN IN ALL-NEW ALL-DIFFERENT AVENGERS #13. --TOM
YOU TRIED TO DAM THE TIMESTREAM.
ADMITTEDLY, A RISK.
YOU ABDUCTED A CHILD.
I BELIEVED I HAD DETERRED A THREAT.
"NONETHELESS, AS I WAS REMINDED BY A... FELLOW TRAVELER, KANG TRAFFICS IN PARADOXES.
"THEY ABOUND IN HIS PRESENCE. I AM GRAVELY DISAPPOINTED THAT MY GAMBIT APPARENTLY FAILED--BUT I AM NOT SURPRISED."

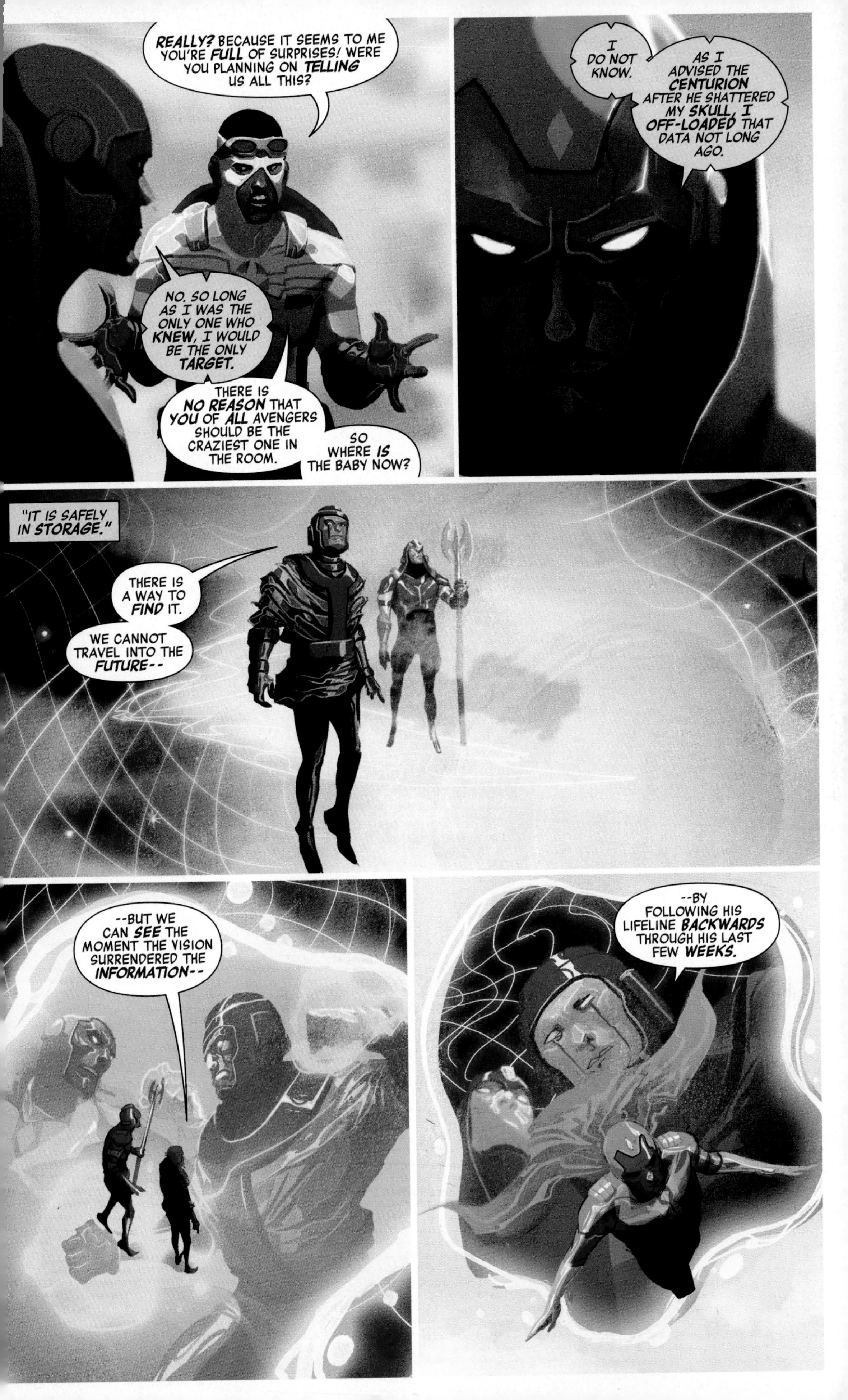
REALLY? BECAUSE IT SEEMS TO ME YOU'RE FULL OF SURPRISES! WERE YOU PLANNING ON TELLING US ALL THIS?
NO. SO LONG AS I WAS THE ONLY ONE WHO KNEW, I WOULD BE THE ONLY TARGET.
THERE IS NO REASON THAT YOU OF ALL AVENGERS SHOULD BE THE CRAZIEST ONE IN THE ROOM.
SO WHERE IS THE BABY NOW?
I DO NOT KNOW.
AS I ADVISED THE CENTURION AFTER HE SHATTERED MY SKULL, I OFF-LOADED THAT DATA NOT LONG AGO.
"IT IS SAFELY IN STORAGE."
THERE IS A WAY TO FIND IT.
WE CANNOT TRAVEL INTO THE FUTURE--
--BUT WE CAN SEE THE MOMENT THE VISION SURRENDERED THE INFORMATION--
--BY FOLLOWING HIS LIFELINE BACKWARDS THROUGH HIS LAST FEW WEEKS.

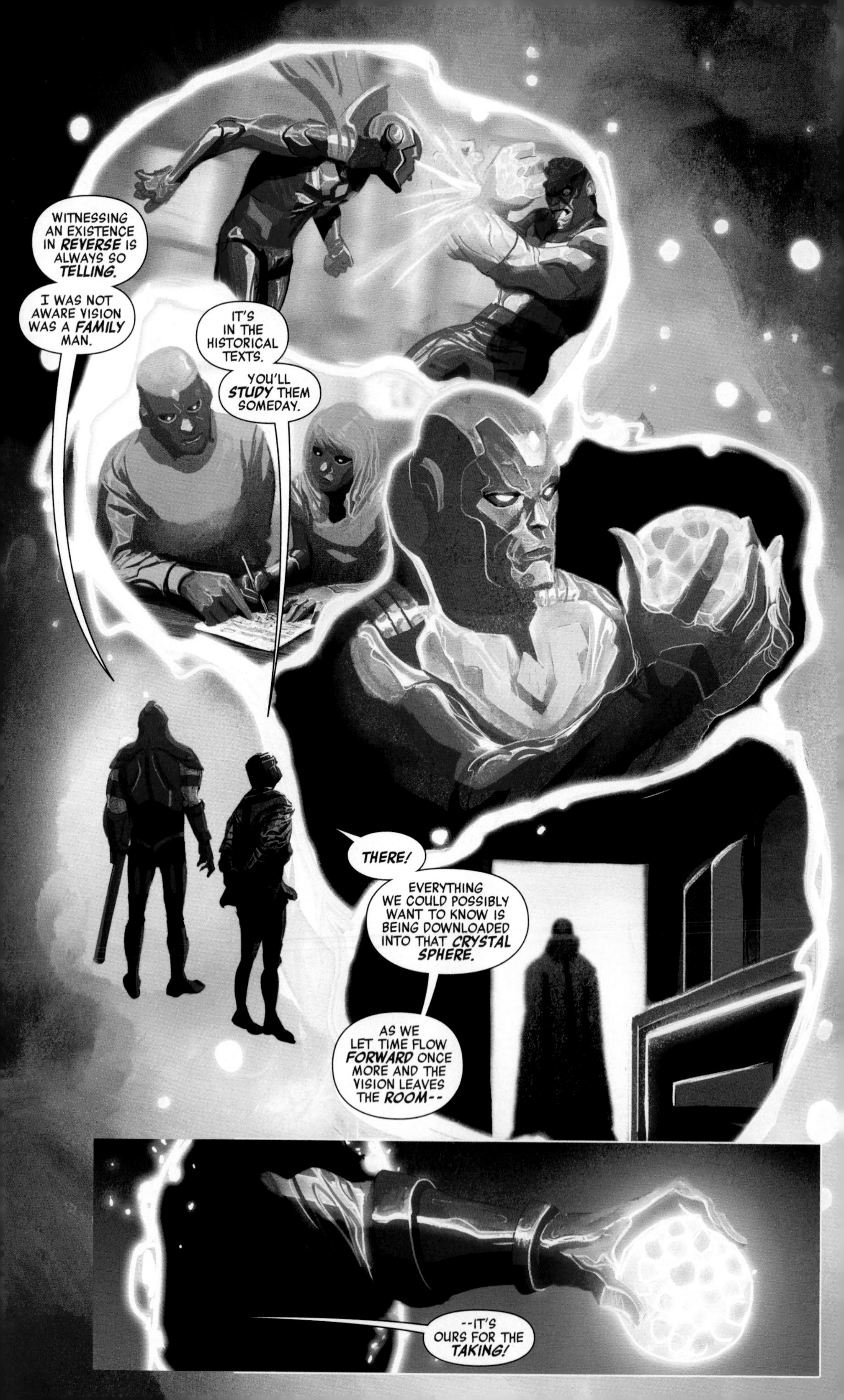
WITNESSING AN EXISTENCE IN REVERSE IS ALWAYS SO TELLING.
I WAS NOT AWARE VISION WAS A FAMILY MAN.
IT'S IN THE HISTORICAL TEXTS.
YOU'LL STUDY THEM SOMEDAY.
THERE!
EVERYTHING WE COULD POSSIBLY WANT TO KNOW IS BEING DOWNLOADED INTO THAT CRYSTAL SPHERE.
AS WE LET TIME FLOW FORWARD ONCE MORE AND THE VISION LEAVES THE ROOM--
--IT'S OURS FOR THE TAKING!

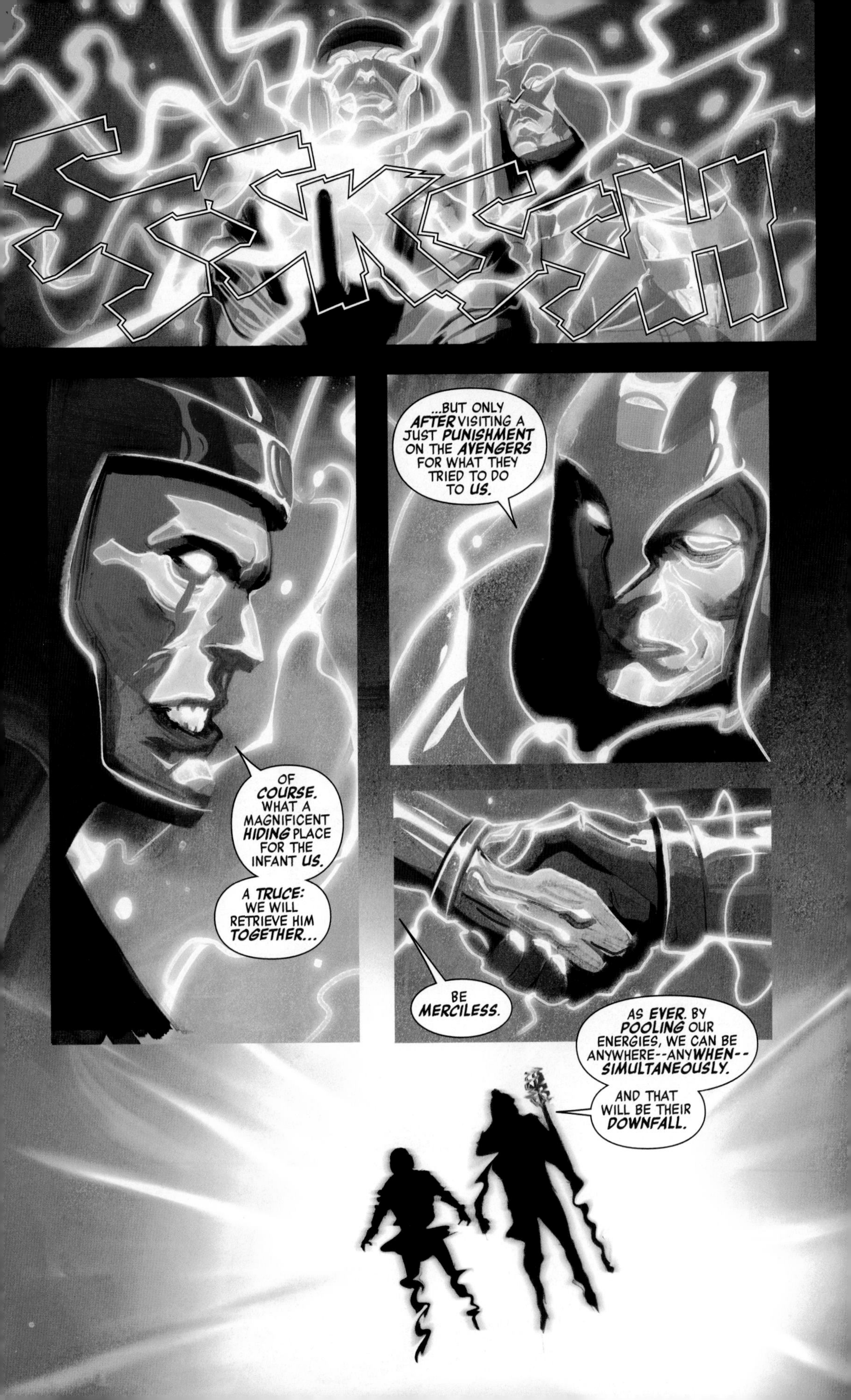
SSKSSHH
...BUT ONLY AFTER VISITING A JUST PUNISHMENT ON THE AVENGERS FOR WHAT THEY TRIED TO DO TO US.
OF COURSE. WHAT A MAGNIFICENT HIDING PLACE FOR THE INFANT US.
A TRUCE: WE WILL RETRIEVE HIM TOGETHER...
BE MERCILESS.
AS EVER. BY POOLING OUR ENERGIES, WE CAN BE ANYWHERE--ANYWHEN--SIMULTANEOUSLY.
AND THAT WILL BE THEIR DOWNFALL.

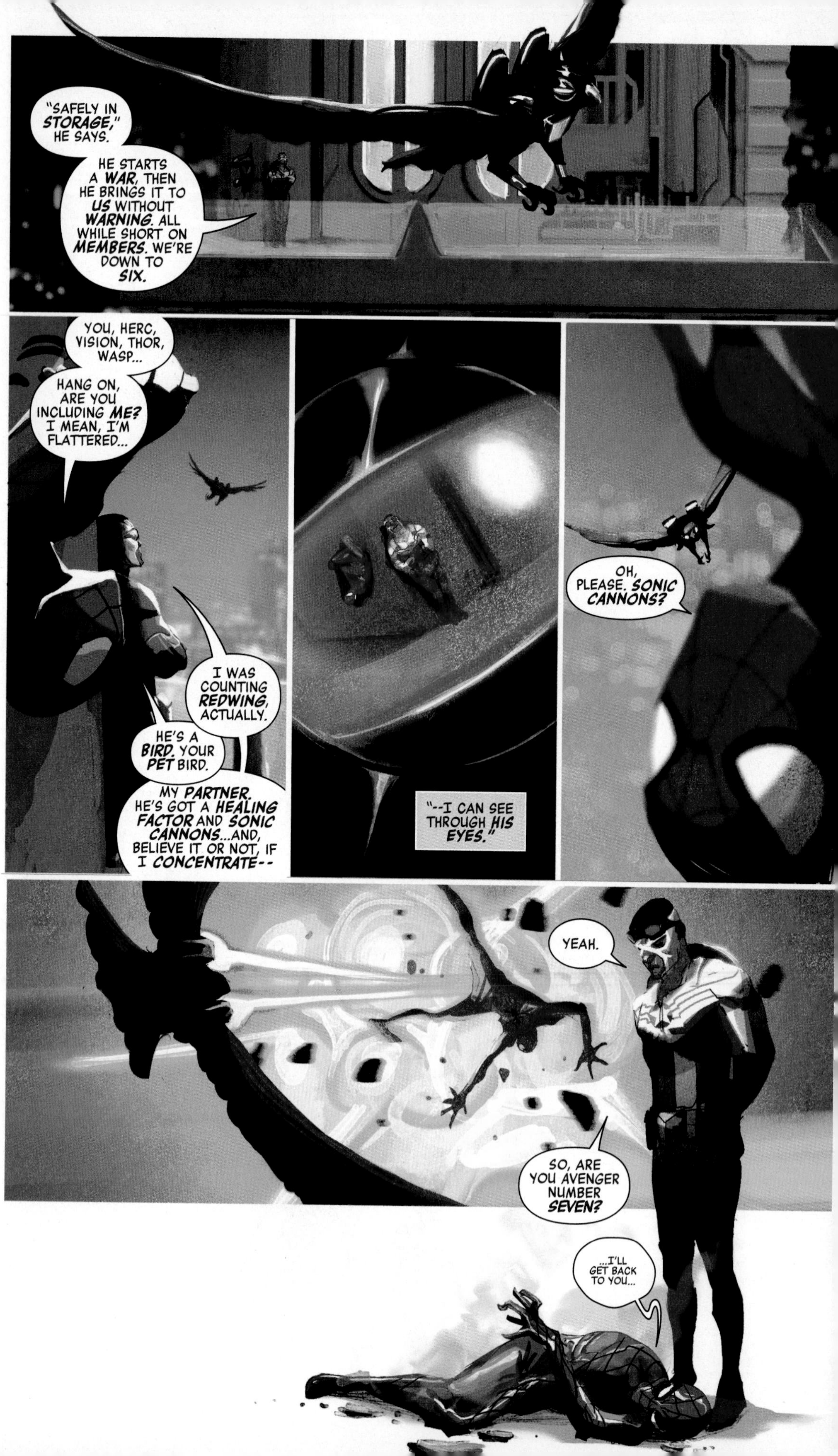

"SAFELY IN STORAGE," HE SAYS.
HE STARTS A WAR, THEN HE BRINGS IT TO US WITHOUT WARNING. ALL WHILE SHORT ON MEMBERS. WE'RE DOWN TO SIX.
YOU, HERC, VISION, THOR, WASP...
HANG ON, ARE YOU INCLUDING ME? I MEAN, I'M FLATTERED...
I WAS COUNTING REDWING, ACTUALLY.
HE'S A BIRD. YOUR PET BIRD.
MY PARTNER. HE'S GOT A HEALING FACTOR AND SONIC CANNONS...AND, BELIEVE IT OR NOT, IF I CONCENTRATE--
"--I CAN SEE THROUGH HIS EYES."
OH, PLEASE. SONIC CANNONS?
YEAH.
SO, ARE YOU AVENGER NUMBER SEVEN?
...I'LL GET BACK TO YOU...

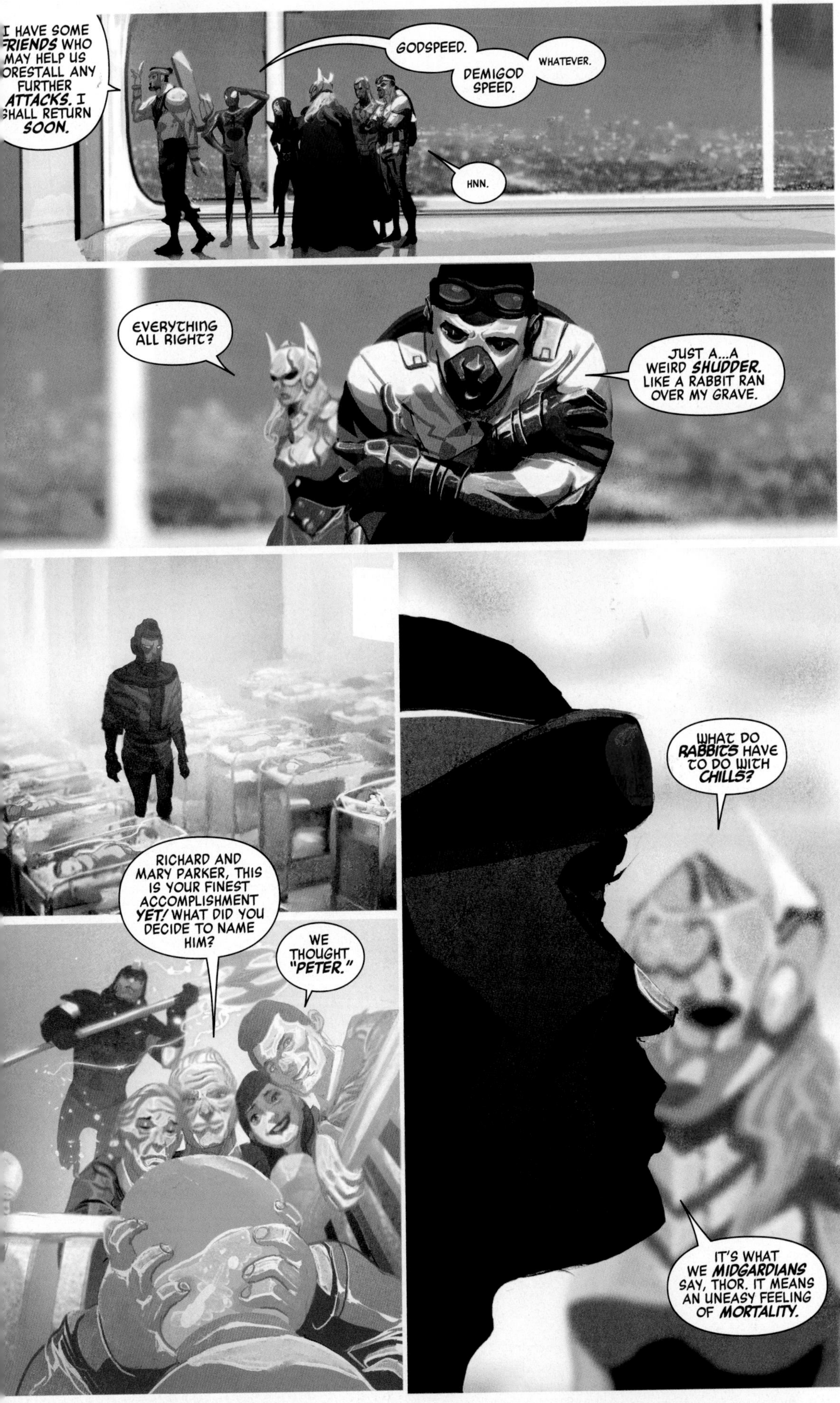
I HAVE SOME FRIENDS WHO MAY HELP US FORESTALL ANY FURTHER ATTACKS. I SHALL RETURN SOON.
GODSPEED.
DEMIGOD SPEED.
WHATEVER.
HNN.
EVERYTHING ALL RIGHT?
JUST A...A WEIRD SHUDDER. LIKE A RABBIT RAN OVER MY GRAVE.
RICHARD AND MARY PARKER, THIS IS YOUR FINEST ACCOMPLISHMENT YET! WHAT DID YOU DECIDE TO NAME HIM?
WE THOUGHT "PETER."
WHAT DO RABBITS HAVE TO DO WITH CHILLS?
IT'S WHAT WE MIDGARDIANS SAY, THOR. IT MEANS AN UNEASY FEELING OF MORTALITY.

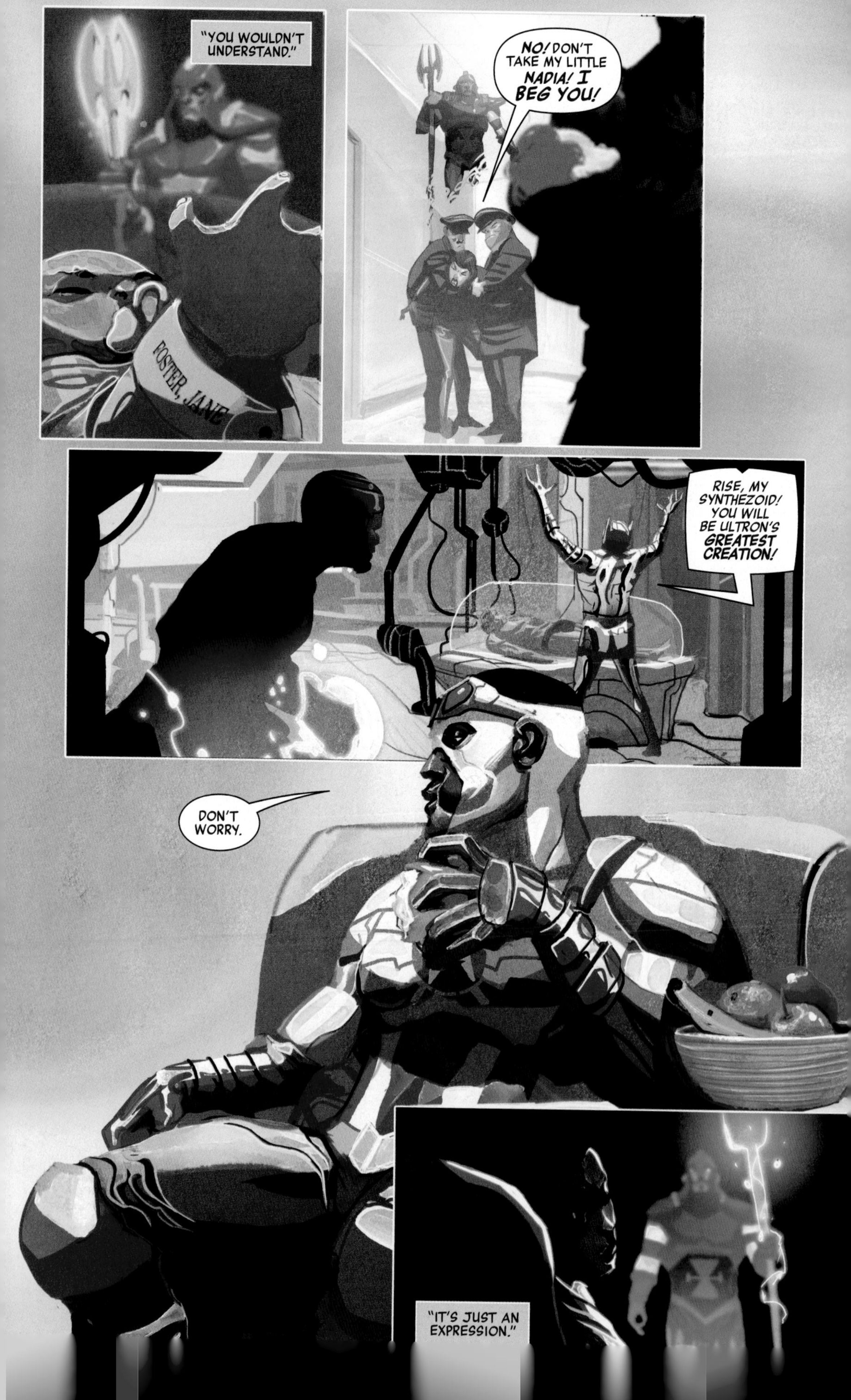
"YOU WOULDN'T UNDERSTAND."
FOSTER, JANE
NO! DON'T TAKE MY LITTLE NADIA! I BEG YOU!
RISE, MY SYNTHEZOID! YOU WILL BE ULTRON'S GREATEST CREATION!
DON'T WORRY.
"IT'S JUST AN EXPRESSION."

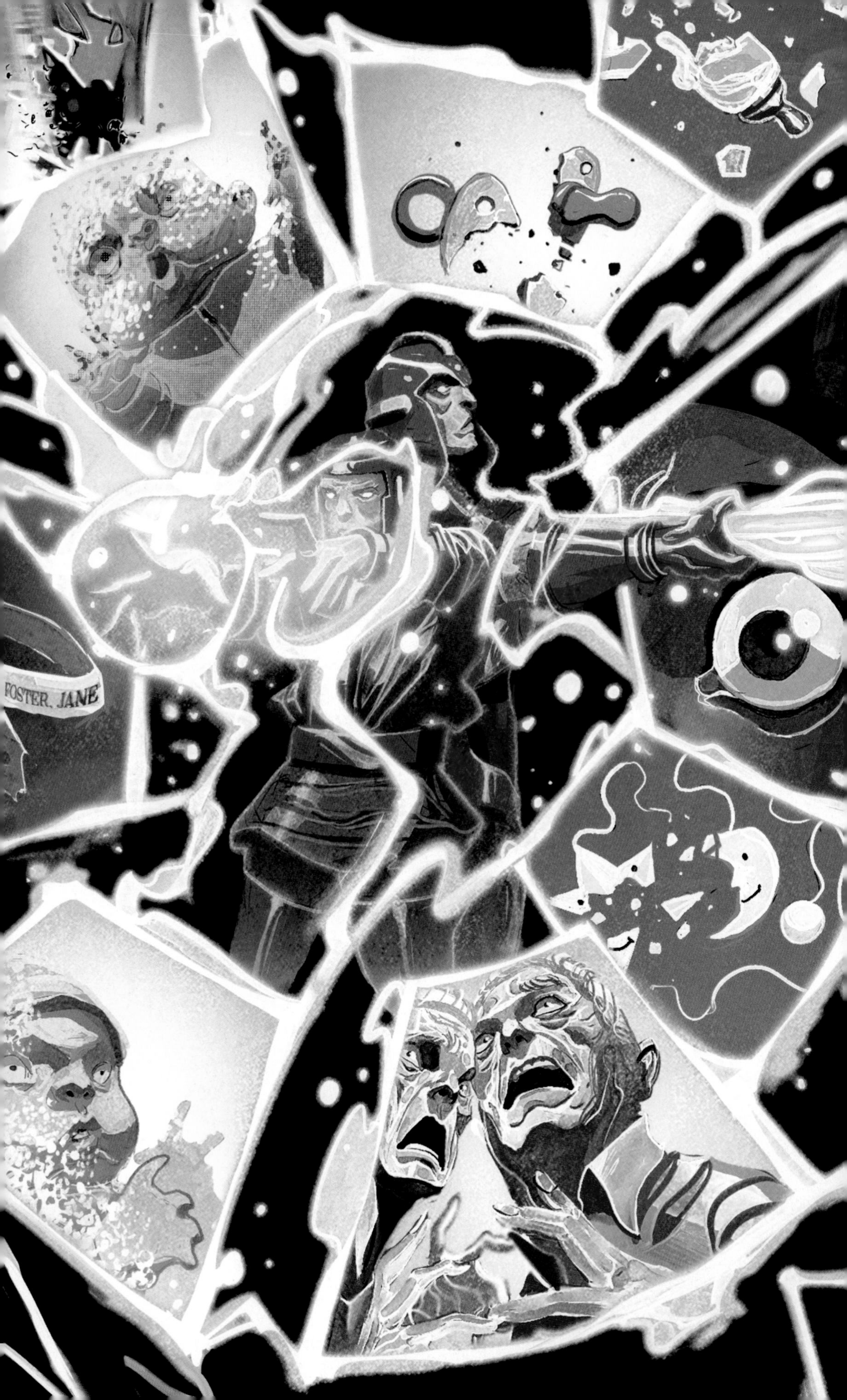
FOSTER, JANE

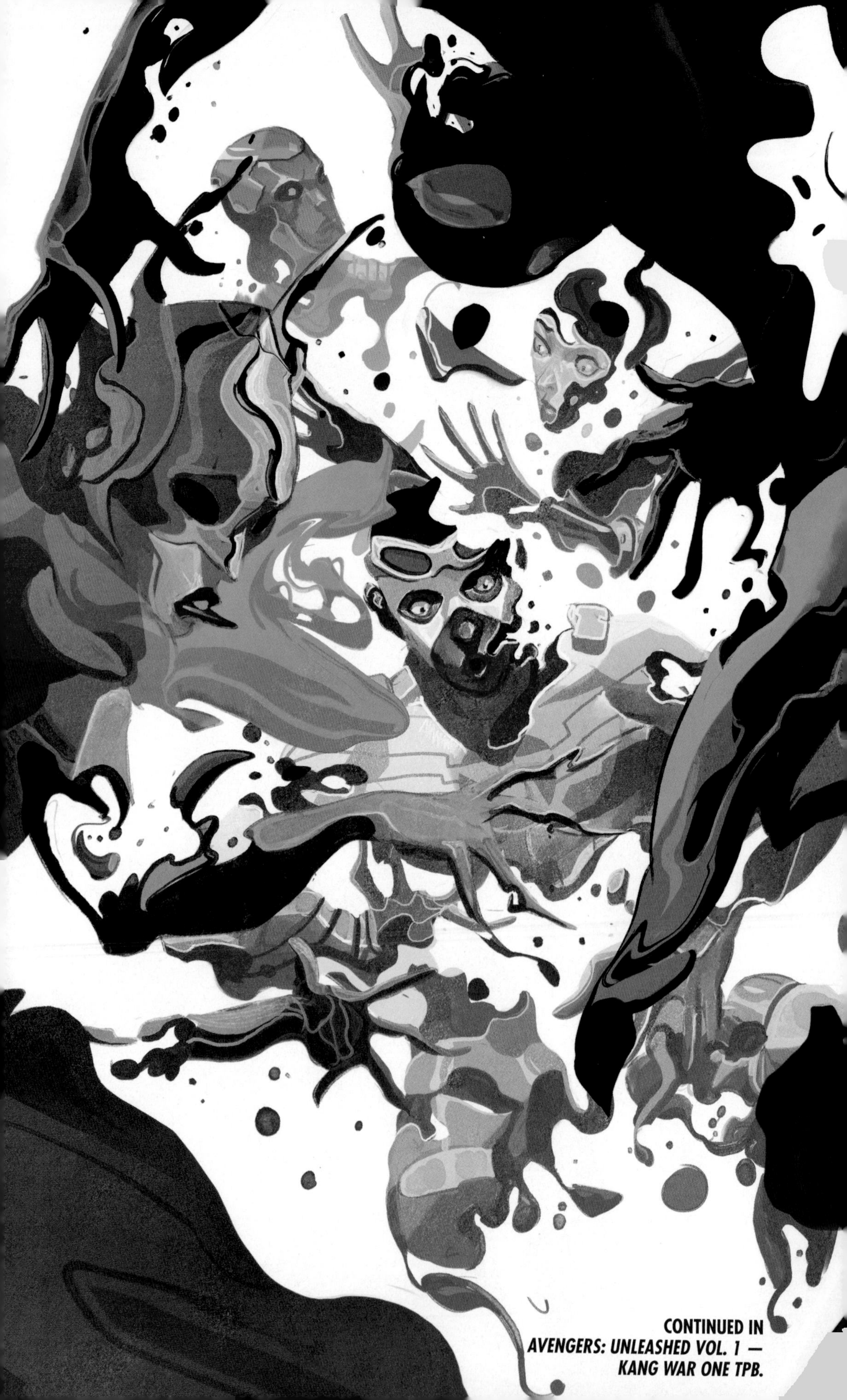

CONTINUED IN
*AVENGERS: UNLEASHED VOL. 1 —
KANG WAR ONE TPB.*

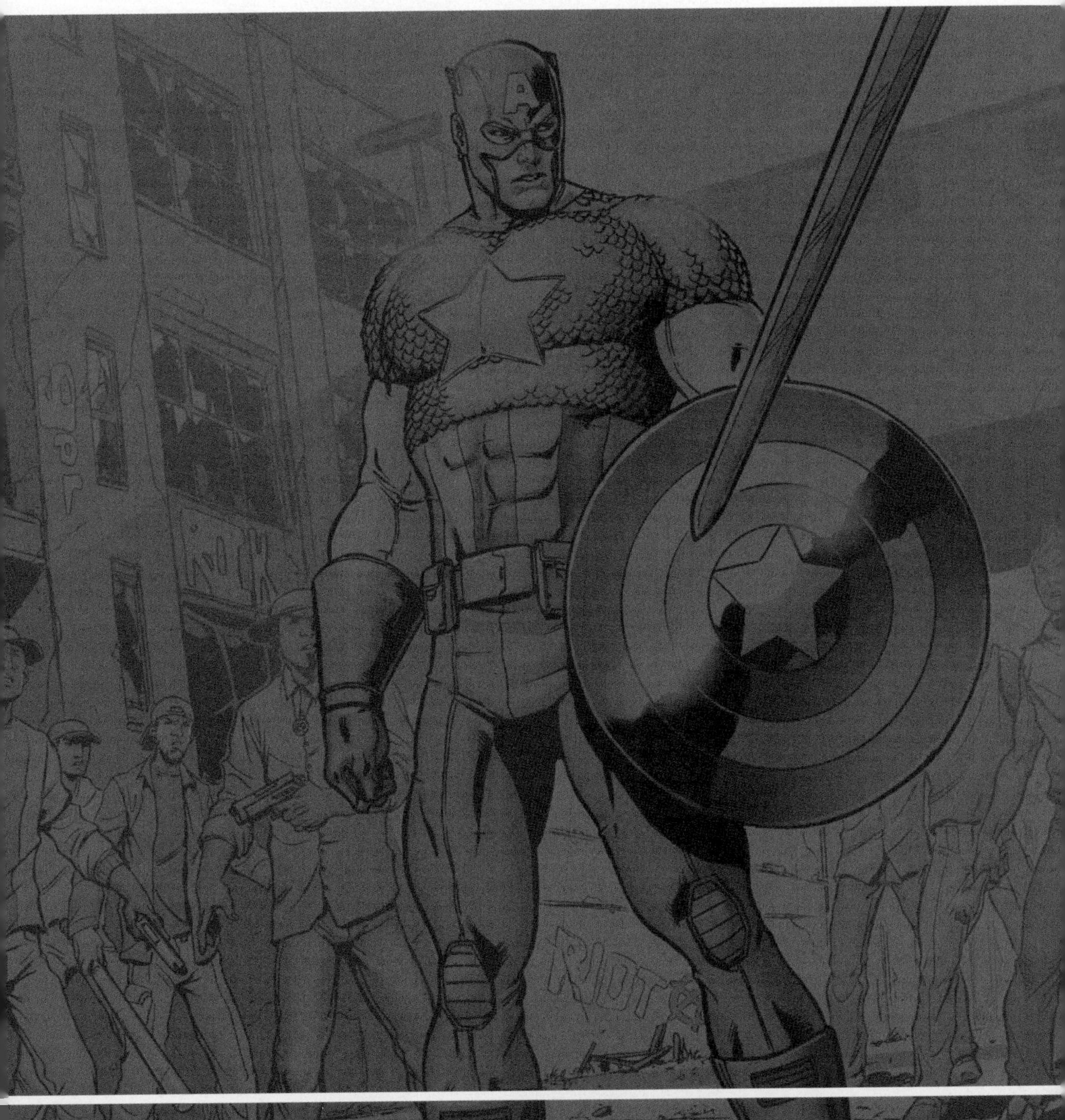
RIOT

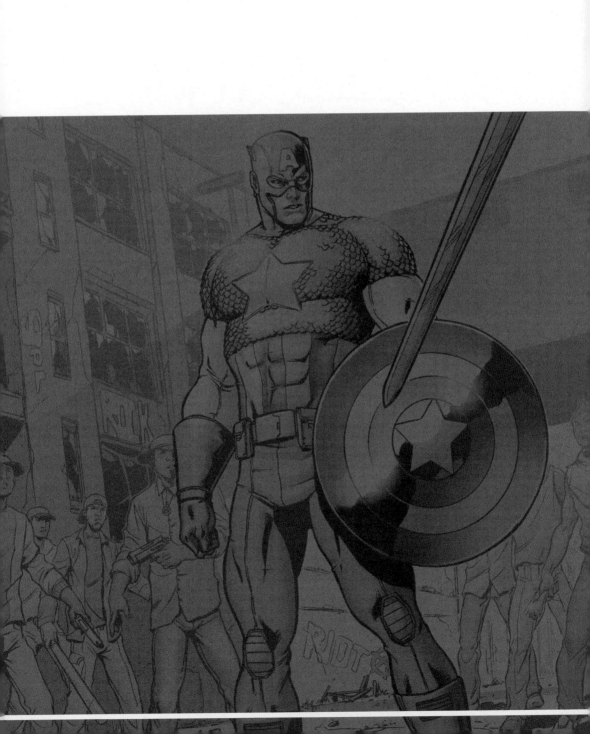

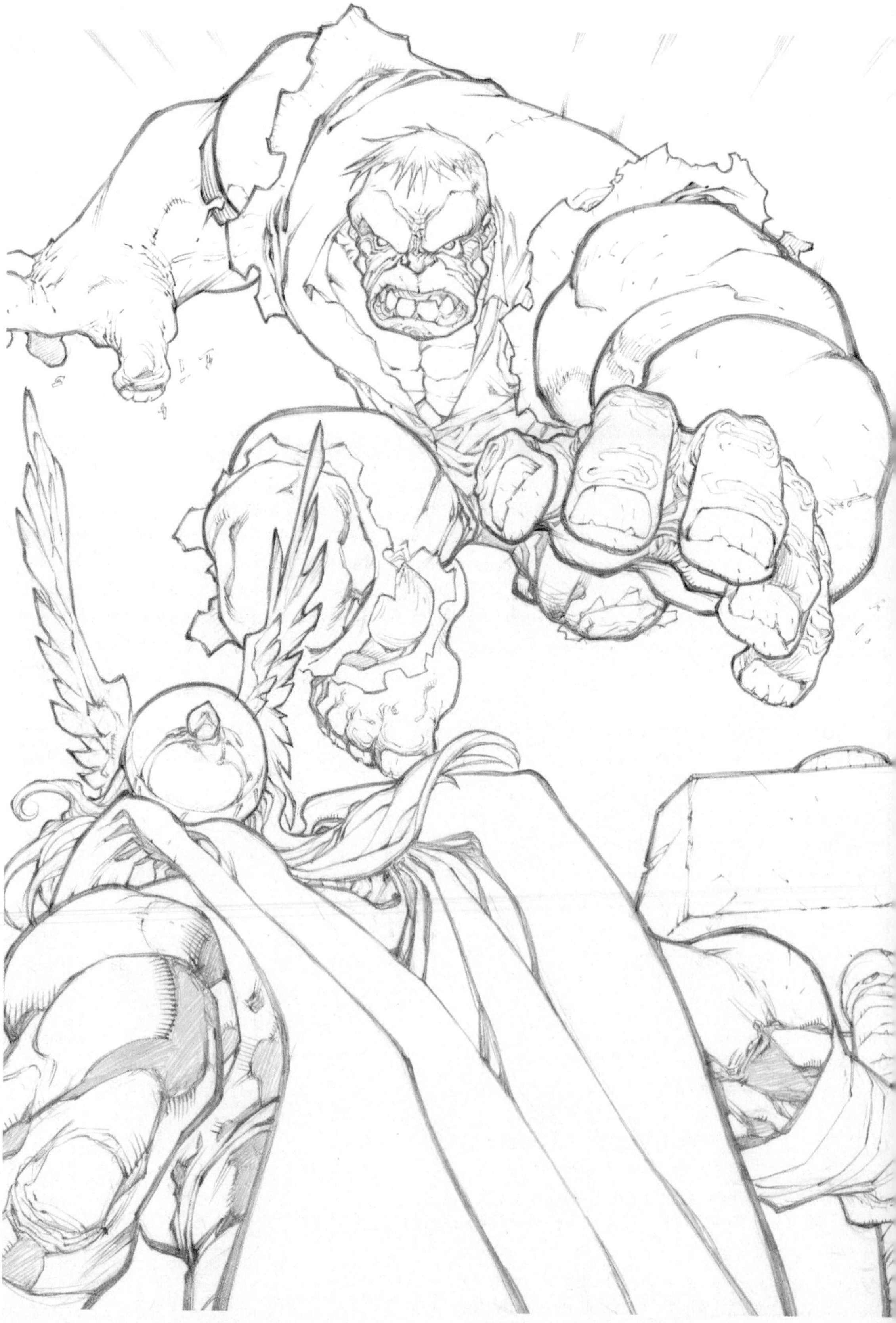

PAGES 1-19

Introduction of LOKI, pissed off while stewing in the Island of Silence. Over these pages we have a recap of the events that led to the formation of the team in the first place, and the discovery of CAPTAIN AMERICA in the ice. He considers each of the major players of the team, stewing over the situation.

CUT TO: IRON MAN is battling the HULK and winds up getting his head handed to him. We then reveal that what we've seen is Tony Stark running scenarios as to how to try to defeat him. Tony also reveals in narrative that he's suspicious of THOR, because he's learned of the existence of shape-changing aliens and is worried that Thor is actually some sort of alien with a hidden agenda, taking the form of a classic mythic hero in order to discourage suspicion. After all, the Avengers have already taken a PR hit thanks to the Hulk; the last thing they need is to be discovered to be harboring an alien spy or worse.

CUT TO: MIGHTY THOR, using his weather powers to bring water to an area that was previously suffering from a drought. A grateful elderly farmer is a WWII vet, and he asks Thor if it's true that Captain America has returned. The old man figures Thor, being a god, is the one to ask about it since it can only be described as a miracle. And this alone starts

Thor wondering, suspicious. After all, what a staggering coincidence it is, that enabled them to find Captain America floating along in the few hours between when the ice would have thoroughly melted in the warm Gulf Stream waters and the point where he would have drowned. Plus, he hardly comes across like the determined, heroic one-man army that legends spoke of. Thor doesn't see how someone who has been given a second lease on life can be moping about "poor Bucky." The teen died heroically. What more can a hero ask than that?

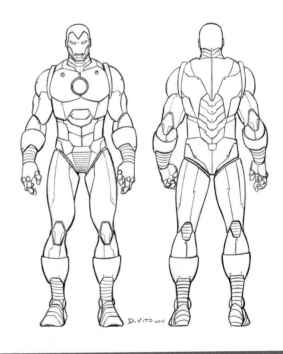

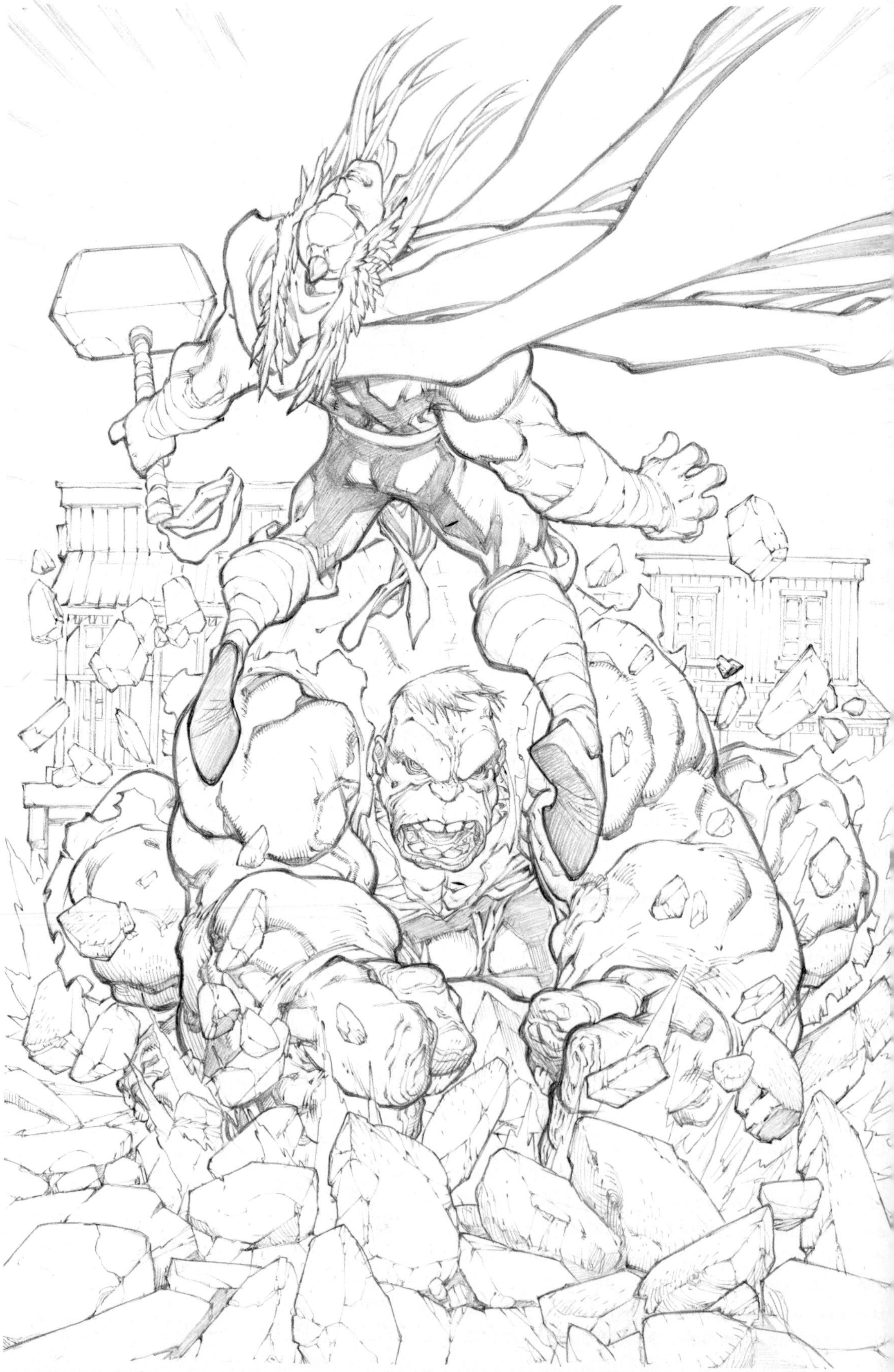

CUT TO: CAPTAIN AMERICA. He intervenes in a gang fight, and lectures them on the futility of fighting each other when all Americans should be united. This doesn't prompt the reaction he'd anticipated as the gang members burst into laughter at how old and out of touch this guy is. They disperse, many of them saying, "Who the hell is Captain America?" They've never heard of him. (If we can have a whole generation that doesn't know who Paul McCartney is, I figure anything's possible.) It leaves Cap wondering who, indeed, Captain America is. Captain America is still grief-stricken over the loss of Bucky, feeling displaced and dealing with survivor's guilt.

The Avengers then receive a communication from NICK FURY (either on panel or not, depending if we want to go with Classic Fury,

Movie Fury or just leave it ambiguous). He informs them that they have reports of the Hulk stampeding around in Nevada and can localize his whereabouts for them. "You're the guys who paraded him around as being rehabbed, only to wind up looking like idiots. I figure you'd want first crack at him."

Jumping in the Avengers Quinjet, the trio heads out (Giant-Man and the Wasp not along for the ride since they have tickets for a cruise and thus are unavailable). The trio is uncharacteristically quiet.

Upon arriving at the Hulk's last known location, the group spreads out so they can cover as much area as possible (Cap on a motorcycle that they brought with them in their plane).

PAGES 20-39

As Cap approaches a small town, he suddenly feels a pinching on the back of his neck, like a mosquito bit him. He loses his balance on his motorcycle and it skids out, but, being Cap, he lands on his feet. The townsfolk approach him in awe, thrilled to see the living legend in their midst. This town is like Main Street in Disneyland. They can't get enough of feting Captain America. There's a parade for him down

DiVITO

the Main Street. Also there's a lovely young girl who is the spitting image of his lost Peggy Carter. He goes on an old-fashioned date with her, everything is wonderful, they're making out...and suddenly he remembers he's supposed to be tracking the Hulk. He has a mission. He'd never turn his back on a mission. That's not who he is; that's not who Captain America is. He fights his way back to awareness and comes to, discovering he's strapped to a table, being experimented on by the Red Skull and his shock troops. The "mosquito" was a knockout dart and the Skull is working on brainwashing Cap in order to make him more controllable, "as per the desires of our billionaire ally," the Skull says to his associates, unaware that Cap's come to. Cap breaks free, battles the Skull and his forces, takes a pounding, but ultimately triumphs. The Skull and his forces escape, and Cap discovers — to his horror — that the equipment used to brainwash him was manufactured by Stark Industries. Then the bunker begins to blow up, and Cap barely escapes, but loses the proof in the process. He is, however, determined to confront Iron Man and ask him what he knows of Stark's apparent association with the Skull.

PAGES 40-59

Iron Man arrives in Reno, arcing over it, and sees people running from "that horrible monster." He angles down, sees a hulking form, assumes it's the Hulk and goes after him. But no: it's MISTER HYDE. Hyde snarls, "About time," and attacks him. He's strong, but he's no match for Iron Man...but just when Iron Man figures, "That was easy," he's suddenly assaulted from all sides by alien Stone Men. These guys are unbelievably tough, and a far ranging battle annihilates an entire casino (sadly, one owned by Tony Stark). Ultimately he manages to drive them off, but he has no idea why they were clearly gunning for him. He goes back to find the unconscious Hyde is just coming around and has morphed back into Calvin Zabo. Zabo, pleading, says he had nothing to do with it; he barely remembers any of it. "I think...they said something about Thor." "About attacking me to get to him?" "No, about...protecting him. That's all I know, I swear!" Patching into S.H.I.E.L.D.'s global monitoring computers (easy enough; they got them from Stark) he finds a photo readout that shows the Stone Men landing on Earth in Norway and then leaving just as quickly...with a satellite photo of Thor watching them go. Holy crap: Thor IS an alien. They dropped him off and somehow Thor figured out that Stark is growing suspicious of him and wanted him taken out.

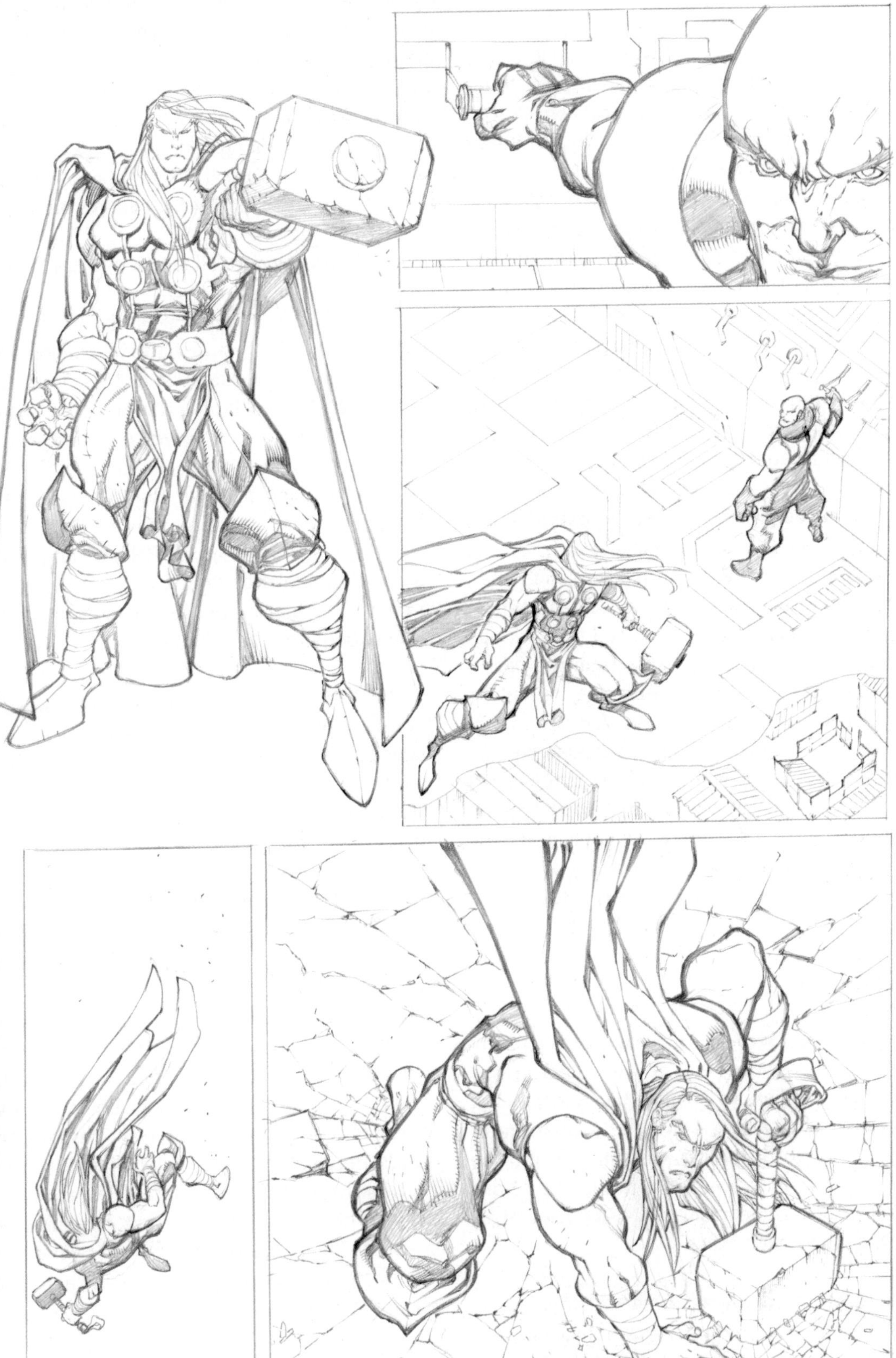

PAGES 60-79

Thor is cruising along when a missile comes screaming toward him. He dispatches it with his hammer and heads for the site from which they were fired, a ghost town. Waiting for him there? ZARRKO the Tomorrow Man, who fires more missiles at him that Thor is able to batter his way past. Zarrko, seeking vengeance for Thor's having defeated his plans before, airily informs Thor that this is just to warm him up and suddenly Thor is under assault by the Hulk. Except...not just one Hulk. Several Hulks, whom Zarrko claims have been taken by him from several different points in the Hulk's past and brainwashed to dispose of Thor once and for all. We have the gray Hulk in tattered clothing, the green Hulk in slacks and the green Hulk in purple trunks, all of them battling furiously. They're battering the living crap out of Thor. He manages to overcome them, and Zarrko, who wasn't expecting that, tries to flee in his vessel, but Thor comes crashing into it. He closes in on Zarrko and sees various video screens trained on Hulks from the past... and then, to his shock, he sees one trained on the 1940s, and there's Captain America. Then, before Thor can take any sort of action, the time ship literally disappears all around him, leaving him alone...and convinced that the Captain America they found, the one with only a sketchy memory of his past, is there courtesy of Zarrko, brainwashed and a danger to everyone.

PAGES 80-100

And now we cut back to Loki, and we reveal the truth: everyone they've encountered has been foot soldiers of Loki's, their true natures disguised by glamours provided by the trickster god. (Hyde, for instance, was the Executioner; the multiple Hulks were rock trolls, etc.) Now, Loki reasons, all he has to do is sit back and let them destroy each other.

Indeed the heroes now come together. Cross accusations are getting thrown around, and fundamental uncertainties about each other rise to the surface and take over. And all it takes is a slight mental nudge from Loki, preventing them

from really "hearing" each other, giving way to their suspicions. Next thing you know, they're battling each other furiously (Iron Man uses magnetic repulsion to separate Thor from his hammer, knocking it into a crevasse, managing to delay its return long enough to inadvertently cause Thor to revert to Don Blake, so he's distracted in trying to get his hammer back).

And suddenly they are all startled to see...

The Hulk. And he's laughing his butt off. Iron Man, Cap and Thor stop battling, seeing the laughing green monster, and he's basically saying, "What a bunch of idiots! You didn't have me to be suspicious of, so you're tearing each other apart!" Immediately the three of them converge on him, and the Hulk battles them while telling them what fools they are. "Don'tcha know anything? Don'tcha LEARN anything? This whole thing stinks of the exact thing that got you guys together in the first place, and you're dumb enough to fall for it again!"

On the Isle of Silence, Loki is freaking out. "I don't believe it! Trust is easily undercut, suspicions flared to full life easily enough. But they are united in their contempt and distrust for him, and thus they lend ear no matter how much I try to turn them away!"

The battle takes them to the Hoover Dam where the Hulk, in battling them, trying to drive them away, brings his hands smashing down so hard that it creates massive vibrations. But Thor sweeps in and slams him with Mjolnir so hard that the Hulk goes crashing into the Hoover Dam. This cracks the dam and water starts flooding through, endangering Boulder City. Three-pronged attack: Iron Man desperately repairs the damage; Thor, using Mjolnir, keeps the floodwaters back; Captain America — through his sheer gosh-darned charisma — is able to keep the people from freaking out and stampeding each other, calming them and telling them to have confidence in the Avengers.

And the Hulk, witnessing this, is angry, saying, "Right; sure. They blame the whole thing on me. Bah," and off he leaps.

oki is cursing up a blue streak and suddenly ecomes aware there's someone behind him. e turns. It's Odin. "All-Father! How did you--?" What part of 'All Seeing' is unclear to you?" ays Odin calmly. "Come here," and he reaches or him and Loki screams.

he heroes come together, the Hulk gone, and ey realize that — ironically — what the Hulk aid made sense. They compare notes and realize they were used. They swear to each other that they will never allow themselves to be so easily manipulated. Iron Man says angrily, "I know he's your brother and all, but I want a piece of him this time." Suddenly the ground rumbles beneath them and Thor says calmly, "I actually believe he's being tended to." Cut to Loki chained to a rock underground, a snake dripping acid on his face, as Odin says coolly, "That should attend to you for a time."

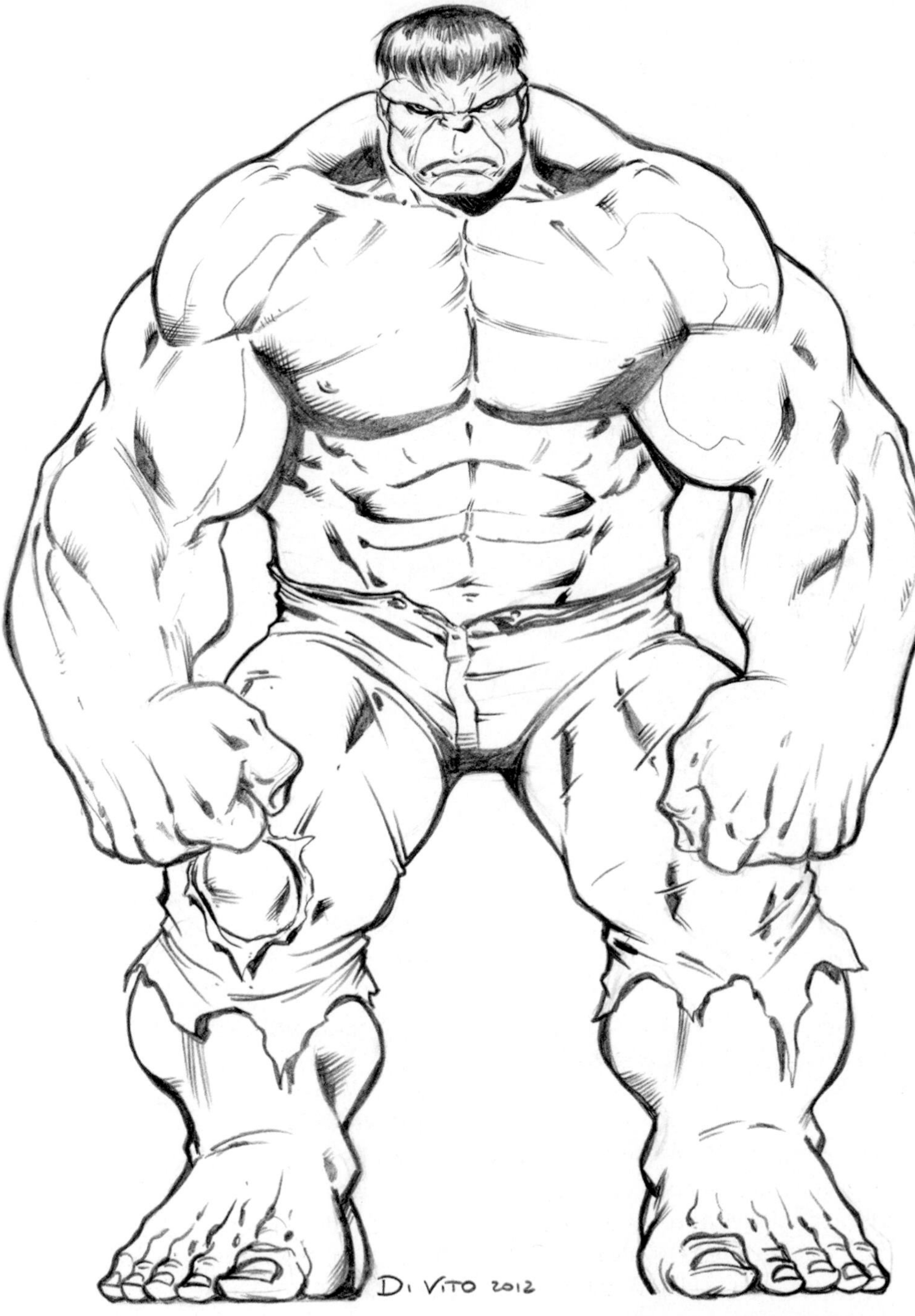
DI VITO 2012

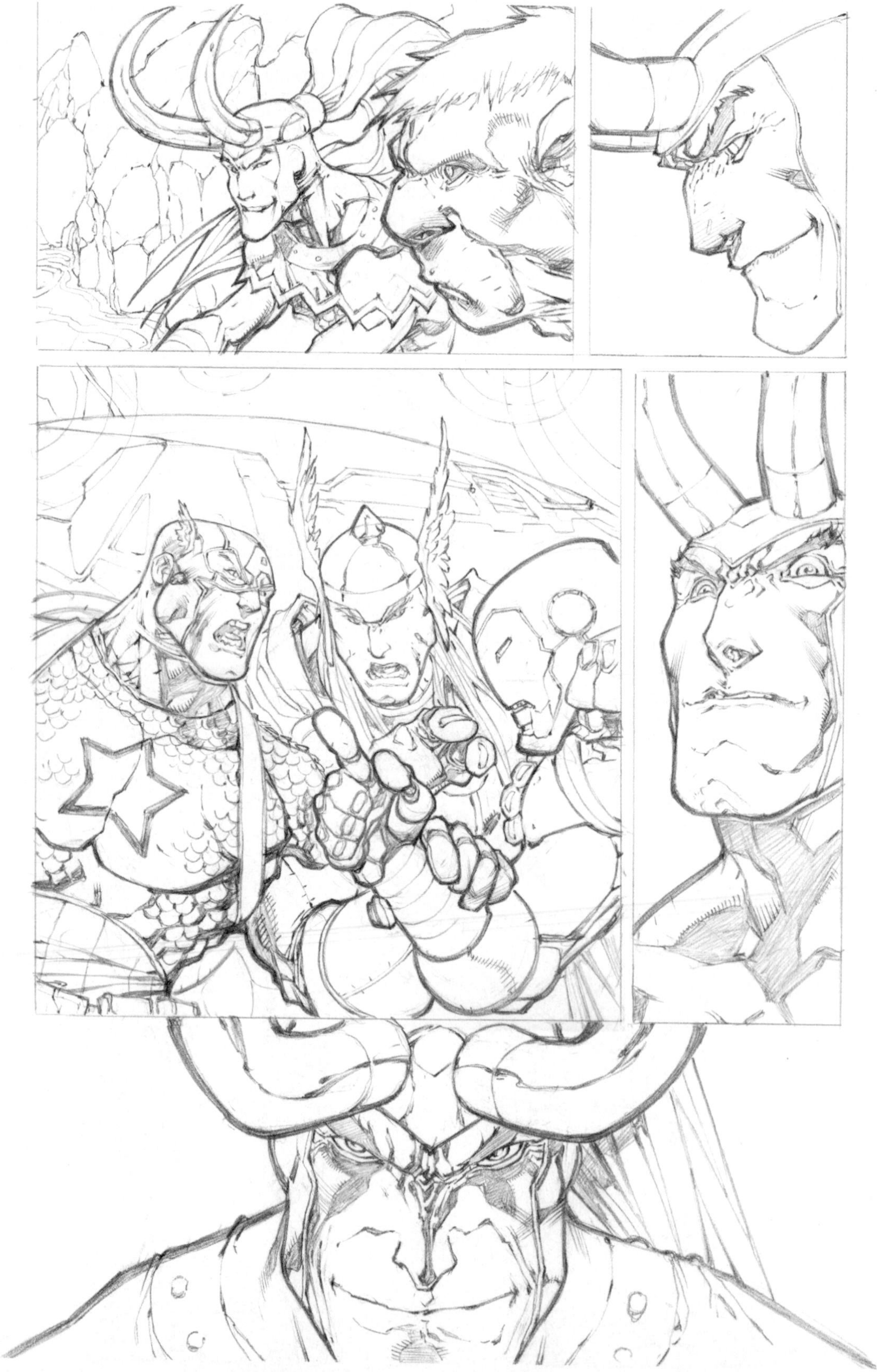

AVENGERS: SEASON ONE PREMIERE HARDCOVER COVER BY **JULIAN TOTINO TEDESCO**

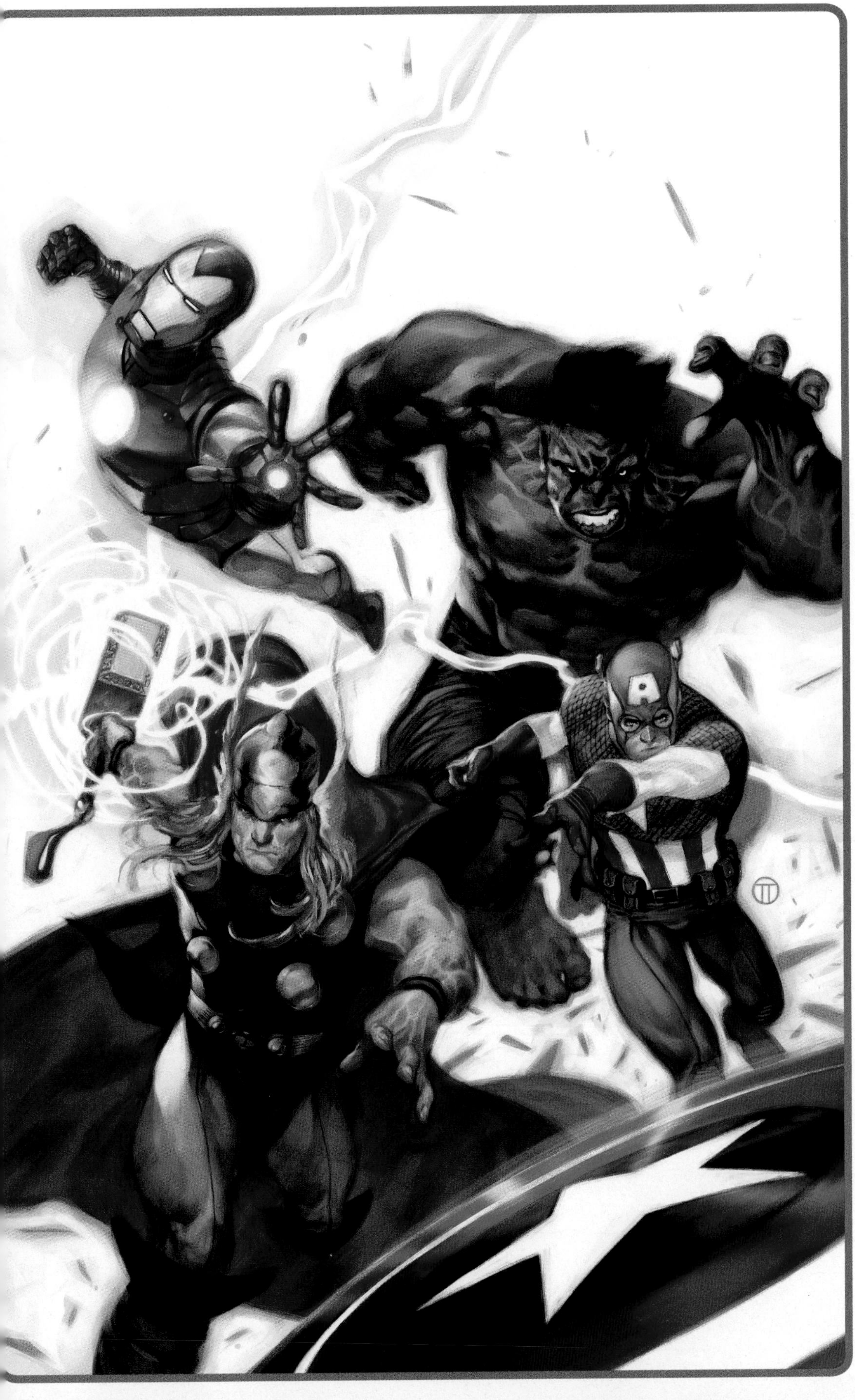

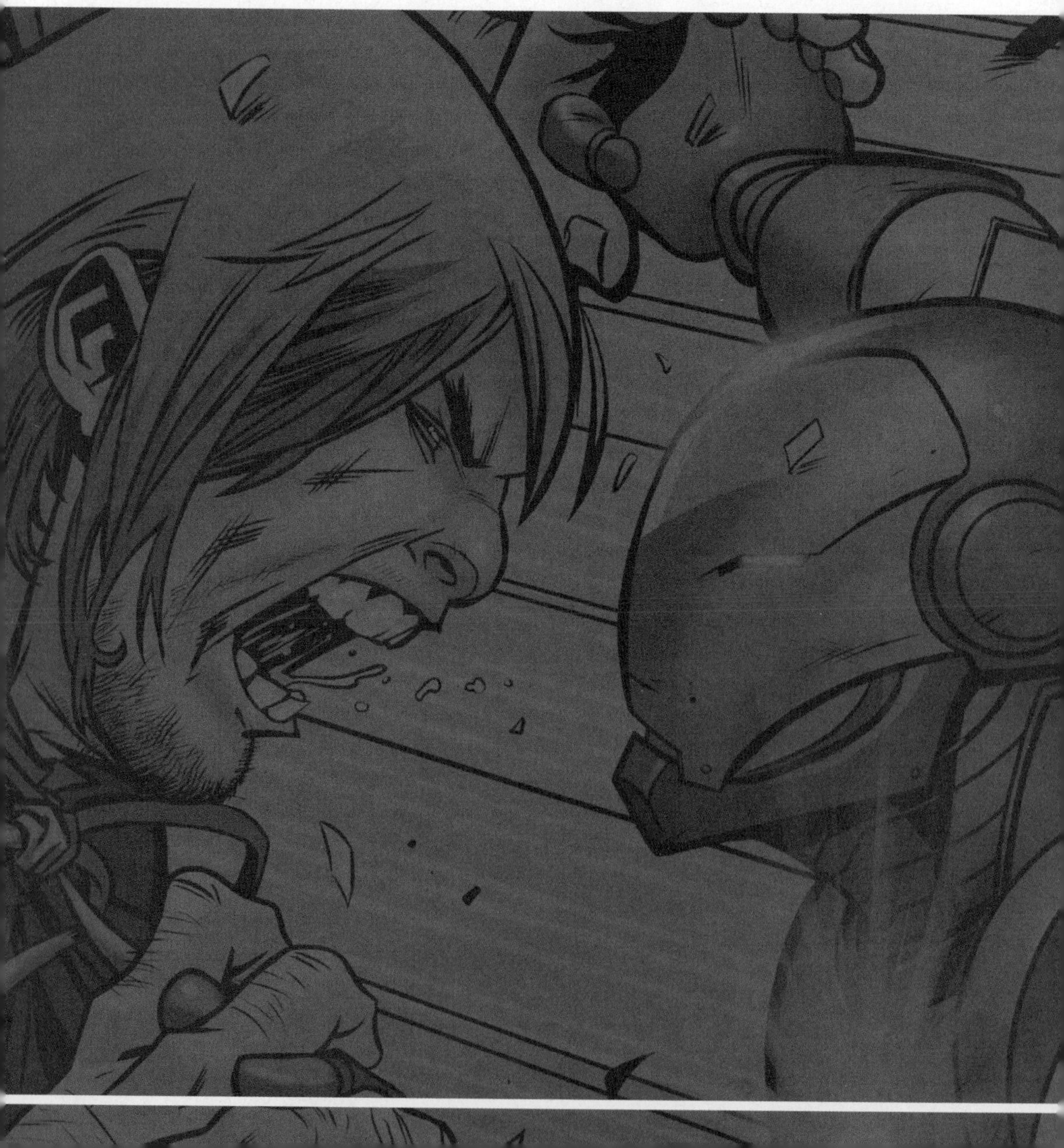

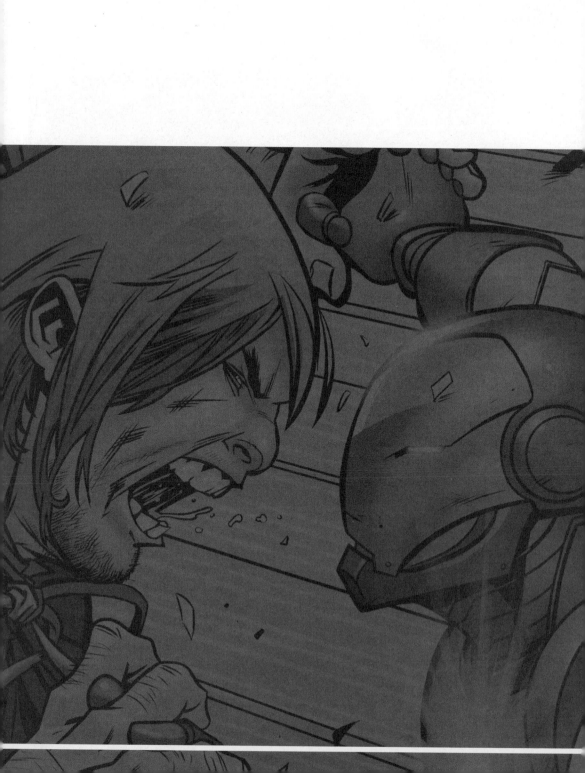